Romantic Affinities:
German Authors and Carlyle

A STUDY IN THE HISTORY OF IDEAS

Romantic Affinities: German Authors and Carlyle

A Study in the History of Ideas

Elizabeth M. Vida

UNIVERSITY OF TORONTO PRESS
Toronto Buffalo London

Reprinted in 2018

Toronto Buffalo London
Printed in Canada

ISBN 0-8020-5012-3
ISBN 978-1-4875-7327-0 (paper)

Printed on acid-free paper

Canadian Cataloguing in Publication Data

Vida, Elizabeth M. (Elizabeth Maximiliana), 1923–
Romantic affinities :
German authors and Carlyle
a study in the history of ideas

Includes bibliographical references and index.
ISBN 0-8020-5012-3

1. Carlyle, Thomas, 1795–1881 – Knowledge – German literature.
2. Romanticism. I. Title.

PR4437.G47V54 1993 824'.8 C93-094602-2

This book has been published with the help of a grant from the Canadian Federation for the Humanities, using funds provided by the Social Sciences and Humanities Research Council of Canada.

In memory of my former teachers
Professors A.S.P. Woodhouse and F.E.L. Priestley,
University of Toronto

Contents

Preface

In any examination of the genesis of Carlyle's literary works his indebtedness to German authors has its part to play. To unravel the tangled strands of German influences is, however, a rather ominous task, as national prejudices and biased opinions have not been altogether avoided in discussions of this topic. Often the question of indebtedness has been denied or affirmed with more fervour than objectivity. Particularly in reference to *Sartor Resartus*, it has been played down by scholars who did not even read the sources in the original before judging them negligible. Neither the events leading up to the Second World War and its aftermath, nor those of the following decades, up to the 1990s, have done much to foster a more impartial view of what is, first and foremost, a literary not a political issue.[1]

A fresh evaluation of Carlyle's relationship to his German sources is called for not only to lift the problem out of a political context, but also to clarify the extent of Carlyle's indebtedness to German Romanticism. These several influences have never before been examined in their entirety. Searching analyses have been written about his debt to transcendental philosophy; but not enough has been said about the combined contribution of poets, novelists, and dramatists of the period on Carlyle the writer. Indeed, the emphasis given German thought has obscured the more obvious literary connections. For this reason R. Wellek rightly demands 'a detailed examination of Carlyle's relation to the German Romanticists.'[2]

This book attempts to expand previous findings and to provide a broader basis for a comparative study in two ways.

First, it offers a wider range of German authors. Besides discussing such well-known literary personalities as Goethe, Jean Paul [Friedrich Richter], Novalis, Fichte, and Schelling, it also introduces Zacharias Werner, Ludwig Tieck, E.T.A. Hoffmann, F. de la Motte Fouqué, Wilhelm Hauff, Franz Horn, and the critic Friedrich Schlegel, all of whom are considered in a variety of combinations.

Second, it presents literary perspectives that have hitherto been neglected, such as fictional techniques, thematic patterns, and character delineations. These could hardly have been overlooked by such a style-conscious writer as Carlyle in search of new approaches for his own 'Kunstwerk,' as he calls *Sartor Resartus* in his *Notebooks.* Grouping influences according to such topical associations will clarify how Carlyle met with recurring themes and concepts in all his German readings, and how their cumulative impact made the Romantic affinities so effective.

The wider scope offered here rules out a purely mechanical approach in critical method that measures influences in terms of correctness. Much ingenuity has been expended elsewhere to show where Carlyle went wrong, where he did not render abstract thought in its precise meaning, where he had misunderstood the system. Such a negative attitude is hardly fruitful for purposes of literary enquiry. It not only disregards the metamorphosis philosophical notions must undergo to find effective expression in another medium, such as literature, but fails to understand the nature of the creative process itself, which moulds and transforms influences prior to their being employed in the author's own works. Whereas Carlyle has been censured for incorrect application of German Idealism, such writers as Thomas Mann and Samuel Beckett have been praised for introducing Schopenhauer's Pessimism and Sartre's Existentialism into their respective works, in at least as vague a manner.

Carlyle uses philosophical insights to create symbolical myth. To observe this transformation taking place should be our foremost concern in any study of this kind. Even if, as M. Storrs claims, Carlyle knew next to nothing about speculative philosophy,[3] he did possess the ability to grasp the essential spirit of Transcendentalism and its ethical implications, with the intention of expressing it in literature 'in a loose and popular manner.'[4] In order to achieve this end, he did not need command of all the niceties of philosophical thought, which would designate him a student of philosophy rather than a literary figure.

Besides this difference in approach, which takes an imaginative treatment of philosophical sources into account, changes in emphasis are made. While Fichte is still recognized as a central influence on Carlyle's brand of Idealism, stress is laid on his popular works rather than on the *Wissenschaftslehre,* directed at a scholarly audience. Accordingly, *Die Bestimmung des Menschen* is included in the investigation as a hitherto untapped source for the central chapters of *Sartor Resartus*. Schelling's *Über die Methode des akademischen Studiums* reveals how far the general temper of his teaching blends in with Carlyle's historical-religious notions applied to Palingenesia, or rebirth of society, while aspects of Novalis's 'Die Christenheit oder Europa' are reconsidered in the context of *Past and Present*.

The study does not intend to give a comprehensive view of German Romanticism as a whole. Important publications appeared in the 1980s in the field, but they do not make a contribution to Carlyle's views on the subject, which constitutes the substance of this book. Here, I focus on particular German literary works that Carlyle confirmably knew or may be presumed to have known on the basis of internal evidence. These works are examined in light of his early writings – such as the *Essays*, *Sartor Resartus*, *Heroes*, and *Past and Present* – but echoes are also traced in connection with Jean Paul and his influence on Carlyle's style.

No attempt is made to derive from the German works in question all the ingredients that went into the making of Carlyle, at the expense of others that also had a bearing on the emergence of his particular genius.[5] It cannot be overlooked, however, that, according to his own repeated and persuasive testimony, they acted as a uniquely stimulating force on his work. Admittedly, any study of sources must to a degree remain conjectural, and cannot be considered as proof, in the sense of a surety-bond. There is no such thing as an 'ultimate point of view.'[6] This book presents suggestions and proof that may or may not convince the reader. One should bear in mind however that although a similarity of ideas and literary methods need not imply a borrowing, a repeated similarity can hardly be judged a coincidence, especially if the source is revealed.

By providing my own translations of material otherwise not available in English, its relevance can now be examined, while in the past positions have frequently been taken on trust. They cover passages from the works of Schlegel, Horn, Tieck, E.T.A. Hoffmann, Hauff, Fouqué, and Schelling, unless otherwise indicated. The German text is contained in the Notes, to enable readers so motivated to check the sources on the spot. Variations in German spelling at a time when it was not as yet standardized, have to be taken into account. Wherever possible, I have used Carlyle's own rendering of German sources, mainly in the case of Goethe and Jean Paul, as presented in *German Romance*, *Essays*, and his translation of *Wilhelm Meister*. For Fichte I relied on W. Smith's approved version of *Die Bestimmung des Menschen*.

Only Carlyle's literary works, not his personal utterances, have been taken into consideration here. His changed approach to his German sources and the different value judgments he passes on them after they have served their purpose make his purely personal statements highly unreliable as critical evidence. Particularly after 1840, when his creed underwent a significant change in the direction of former Puritan affinities and his concern with problems of faith gave way to a preoccupation with social conditions, his initial enthusiasm for German literature began to flag. He exhibits from then on a growing tendency to belittle all previous stimuli, with the result that his judgment becomes erratic. German Idealism, which at one time had opened up a New Heaven and a New Earth, is termed 'a kind of disease.'[7] Fichte, once 'the adamantine spirit,'[8] turns into 'a thick-skinned fellow.'[9] The wise Goethe, the heavenly Jean Paul, give up their front-row seats in the literary arena to Cromwell, Baillie the Covenanter, and John Knox.

Those among us who have undertaken a study in the history of ideas on a larger scale will know the difficulties the mariner encounters who sails on the sea of thought, eager to find a passage on his voyage of discovery. Besides surf-beaten rocks, sometimes submerged by swelling waves, he believes to see stars, half-hidden by clouds, illuminating the watery darkness. Rarely does he enjoy the motionless sea, while stretched out on a sunny quarter-deck, giving himself up to a sense of direction and fulfilment. By way of analogy, I may state that I found my material partly by painstaking investigation of sources and wide background reading, partly by sheer luck. The task of translating works never before rendered into English – those by Friedrich Schlegel and Jean Paul among them – was demanding but stylistically a most rewarding effort. Above all I tried to do justice to Carlyle's admired Jean Paul, attempting not only to settle the much-disputed similarity of style question in a more satisfactory manner, but also to reveal the critical impact of this author's aesthetic theories on Carlyle's concept of the idyllic and the humorous in fiction. The greatest challenge was to present such diverse material in readable form, that is, as a synthetic whole.

My gratitude goes to the late Professor A.S.P. Woodhouse. Without his classes on Nineteenth-Century Thought and Romanticism – the latter given jointly with Professor F.E.L. Priestley – I would have been ill-equipped for my project, which Woodhouse himself had planned to undertake in future years.

On a more personal level, I would like to deviate from the usual laudatory comments on assistance received from various intellectual and material sources, beyond the obligation expressed to the two scholars to whom I dedicate this book. It is also evident that I could not have undertaken my study without the critical foundations provided by the impressive research done in the past, listed in the select bibliography. The tendency today is to curtail rather than expand bibliographical citation, omitting those sources that do not have a direct bearing on the topic. For this reason, many outstanding books and articles in English on historiography and related subjects had to be deleted from my original list. My direct predecessor is still C.F. Harrold, whose work I wished to update and expand. However much I appreciate the interest kept alive over many years in Toronto circles – Professor Peter Morgan of University College will have to stand for all – as well as the Canada Council grants I received at the early stages of my research, my work found little furtherance at the University of Saskatchewan, geared to promoting more tangible endeavours, with immediate practical results, rather than the time-consuming investigation of the kind I was undertaking. The only colleague who showed unflagging concern was Professor L.M. Findlay, whom I would like to thank for reading and discussing the manuscript with me. Inadequate library facilities resulted in endless delays in the Inter-Library Loan system. In spite of this severe drawback, I am grateful to the staff of the Reference Department of the Murray Memorial Library, especially Victor Wiebe and Mary Dykes, for their assistance. I am happy to acknowledge my debt to the Canadian Federation for the Humanities. It was with their aid that this book was published, using funds provided by the Social Sciences and Humanities Research Council of Canada.

Without the moral support of my husband, Dr Joseph L. Vida, who did not live to see my book in print, it would not have reached the final stage. As a German scholar in his own right, his wide-ranging knowledge of European literature, his expertise in research methods, penetrative comments, and invaluable advice helped me to find solutions to many intricate problems that appeared insoluble. His confidence in my ability to put the mosaic together never failed me.

I cannot expect that all chapters of this study will be of equal interest or value to my readers, but I believe that in the case of Carlyle to trace influences is to understand him better. Anyone who has wrestled with his meaning knows only too well that he does not set an example for lucid exposition and tidy thought associations. Much is left unsaid or is implied by mere hints, perhaps because certain premises that had become part of his own background he wrongly presumed to be known to others as well. Readers are inclined to have, in J. MacCunn's words, 'an imperfect notion of the connection of the whole, though they recognize the splendour and force of the passages.'[10] This study may be able to suggest solutions by pointing to similar manifestations from the larger field of German Romantic literature.

Romantic Affinities:
German Authors and Carlyle

Introduction

> In affirming that any vestige, however feeble, of this divine spirit, is discernible in German poetry, we are aware that we place it above the existing poetry of any other nation.
>
> (Carlyle, 'State of German Literature')

To ascertain Carlyle's approach to his German Romantic sources must be the starting-point for their revaluation. Did Carlyle have a unified view of the essence of German Romanticism, and, if so, what were the tendencies that struck him as new and most noteworthy?

Carlyle saw continuity rather than opposition in the relationship between the German Classics Goethe and Schiller and the evolving Romantic movement.[1] In the preface to his translations from Tieck in *German Romance*, he is quite explicit on the subject. Attempting neither a description nor a judgment regarding the 'New School', he rejects the epithet 'School' altogether and denies that the great change was brought about solely by three young men, living in the little town of Jena: 'The critical principles of Tieck and the Schlegels had already been set forth in the form both of precept and prohibition, and with all the aids of philosophic and epigrammatic emphasis, by the united minds of Goethe and Schiller in the *Horen* and the *Xenien*. The development and practical application of the doctrine is all that pertains to these reputed founders of the sect' (*German Romance I*, 260).

For Carlyle then, German Romanticism issued forth from Goethe's and Schiller's efforts to challenge rationalistic tendencies of the Enlightenment, an undertaking that eventually resulted in the third great period of German literature, 'full of rich prospects of spirituality, faith, reverence, freedom, and fusion of art and religion.'[2] Grouping all poets who followed the new trend under the watchword 'Moderns' – a term

Carlyle was familiar with from English literature – he believed writers such as Tieck, E.T.A. Hoffmann, Fouqué, and Zacharias Werner to have built on these solid foundations of the 'German Classics.'

Accordingly, he recommends for a study of the principles of German aesthetics certain treatises by Kant, Schiller, Jean Paul, and the Schlegels – a mixture that would hardly please some German literary critics of today. However, contemporary evaluations of new literary phenomena do not always fall in line with a strict classification into literary periods. That Carlyle, with little critical precedence to go by, arrived at conclusions that differ from those of critics of our own time does not prove his judgment invalid. Justifiably M. Joachimi points out that Classicism and Romanticism are not necessarily to be conceived of as strict opposites but may well complement each other.[3] Goethe, a Shakespeare enthusiast in his Storm and Stress years, found inspiration in Classical aspects of art, before returning to *Faust*; Schiller wrote *Die Braut von Messina*, as well as *Die Jungfrau von Orleans*, subtitled 'a romantic tragedy.'

Carlyle's great admiration for Goethe most likely determined his attitude to German literature as a whole, which he judged in the light of illumination he had received from such works as *Faust* and *Wilhelm Meister*. What he repeatedly stresses in his essays on the subject is Goethe's timelessness or, as Carlyle prefers to call it, his modernity: 'Poetry of our own generation; an ideal world, and yet the world we even now live in.'[4] In *Werther*, otherwise not one of Carlyle's favourites, Goethe is 'deeply important to modern minds,'[5] as a poet who embodies 'the Wisdom which is proper to this time.'[6] Besides, Goethe had proved his relevance for Carlyle himself, by helping him solve his own spiritual problems as a kind of poetic mentor.

Setting aside the complicated matter of the origins of German Romanticism, it must be admitted that, without Goethe's *Wilhelm Meister*, the Romantic Movement in Germany would have lacked a model to illustrate effectively the poetic theories Friedrich Schlegel was in the process of evolving in his periodical *Athenaeum* in the first phase of his critical activity. It was he who, in his review 'On Goethe's *Meister*,' set up this novel as worthy of emulation, indeed as a standard of excellence. Mainly on the basis of its Classical aloofness, which could be taken as a manifestation of Romantic irony, it was hailed as 'a divine growth.'[7] Nor did Friedrich Schlegel's praise abate two years after the initial review, for in his 'Conversations on Poetry' he reiterates his conviction that this work manifested 'the classical spirit in modern form', bringing about 'the harmony of the classical with the romantic.'[8]

This repeated emphasis on both the Classical *and* the Romantic features of this epoch-making *Bildungsroman* must be connected with the background peculiar to the Schlegels. Both brothers had taken their starting-point in criticism from a deep appreciation of classical antiquity, its literature and art, before applying their ingenuity to the new Romantic field. If the designated founders of the new movement proclaimed in this manner an inner continuity, Carlyle's doing so can hardly be considered out of tune with developments. He had not only read Friedrich Schlegel's famous *Meister* review, but also knew of the Schlegel's Classical origins in criticism.[9]

In spite of later value judgments Goethe made on the movement, linking Romanticism to a state of disease, as opposed to the health expressed in Classicism,[10] he never erected insurmountable barriers between Classical and Romantic literature. On the whole he was not displeased by the tribute the younger generation paid him, prior to Novalis's attempt to outdo *Wilhelm Meister* in his own novel *Heinrich von Ofterdingen*. Goethe even believed, rightly or wrongly, that he and Schiller had unwittingly introduced the terms into German literature: 'The concept of classic and romantic poetry, now spread over the whole world and causing much commotion and division, originated from Schiller and myself ... Schiller even proved to me that I myself was, if unconsciously, romantic ... The Schlegels took up the idea and carried it further so that it has now spread over the whole world and everybody speaks of Classicism and Romanticism, unheard of fifty years ago.'[11]

In his *Faust*, Goethe had used the Classical-Romantic linkage with great effect for his Helena episode, the first fragmentary continuation of his tragedy, which Carlyle had reviewed.[12] By employing the subtitle 'klassisch-romantische Phantasmagorie,' Goethe suggested a concept Carlyle regarded as valid. Beyond this phrase – the model for Carlyle's several 'phantasmagoria' references in *Sartor* – an interpretative hint lay in the episode itself: the union between Classical form, represented by Helena, and the medieval spirit of the North, in the person of Faust, produces as offspring the new spirit of Poetry, personified in the youthful Euphorion, modelled on Byron. Carlyle interprets the episode along these lines: 'Our readers are aware that this Euphorion, the offspring of Northern Character wedded to Grecian Culture, frisks it here not without reference to Modern Poesy, which had a birth so precisely similar' (*Essays I*, 191).

Jean Paul left just as important a mark as Goethe's on the evolving theories of the day. In his *Vorschule der Ästhetik* (§25), he presents Schiller and Goethe as Romantics – especially the latter, in connection with the episodes relating to Mignon and the Harper in *Wilhelm Meister*, which impressed themselves as images with a strong Romantic flavour on the minds of the contemporary reader. F. Schlegel then set another literary precedent by advocating that Jean Paul's own formless novels were a congenial prototype of Romantic fiction. According to his later views, Romanticism consisted in 'sentimental material presented in a fantastic form,'[13] a definition that fitted Jean Paul's arabesque style perfectly. It seems indeed remarkable that German Romantic theory, emerging prior to actual works written in the style, turned to the immediately preceding generation to find suitable literary models in its formative period.

Another critical voice that joined the Schlegel chorus on a lesser level also helped shape Carlyle's judgment on Classical-Romantic relationships. This was Franz Horn, whose opinions Carlyle followed closely in his emphasis on the role of the *Xenien* as being directed primarily against the Enlightenment. Horn names both Schiller's periodical *Die Horen* and the *Xenien* epigrams written in collaboration with Goethe as epoch-making publications, aimed at 'the destruction of irreligious, anti-philosophical and anti-poetical Philistines' who, subscribing to the narrow doctrine of utility, 'did not blush to invest even the Highest Being with mediocre aims.'[14]

Carlyle also shares with Horn the view that the Schlegels' so-called School of Poetry was no school at all, and adds broadening implications, lacking in Horn, when he sees the change as originating 'not in the individuals but in the universal circumstances, belonging not to Germany, but to Europe,'[15] an opinion that proved to be right. As a foreigner he was in a better position to judge literary tendencies from outside the purely national pale.

If a unified view of German literature is basic to Carlyle's approach – and reasons for this view have been suggested – it also applies to the values he found expressed therein. As an expositor of the higher literature of Germany to British readers more or less unacquainted with the field, Carlyle felt inclined to stress unity rather than diversity, particularly as he had to do away with the scarecrow of 'Mysticism'.

What struck Carlyle as unique in all his readings was the spiritual, quasi-religious note: 'In the higher Literature of Germany there lies, for him that can read it, the beginning of a new revelation of the Godlike.'[16] This theme he repeats in several variations, for example, 'Their Literature, alone of all existing Literatures, has still some claim to that ancient 'inspired gift,' which alone is poetry.'[17]

The tribute of having first drawn attention to this characteristic goes to Madame de Staël. Not only did she notice that in Germany at the time a fund of new ideas was being tapped, 'which the other nations of Europe will not for a long time be able to exhaust',[18] but she was also aware of its illuminating qualities in things transcendental: 'When I began to study German literature, it seemed as if I was entering on a new sphere, where the most striking light was thrown on all that I had before merely perceived in a confused manner ... the peculiar character of German literature is, to refer everything to an interior existence' *Germany*, II, 271–2).

This alliance between religion and genius did not escape Carlyle's own observation. His enthusiastic comments, too well known to have to be cited, confirm the rewarding nature of his search. He states and restates his 'New Evangel,' and shows how it grows from a dual root, the fusion of poetry with philosophy. From here evolves the ideal of the philosophical poet: 'To seize a character in its life and secret mechanism, requires a philosopher; to delineate it with truth and impressiveness, is the work of a poet.'[19]

In view of this insistence on the union of poetry and thought, it seems evident that the value of German literature was, for Carlyle, never restricted to thought-content alone. This perspective derives, in part, from his notions about the emblematic nature of language, which contributes decidedly to the idea taking shape in the reader's mind. He himself depended for effectiveness in his own writing on this very quality of language.

Thought embedded in poetry or 'the infinite clothed in the finite' – in Friedrich Schlegel's famous phrase – forming a harmonious whole is a particular quality of the writing of Goethe, the epitome of the poet-prophet for Carlyle. Because the linkages of this unity are so closely knit, C.F. Harrold, in *Carlyle and German Thought*, experiences difficulties in trying to extract thought from poetic vision. Carlyle, in contrast, refrains from attempting to tear it apart, but treats it as a significant trait of this new type of literature. Those who followed it were Romantics for him. In all the biographical delineations of the German poets, mainly in 'Goethe' and 'Jean Paul Richter,' this ability to combine both faculties is sharply brought into focus. Carlyle considers Goethe to be 'a richly educated Poet ... a master both of Humanity and of Poetry; one to whom Experience has given true wisdom, and the "Melodies Eternal" a perfect utterance for his wisdom.'[20] Jean Paul, too, is characterized in this manner as 'a moralist and a sage, no less than a poet and a wit.'[21] Novalis and Werner also fall in line with this ideal: 'As a Poet, Novalis is no less Idealistic than as a Philosopher.'[22] Werner strives 'earnestly not only to be a poet, but a prophet.'[23]

Whichever aspect – thought or poetry – is stressed, the uniqueness of German literature consists in this combination and forms, in Carlyle's view, the strongest bond among all German poets.

ONE

Critical Inroads (Essays, German Romance)

God Almighty's own theatre of Immensity, the INFINITE made palpable and visible to me.

(Carlyle, letter, 14 Oct. 1869)

The Effect of Friedrich Schlegel on Carlyle as Literary Critic

The critical foundations of German Romanticism, briefly touched upon in the introduction, warrant a closer investigation regarding the effect of Friedrich Schlegel on Carlyle. In the past, criticism has remained peculiarly silent about this influence. Either it was taken for granted in a rather nebulous way, or it was dismissed in a summary fashion. The reader was simply informed that Carlyle's dependence on this critic 'did not require any proof,'[1] or that he 'need go no further than Fichte and Goethe for German critical ideas to which Carlyle was so largely indebted.'[2] Whichever way scholarly opinions tended, critics appeared to stop short of presenting the necessary evidence for the pros or cons of critical affinities in Carlyle's works. The reason for this hiatus may be that the overall impact of Friedrich Schlegel's teaching is hard to pinpoint. He himself considered the accumulated mass of new ideas he had spread, as a common possession, the basis of all Romantic literary productions, urging his friends to philosophize on them together (*symphilosophieren*) and to use them according to their specific talents in their own works.[3]

To what degree was Carlyle acquainted with the literary principles of one of the leading theorists of the German *Frühromantik* or early phase of the movement laid down in such diverse publications as *Athenaeums-Fragmente, Charakteristiken und Kritiken, Vorlesungen über die Geschichte der alten und neuen Literatur,* and *Philosophische Vorlesungen*?

In all probability Carlyle was introduced to the Schlegels through the writings of Mme de Staël. In *Germany*, she dedicates a whole chapter to the literary renown of August Wilhelm and Friedrich, characterizing the latter as the more philosophically inclined of the Schlegel brothers, and praising him for the originality of his far-reaching speculations.[4] This appraisal appears natural enough if we consider that it was Friedrich who had given her private lectures on the topic of transcendental Idealism and its application to literature – one of the most pressing concerns pertaining to her book. But there is more than subjective truth to this pronouncement; the breadth of Friedrich's intellectual activities, ranging from literary criticism to philosophical-historical presentations in his lectures, far exceeded A.W. Schlegel's more restricted contributions, primarily related to the development of drama, on which his fame rests.

In Carlyle's early *Essays* and prefatory comments to his translations in *German Romance*, mention is most frequently made to both brothers, but the three quotes that have so far been identified can be traced back to Friedrich: the first one, from the 'Ideen-Fragmente,' appears unacknowledged in *Sartor Resartus*; the second one, from the *Charakteristiken*, is correctly attributed to its source; and the third one, from the *Geschichte der alten und neuen Literatur*, is wrongly attributed to A.W. Schlegel – a pardonable error if we take into consideration that two of the most influential works of the Schlegels, the journal *Athenaeum* and the *Charakteristiken*, were published jointly. Also in Carlyle's *Notebooks* several references are made to Friedrich Schlegel, dealing specifically with his ideas, while his brother is mentioned only once.[5] It follows that Carlyle was, at least, acquainted with three important aspects of Friedrich Schlegel's work: his Romantic critical theory, his practical criticism, and his lectures on literature. Of these three sources, the first two are most significant for the critical notions Carlyle himself develops.

Friedrich Schlegel's 'Ideen,' from which Carlyle's unacknowledged quote in the chapter 'Symbols' is taken (*Sartor*, 217), constitutes part of the critical fragments published in the literary journal *Athenaeum* (1798–1800), founded by both brothers. These fragments of thought, as they might be called, contained brief aphorisms, in Chamfort's style, on art, philosophy, and literature, defined by Friedrich's fellow Romantic Novalis as 'literary seedbeds' (*literarische Sämereien*).[6] They were to announce 'a new Evangel' and popularize among lovers of literature a revolutionary way of seeing and appraising aesthetic values. The fragment from the 'Ideen' that Carlyle chose deals with the imagination as 'being the organ of the Godlike,'[7] a notion the English editor of Teufelsdröckh's papers considers to be both mysterious and impalpable. This observation is followed by a reference to the nature of symbols in the same chapter: 'The Infinite is made to blend itself with the Finite' (*Sartor* 220), which, so far undetected, is an adaptation of Schlegel's central pronouncement of 'the Infinite revealing itself in the Finite' (*Athenaeum*, vol. 3, 21).

In the 'Ideen,' consisting of thirty pages of fragments, Carlyle would have familiarized himself with a variety of aphoristic utterances on the nature of the poet as divinely inspired and other basic notions of *Universalpoesie*, such as the symbolic and allegorical aspects of literature and the part mythology had to play in it, resulting in a feeling of reverence (*Andacht*) as an emotional response. Because mere entertainment and usefulness are no longer considered as elements by which to judge poetry, the poet must be inspired and cannot be a 'breadartist' alone, who works foremost for gain. This leads up to the most important point about the union between philosophy and poetry, with added religious elements in literature, also called transcendental verities. The following selection from the 'Ideen' may convey a general impression of their message and might reveal to some readers the similarity in thought associations between Friedrich Schlegel and Carlyle:[8]

Only in relation to the Infinite there is substance and profit; whatever is unrelated to it is quite empty and useless. (no. 3)

Therefore spread sacred seed into the soil of the mind without artistry and empty puffing. (no. 5)

Just as the merchants in the Middle Ages, artists should unite to form a Hansa [guild] to protect each other to some extent. (no. 142)

The universe cannot be explained, nor can it be understood. It must be contemplated and revealed. Cease to call the empirical system the universe, and learn to [fathom] its true religious idea. (no. 150)

Oh, how poor are your notions of genius – even of the best among you. Where you find genius I find more often the fulness of wrong tendencies, a centre of bunglers. (no. 141)

Only such a confusion may be termed a chaos out of which a new world can be shaped. (no. 71)

The new eternal Evangel will appear as a Bible as Lessing prophesied ... This it cannot do without the godhead wherein the esoteric notion falls together with the exoteric. (no. 95)

You are astounded about the age, that fermenting gigantic power, these upheavals, and do not know what new birth to expect. (no. 50)

A spiritual man is he who lives only in the invisible; for whom everything that is visible only contains the truth of an allegory. (no. 2)

Poetry and philosophy are ... different spheres or forms of religion ... Try then to combine them truly and you will receive nothing else but religion. (no. 46)

He who has religion shall speak poetry. But to seek it and discover it philosophy is the tool. (no. 34)

The last fragment of the 'Ideen,' addressed to Novalis, once more presents one of Friedrich Schlegel's most cherished tenets, relating to the religious element in literature: 'You no longer hover on the borderline, but in your spirit poetry and philosophy have undergone an intimate fusion' (no. 156).

Central to both F. Schlegel and Carlyle is man's relationship to the Infinite (*das Unendliche*), over and above the visible Finite which only contains the truth of an allegory. Religion constitutes man's awareness of the world-soul in some form or other, but only the higher imagination (*Fantasie*) of the poet brings the Infinite to this world. Such views shaped the transcendental climate Carlyle valued above all in German literature of his time, a preference which determined his critical position in future years.

In his expository essay 'State of German Literature,' he acquaints his readers with these new standards: 'Criticism has assumed a new form in Germany; it proceeds on other principles, and proposes to itself a higher aim' (*Essays I*, 51). Carlyle explains this aim as a shifting of values away from quality of diction and metaphor to questions of essence. No longer is the garment or body of poetry a primary concern; instead, its soul and spiritual existence are central: 'The science of Criticism, as the Germans practise it, is no study of an hour; for it springs from the depth of thought, and remotely or immediately connects itself with the subtlest problems of all philosophy' (ibid., 55).

What was theoretically expressed in the 'Ideen' took the form of practical criticism in the *Charakteristiken und Kritiken* presenting character sketches of contemporary literary figures relative to other works, praised highly by Carlyle: 'Take for instance the *Charakteristiken* of the two Schlegels ... and say whether in depth, clearness, minute and patient fidelity, these *Characters* have often been surpassed, or the import and poetic worth of so many poets and poems more vividly and accurately brought to view' (*Essays I*, 'State of German Literature,' 61). This comment does not appear to be the judgment of a critic who merely skimmed through the pages but rather of one who studied the work with care and diligence, bearing aspects of its technique in mind.

It becomes obvious to any reader that F. Schlegel's contributions to the *Charakteristiken*, consisting mainly of reviews on Jacobi, Forster, Lessing, and Goethe's *Wilhelm Meister*, overshadow A.W. Schlegel's shorter critiques of minor works. Carlyle had read F. Schlegel's *Meister* essay, as he quotes Friedrich's opinions in the preface to the translation of the book (*Wilhelm Meister I*, 7). He even promised his readers to translate it, if only to show English critics how to undertake such a task.[9]

In this epoch-making review, F. Schlegel presented his view of the importance of biography for the evaluation of any literary achievement. The 'biography' he values, however, does not deal with facts; he sees in Goethe's novel the unfolding of a striving mind, a presentation of a moral struggle for values, not necessarily characterizing its hero, Wilhelm, but rather expressing the experience of Goethe himself. Only a writer of Goethe's breadth of vision is capable of presenting emotions that touch upon the Infinite. Friedrich Schlegel claims that the reader submits to the poet's magic whose personality is indirectly revealed within the rich context of art, theatre, and poetry. Goethe emerges as a divine poet and philosopher, who looks at his own protagonist through a lens of benevolent irony. Various levels of mellow harmonies merge together, presenting the true spirit of poetry.

In the three remaining characteristics Friedrich's biographical method can be studied even more fully, in accordance with principles laid down elsewhere in the book: 'We know that we are doing something which is not insignificant and not unworthy, if we characterize with care the peculiarities of an original mind; relive his life in our imagination and participate in the broadening and limiting experiences his personality underwent. We do not seek to hide his failures ... The genius of a poet can often be confirmed and presented through his wrong tendencies, as much as and ever more than through his most successful works.'[10] This idea of reviewing the works as a manifestation of the whole man constitutes an innovative venture in practical criticism.[11]

In his criticism of Friedrich Jacobi's *Woldemar*, F. Schlegel seeks out the unity of the novel by investigating the spirit in which it was written. For this reason he deems it necessary to become thoroughly acquainted with the character and the history of the author's mind.[12] Jacobi 'is not a philosopher by profession but by character.'[13] The novel expresses earnest striving for the Infinite and counteracts disbelief: the invisible God is made visible as through a shroud of light. This basis in belief, he considers the most valuable aspect of the book. Reviewing the rationalistic attitude of the previous generation of the Age of Reason (*Aufklärung*), Schlegel chastizes their unbelief as 'the nonsense of cold reasoners without sense, heart and judgment.'[14] Mostly possessed of mediocre minds, such limited personalities forever doubt the existence of what they themselves cannot fathom, classing it as 'Mystizismus! Schwärmerei!' (*Kritische Ausgabe*, II, 58). Carlyle chooses the same approach in his very effective discussion on transcendental values in 'State of German Literature,' to answer the charge of Mysticism against the Germans (*Essays I*, 70).

According to Schlegel, assertions of spiritual vision are, however, counterbalanced by weakening factors inherent in Jacobi's personality. His striving for the Infinite does not result in action (*Tätigkeit*), as it should, but merely ends in distrust and despair. This is attributable to Jacobi's lack of inner harmony, without which a successful union of contraries cannot be achieved, and is ultimately the cause of Jacobi's failure as a writer. Throughout the review, interest in Jacobi the man, who had received his 'fire baptism' (*Kritische Ausgabe*, II, 59), yet lacked the inner stability to act upon his insights, is sustained.

Whereas Schlegel regrets the lack of moral fibre in Jacobi, he does not find Georg Forster[15] deficient in this virtue: 'Not only this or that opinion, but the overruling mood of all his works is truly moral.'[16] This author does not follow 'the deceitful picture of happiness' (*Kritische Ausgabe*, II, 83); he reaches out directly for his set goal: 'Every pulsation of his ever active being strives *forward*. Among the great diversity of opinions of his rich and profuse mind, perfection was the solid concept of his whole literary career.'[17] Forster's transcendental tendencies include an earnest occupation with the Infinite ('stetes Streben nach dem Unendlichen,' 82) in the ideals he presents and the perspectives on life he opens up. Schlegel sees in Forster not only a gifted prose writer but a polyhistor and, lastly, a philosopher who achieves inner harmony, because his moral character and intellectual expansion are proportionate. Indeed, the vastness of his mind lends his works traits of true sublimity, while his appreciation of genius results in admiration for great men, such as Mirabeau, Franklin, and

Frederick the Great. Most laudable are his ideas on the dignity of man which he applies to his own life in the form of *Selbsttätigkeit*, a concept of spiritual self-improvement. What appears as involuntary irony in this characteristic is the ingenuity F. Schlegel expends to present the world-view of a writer remembered for this criticism of him rather than for his overrated works.

In 'Über Lessing,' Schlegel sets himself the task to characterize Lessing's mind in its totality which is revolutionary in essence. This revolutionary spirit provides the key to all his works in literature, criticism, and theology, revealing itself as well in his manly maxims, disregarded by an age incapable of appreciating moral superiority. Schlegel undertakes to list every remarkable quality he finds in Lessing in a sentence that runs on for thirty-one lines, interrupted by semicolons, much in the style of Carlyle's long paragraphs in his essays on Jean Paul, Fichte, and his own evaluation of Lessing.[18] Among the character traits contained in this catalogue of excellence, F. Schlegel mentions Lessing's free lifestyle; his upright friendliness; his hatred of lies and intellectual sloth; his warm reference to all that furthers intellectual growth; and his divine restlessness, the desire to become active that emerges from an inborn sense of the Infinite. He concludes that Lessing 'was worth more than all his talents,'[19] equating his character with that of Nathan the Wise and claiming that only an outstanding man could have such virtues, such emotions, and such strength of mind.

Carlyle generally confirms Friedrich Schlegel's approach in *Sartor Resartus*, while specific application is made in his prefaces to *German Romance* and above all, his early *Essays*. Basic ingredients of a spiritual biography are even carried over into some of his essays on the English poets, a feature which had been conspicuously absent from his previous biographical sketches, written for *Brewster's Edinburgh Encyclopaedia*. Indeed, one could say that the fusion of religion and philosophy in literature, and the emphasis on aspects of the author's personality that helped or hindered in shaping his work, run like a thread through the fabric of Carlyle's criticism. Hofrath Heuschrecke postulates that Carlyle's view of biography is essential for a deeper understanding of an author: 'no Life-Philosophy (*Lebensphilosophie*) ... can attain its significance till the Character itself is known and seen; "till the Author's View of the World, (*Weltansicht*), and how he actively and passively came by such a view, are clear: in short till a Biography of him has been philosophico-poetically written, and ... a complete picture and Genetical History of the Man and his spiritual Endeavour lies before you"' (*Sartor*, 75).

In the order of importance as proof for Schlegelian influences, the

Essays rank first. Carlyle's Goethe image is clearly shaped by a transcendental alignment that shows 'some touches of that old divine spirit' (*Essays I*, 'Goethe,' 208). He begins his critical appreciation of his paragon with the question: 'What manner of man *is* this?' (ibid., 199), which leads to the unfolding of 'the man himself, and his own progress and spiritual development' (ibid., 202). Not unlike F. Schlegel in his essay on Georg Forster, Carlyle stresses Goethe's sense of harmony, expressed in his personality and his work. Goethe's poetry is not mere handicraft 'but the voice of the whole harmonious manhood' (ibid., 208). As the man and his work are one, the critic must consider 'his opinions, his creations, his mode of thought, his whole picture of the world as it dwells within him' (ibid., 243).

This harmony is, for Carlyle more so than for F. Schlegel, the outcome of a life-long struggle that he depicts in all his biographies, with more or less intensity. In his evaluation of Goethe, he presents a spiritual biography of a strangely familiar kind. Goethe too 'has struggled toughly' (ibid., 209), living a life of 'earnest toilsome endeavour after all excellence' (ibid., 210). The result is victory: 'At one time we found him in darkness, and now he is in light; he was once an Unbeliever and now he is a Believer' (ibid.). Carlyle probes even greater into the genesis of this spiritual transformation by following up this statement with a searching question: 'How has this man, to whom this world once offered nothing but blackness, denial and despair, attained to that better vision?' (ibid.). He insists that *Werther* and *Wilhelm Meister* are spiritual documents of Goethe the man: 'The problem which had been stated in *Werter* with despair of its solution, ... is here solved [*Wilhelm Meister*]' (ibid., 224).

This transfer of problems dealt with in fiction onto the personality of the writer is notable indeed – a feat Schlegel had also accomplished in his critical evaluation of Jacobi. In the process, Werther and Wilhelm fade into the background and merely document Goethe's own spiritual development, which is made to follow the doubt–faith pattern; 'A great change had taken place in the moral disposition of the man a change from inward imprisonment, doubt and discontent, into freedom, belief and clear activity' (ibid., 242–3).

Carlyle's essay 'Goethe' shares another feature with Schlegel's review of Jacobi: the spirited attack on the old set of values established by the Age of Reason as represented by Voltaire. In this connection he speaks of Goethe as counteracting the anti-religious time-spirit: 'In such a state of painful obstruction, extending itself everywhere over Europe ... lay the general mind, when Goethe first appeared in Literature. Whatever belonged to the finer nature of man had withered under the Harmattan breath of Doubt' (ibid., 216).

The first essay on Jean Paul Friedrich Richter starts off by seriously finding fault with Döring, Jean Paul's previous biographer. Carlyle is dissatisfied with the want of spiritual unity in Döring's account. He claims that such a composition, 'pointing everywhere but to the zenith ... cannot well be what critics call harmonious' (*Essays I*, 3). Part of this harmony is an eternal one: Jean Paul's natural religious spirit, pulsating in his works as in his personality. In his books we are 'wandering through Infinitude ... in its dim religious light' (ibid., 14), while as a man he shows reverence, the first and last aim of all true culture. A detailed characteristic of Jean Paul's traits, akin to the one Friedrich Schlegel presented in 'Lessing,' stretches over half a page. The following may serve as a sample: 'He is a man of feeling in the noblest sense of that word; for he loves all living things with the heart of a brother; his soul rushes forth, in sympathy with gladness and sorrow, with goodness or grandeur, over all Creation: every gentle and generous affection, every thrill of mercy, every glow of nobleness, awakens in his bosom a response; nay, strikes his spirit into harmony' (ibid., 15). He too has experienced hardships, which have purified the fiery elements in his nature. The outcome of this struggle is rendered according to the usual pattern: 'He has doubted, he denies, yet he believes' (ibid., 22). The stress on faith brings the essay back to the beginning, closing the circle; Carlyle finds in Jean Paul 'that which does not die' (ibid., 24).

In 'Jean Paul Friedrich Richter Again,' Friedrich Schlegel's notions surface once more in their ideal form. Not only is Jean Paul 'a man of wonderful gifts in whom Philosophy and Poetry are not only reconciled, but blended together into the purer essence of Religion' (*Essays II*, 100), but Carlyle considers the life of such a man '"in itself a Bible"' – a reminiscence in quotes from Schlegel's 'Ideen,' referring to the New Evangel (no. 95) in a slightly changed version.

In the essay 'Life and Writings of Werner,' Carlyle sums up this mystical playwright as 'a gifted spirit, struggling earnestly amid the new complex tumultuous influences of his time and country' (*Essays I*, 88). He is limned as the would-be moral man who fails to reach his mark – a personality who aroused Carlyle's interest, if not his esteem. Werner lacks force; he is involved in a struggle for harmony he can never win. In this he shows a certain affinity with Jacobi, who also had not accomplished his goal. The ill-fated Werner leads an inconstant and feverish life: 'The strange chaotic nature of the man ... his baffled longings, but still ardent endeavours after Truth and Good ... through the pathless infinitudes of thought ... is more than a rhapsodic effusion; the outpouring of a passionate and mystic soul' (ibid., 95). Again, the man and his work enter into a complete fusion, or, in this case, a chaotic confusion.

The essay 'Novalis' is most often referred to by English scholars because it contains Carlyle's comments on the role of the critic. He defines his role as Schlegel does, in terms of the priest of Literature and Philosophy, to interpret their mysteries to the common man' (*Essays II*, 7). The themes of harmonious vision and earthly struggle are presented in a more sanguine manner than in the Werner essay. Largely based on Ludwig Tieck's account of Novalis, (some of it unacknowledged)[20] the poet is not found lacking in transcendental substance; his poems are 'breathings of a high devout soul' (ibid., 29). Critical maxims concerning Infinitude are part of the character delineation. Here a chosen man is found with unique powers of abstract meditation, a poet as well as a philosopher to whom 'Nature is no longer dead, hostile matter, but the veil and mysterious Garment of the Unseen' (ibid.). The religious note is of primary importance in the interpretation of Novalis's poetry, which is enigmatic but thought-provoking in its presentation of eternal verities.

The prefaces to *German Romance* reveal the same critical ingredients, not treated at that length but quite as diversified. Carlyle's characterization of Tieck answers most fully the problem of initial failure to respond to the quest and simultaneously of victory over doubt and despair. Much is made of 'the image of a high passionate mind interrogating Fate, and receiving no answer, but the echo of his own questions reverberated from the dead walls of its vast and lone imprisonment' (*German Romance I*, 257). Tieck does not, however, find a permanent abode on the stage of naked despair, but seeks a way out of this spiritual confinement into a more harmonious spiritual existence. What follows stands out among the rest of the *German Romance* biographies as a miniature *Sartor Resartus*, a forerunner of Teufelsdröckh's wrestlings with the same problems: 'He had begun to see that there were things to be believed, as well as things to be denied; things to be loved and forwarded, as well as things to be hated and trodden under foot. The active and positive of Goodness was displacing the barren and tormenting negative; and worthy feelings were now to be translated into their only proper language, worthy actions' (ibid., 258). Inner harmony has finally been achieved on moral grounds.

As a counterpart to this victorious struggle for perfection, E.T.A.

Hoffmann, with whom Carlyle was decidedly out of tune, appears as a character who never attained perfection, in spite of elements of moral worth. This writer of some of the finest Romantic novels and tales 'unhappily had found no sure principle of action; no Truth adequate to the guidance of such a mind ... his wayward spirit was without fit direction or restraint, and its fine faculties rioted in wild disorder' (*German Romance II*, 17). In this inability he falls into the same category as Werner for Carlyle.

Although Carlyle primarily adopts Friedrich Schlegel's critical approach in the German essays, he carries remnants of it into his evaluation of the English poets, such as Burns, Johnson, and Sir Walter Scott. Thus, in 'Burns,' the reader is being reassured that 'true and genial as his poetry must appear, it is not chiefly as a poet, but as a man, that he interests and affects us' (*Essays I*, 264). In connection with biographical facts, a variant of the question posed in the Essay on Goethe is being asked: 'How did the word and man's life, from his particular position, represent themselves to his mind?' (ibid., 261). Carlyle comes to the conclusion that, in spite of Burns's lasting impact on the literature of Scotland, all that remains of him are 'brief and broken glimpses of a genius that could never show itself complete' (ibid., 266). Not unlike Werner and Hoffmann, Burns too wasted himself 'in a hopeless struggle with base entanglements' (ibid., 264).

In 'Boswell's Life of Johnson,' the prophet of truth ranks above the man of letters, an evaluation that strangely runs parallel with Friedrich Schlegel's pronouncement that Lessing the man was worth more than all his talents. Johnson is 'a noble man, resolute for the truth, to whom Shams and Lies were once for all an abomination' (*Essays III*, 109). He struggles successfully to gain his beliefs and endures with heroic faith: 'But in his sorrows and isolation, when hope died away, and only a long vista of suffering and toil lay before him to the end, then first did Religion shine forth in its meek, everlasting clearness' (ibid., 111). As a bonus Carlyle adds a perfectly precise definition of Schlegelian criticism: 'Critics insist much on the Poet that he should communicate an "Infinitude" to his delineation; that by intensity of conception, by the gift of "transcendental Thought", which is fitly named *genius*, and inspiration, he should *inform* the Finite with a certain Infinitude of significance; or as they sometimes say, ennoble the Actual into Idealness. They are right in their precept' (ibid., 78).

How far these German Romantic standards are still part of Carlyle's critical tools manifests itself once more in 'Sir Walter Scott.' He expresses the stern conviction that Scott did not live up to spiritual notions

Carlyle demanded as a prerequisite for great literature. He growls that Sir Walter missed the boat destined for transcendental waters, and for this reason he does not even undertake to judge the author's work as an expression of the man. As far as poet as prophet is concerned, Carlyle is bothered by the absence of spirituality: 'The great Mystery of existence was not great to him' (*Essays IV*, 36). For those readers who cannot follow these veiled allusions, he adds: 'A great man is ever, as the Transcendentalists speak, possessed with an idea' (ibid., 23). Where Werner failed but struggled, Scott did not even try. That this way of life was not wise is the *facit* Carlyle derives from an *un*-spiritual biography.

Regarded in this light Scott's work is negligible, as it is neither the outcome of a search for inner values nor the expression of an ideal. Carlyle nowhere asks himself whether it is fair to apply this yardstick of supernatural worthiness to Walter Scott. In this he does not live up to the praise-worthy critical maxim set down in his preface to the *Wilhelm Meister* translation, insisting 'that the work be not condemned for wanting what it was not meant to have' (*Wilhelm Meister I*, 10). No attempt is made to expose the antiquarian spirit as a key to Scott's novels. Carlyle chooses to see external trappings only: 'Buff-belts and all manner of jerkins and costumes are transitory; man alone is perennial' (*Essays IV*, 77). This pronouncement fitted his own Philosophy of Clothes admirably, but how true a judgment of Scott's work is it? Where there is no prophet, no teacher, no revealer of the 'Divine Idea' in sight, Carlyle turns a cold shoulder in bitter disappointment. In this negative application of German critical concepts, the limitations of his biographical method are all too evident.

From the above comparison of Friedrich Schlegel's with Carlyle's critical approach, the following similarities evolve:

1 the transcendental relationship is stressed, by both authors, as an important overall aspect in the work under review; that is, the impact of religious and philosophical thought is viewed as a significant critical tenet;
2 the literary work is an expression of the whole man, who must accordingly be evaluated as a personality including his moral impact;
3 a dominant trait is singled out as a standard against which the poet is measured. In the case of Schlegel this trait is the desire to achieve harmony. Carlyle links the quest for harmony more directly to mental struggle, oftentimes bringing about the transition from doubt to faith, which he tries to trace in all writers.

It is apparent that Friedrich Schlegel's critical theory, as developed in his 'Ideen,' and its practical application to specific poets, in the *Charakteristiken*, constitute the most significant influence Carlyle received from this source.

There are other peripheral points of contact where Schlegel acted as a mediator in a more general sense on Carlyle the literary historian. The following Friedrich Schlegel statement on Hume confirms the fact that Carlyle knew the *Geschichte der alten und neuen Literatur*:[21]

F. Schlegel	*Carlyle*
Because since Hume nothing more has happened than to ward off by way of various fortifications the harmful practical influence of this sceptical way of thinking, and by various supports and make-shift aids to prop up and preserve the edifice of all necessary moral conviction. (*Geschichte*, 342)	British philosophy, since the time of Hume, appears to them nothing more than a 'laborious and unsuccessful striving to build dike after dike in front of our Churches and Judgement-halls, and so turn back from them the deluge of Scepticism, with which that extraordinary writer overflowed us, and still threatens to destroy whatever we value most.' (*Essays I*, 'State of German Literature,' 80)

The passage in Schlegel's and Carlyle's versions shows how the latter gains in emphasis what he loses in literal accuracy – a typical feature of his translations at their best.

In the *Geschichte* Friedrich Schlegel successfully presented a new Romantic history of literature. Based on a series of lectures delivered in Vienna (1812) it was hailed as having broken new ground by setting before the reader's mind a truly comprehensive review of literature, old and new. Enlightening, but not tediously so, it served the needs of the educated reading public. Schlegel visualized literature as a dynamic ever-changing whole, surveyed with historical perspective. He insists, as Herder had done before, the central ideas are reflected in literary productions through the ages; for great works of art, however unique in themselves, nevertheless have a certain place in history. Therefore literature must be examined in the light of its becoming. A comprehensive painting (*Gemälde*) of the literary culture of Europe, including Greece and Rome, was here, for the first time, attempted and partly achieved. Philosophical thought is tied in with poetry because both philosophers and poets reflect the essence of the intellectual life of a nation, including memories that reach back to its dim origins. As a typically Romantic tendency, Schlegel added ethical and religious evaluations: if the poet was indeed a spokesman of God, and literature a manifestation of the Infinite in the Finite, such perspectives would also manifest themselves in its historical development. These assumptions endeared the book to Carlyle.

Carlyle not only shared these general notions but partly reiterated them in his own lecture series (in 1838), posthumously published as *Lectures on the History of Literature* (1892) where the selection of material is influenced by Schlegel's work. The same holds good for his *Unfinished History of German Literature* (1830) in which Carlyle skirts around Schlegel, especially in the introduction as well as in the lengthy footnotes. Both are peripheral works that can be related to general, not specific influences. They are therefore not included in this investigation, especially as valuable scholarly insights have already been published – by R. Wellek (*Confrontations*) and Hill Shine (*Carlyle's Unfinished History of German Literature*) – in this less important field.

Franz Horn's Critical Function

Scholarship is indebted to W. Leopold for first having drawn attention to the not altogether negligible influence of the Romantic critic and novelist Franz Horn on Carlyle.[22] Carlyle used Horn's history of literature *Die Poesie und Beredsamkeit der Deutschen* (3 vols., 1822–4), as well as the *Umrisse zur Geschichte und Kritik der schönen Literatur Deutschlands* (1819) for the prefaces to *German Romance* (1826–7) and his essay 'State of German Literature' (1827), which purports to review the above works.[23] According to Leopold's findings, Carlyle not only extracted facts from Horn, but also made brief verbal borrowings including those related to the garment metaphor and the blessing of half-sleep, as well as the phrase for the 'Everlasting No' and the 'Everlasting Yea' ('das ewige Nein und das ewige Ja') so effectively employed in *Sartor*. Furthermore, Leopold points out the general similarity of Horn's and Carlyle's outlook and idealistic concept of literature, but rejects the possibility of Carlyle's having received any ideas from Horn.

Was Horn more than the author of a literary handbook for Carlyle, and which of Horn's several other works did he read? The fact that Carlyle reviewed some of Horn's books does not rule out the possibility of his having read others at a later or earlier date. This possibility is certainly substantiated by his use of Horn's early *Geschichte und Kritik der deutschen Poesie und Beredsamkeit* (1805), so far overlooked by scholars,[24] and may also hold true for the fourth volume of *Die Poesie und Beredsamkeit der Deutschen*, published in 1829, several years prior to *Sartor*.

Carlyle's comments on Horn are far less censorious than Leopold leads his readers to believe; he was never known to be particularly charitable as a reviewer, but he was basically not unfair. Horn was one of the guild of upcoming *literati* who possessed the gift of presenting literature in a conversational mood, creating a fireside atmosphere we also find in the familiar essays by the English Romantics Lamb and Hazlitt. Carlyle praises him for his candour and tolerance, and remarks appreciatively that Horn adopted the best ideas of his contemporaries. He rebukes Taylor (*Essays II*, 'Historic Survey of German Poetry,' 350) for having left this source untapped, and praises Horn's account of Goethe's and Schiller's *Xenienkämpfe* in a footnote to the revised edition of his *Life of Schiller* (1845, 107), incorrectly giving *Die Poesie und Beredsamkeit* as the reference instead of *Umrisse* (ibid., 74). He furthermore mentions him in his *Notebooks* (120), which also contain Horn's selections from the poets Logau and Brant (ibid., 118), together with Carlyle's own translations. What he objects to is Horn's rather affected but readable style, his too zealous advocation of Christianity, and his habit of 'talking too often about representing the infinite in the finite' (*Essays I*, 'State of German Literature,' 27), obviously unaware of his own abundant use of Friedrich Schlegel's term. Compared with the 'almost frightful laboriousness' of literary historians like Bouterwek and Eichhorn, he describes Franz Horn as a 'valuable guide' (*German Romance II*, 128 fn.; *Essays I*, ibid., 26).

The form this guidance takes ranges from reading suggestions and judgments on writers to verbal borrowings that Carlyle incorporated into his own work – by no means acknowledging them all.[25] Among the suggested readings are some that Carlyle might have found in other literary aids he used,[26] but some specific recommendations are Horn's alone. He praises the *Charakteristiken* without reservation as the best among contemporary works of criticism, and dwells on Friedrich Schlegel's mental struggles in a remarkable manner: '– Looking around in all directions – Aesthetic cosmopolitanism – Pause – Rooting in his own Self – Rebirth – Serious deep Catholicism – [which is followed by] A pure concept of God and Christ.'[27]

Horn writes warmly on Goethe's *Faust* and *Wilhelm Meister*, both usually classed very deliberately by critics as works of his old age, and makes a point of defending Wilhelm's passive character as suitable for conveying his impressions and opinions (*Umrisse*, 227). As far as his favourite, Jean Paul, is concerned, he recommends the *Auswahl aus des Teufels Papieren*, *Hesperus*, and *Siebenkäs* from among his novels, and *Fixlein* and *Schmelzle* as humorous shorter pieces, besides dwelling on his autobiography, *Wahrheit aus Jean Pauls Leben*. Horn also devotes considerable space to the discussion of Tieck's 'Der Gelehrte' and *Peter Lebrecht*, part of which Carlyle used for his preface on Tieck (*German Romance I*, 257). Hauff's *Memoiren des Satan* is mentioned as an example of a youthful satirical talent.

Several lesser-known works of previous periods of German literature, especially of the sixteenth and seventeenth centuries, with which Carlyle shows familiarity, he may have read because of Horn's recommendations, such as Luther's pamphlet 'Wider Hans Wurst,' in which the word 'Teufelsdreck' appears, and the cobbler-poet Hans Sachs's Shrovetide plays *Das Narrenschneiden* and *Der Schneider mit dem Panier*, both relatively unknown *Schwänke* for which Horn shows a predilection.

Not infrequently Carlyle shares Horn's critical opinions on writers. Both show great admiration for Fichte, with Horn providing occasional comments on the 'Divine Idea' in a watered-down version (*Umrisse*, 53). Horn describes Goethe as a renunciant, in which connection he speaks of *Selbstüberwindung* in order that a higher form of Self may emerge through life in God (*Poesie*, IV, 130).

There are negative judgments as well. Horn belittles the Austrian playwright Franz Grillparzer, ridiculing his drama *Die Ahnfrau* (*Umrisse*, 278), a critique Carlyle paraphrases closely in 'German Playwrights' (*Essays I*, 364). Zacharias Werner does not fare much better, as he 'replaces undesirable Rationalism (*Aufklärung*) with undesirable Mysticism' (*Umrisse*, 186), thus spoiling a basically appealing message. Remarkable are his judgments on Sir Walter Scott and Byron, neither of whom find favour in Horn's eyes. While there is no idea or artistic depth to be found in the novels of the former, the latter suffers from an excessive personality cult in his drama *Manfred*.

Horn is also aware of the entertaining factor in presenting literary material – a rare manifestation among scholars of his time. He frankly tells his readers (*Poesie und Beredsamkeit*, IV, Introduction) that he serves up a mixture of seriousness and humour, but that he nevertheless attempts to convey unity of sentiment and judgment. He includes paragraphs on 'writing as an action,' discussions of journals and their intrinsic value, 'biography in creative writing,' 'literary fashions,' and the shallowness of the dandiacal novel. Such topics, partly treated with humour, may have acted as a stimulus to Carlyle's thought, if only by way of explanation and elaboration.

In 'State of German Literature' Carlyle uses Horn's approach to open up the theme of German literature and its values. The question of whether a German could be a *bel esprit* is also asked by Horn for the same purpose. This parallel is all the more amusing as Carlyle summarily dismisses Horn, declaring that 'our chief business ... is not with Franz Horn or his book' (*Essays I*, 28):

Horn	*Carlyle*
A certain Father Bouhours ... had a dialogue printed in which the question 'if a German could be a *bel esprit*' was propounded and ... answered negatively.[28] (*Poesie*, II, 105)	The Père Bouhours propounded to himself the pregnant question: *Si un Allemand peut avoir de l'esprit?* ... to decide, negatively, that a German could *not* have any literary talent. ('State of German Literature,' 28–9)

Carlyle was evidently so intrigued by this pronouncement that he used it twice more, without once acknowledging its source.[29]

This is not the only case in which Carlyle refuses to give Horn due recognition. Besides the three acknowledged quotes, on Richter (*German Romance II*, 128), Lessing, and Erasmus (*Essays I* 'State of German Literature,' 48, 28), as well as a fourth, so far overlooked,[30] the samples below constitute borrowings that amount to plagiarism by modern standards of scholarship:

Horn	*Carlyle*
Rightly Friedrich Richter therefore called this poet [Fouqué] in the famous review of this work (in the *Heidelberger Jahrbücher*), the *Tapfere* and this has ever been confirmed later, that this virtue lay at the core of his poetry. (*Umrisse*, 175)[31]	... had the honour to be criticised in the *Heidelberger Jahrbücher*, by no meaner a person than Jean Paul Friedrich Richter, who bestowed on the poet the surname of *Der Tapfere*, or *The Valiant*, an allusion to the quality which seemed to be the soul of his own character, and of the characters which he portrayed. (*German Romance I*, 210)

Whether we agree with the principles of the *Wissenschaftslehre* or not, every literary historian must not only acknowledge Fichte's great philosophical merit, but must see in him one of the first heroes of the new era. (*Umrisse*, 54)[32]	Fichte's opinions may be true or false; but his character as a thinker can be slightly valued only by such as know him ill; and as a man approved by action and suffering ... he ranks with a class of men who were common only in better ages than ours. (*Essays I*, 'State of German Literature,' 77)

In his essay 'German Playwrights' Carlyle adopts Horn's satirical observations on Grillparzer's *Ahnfrau*:

Horn	*Carlyle*
A being clad in ghostly apparel, she awakens the poor old Count Borotin ... in the evening with senseless cruelty, just when he is about to take his nap. (*Umrisse*, 278)[33]	She is seen with other ghost-appurtenances ... to the terror of old Count Borotin ... whose afternoon nap she, on one occasion, cruelly disturbs. (*Essays I*, 'German Playwrights,' 364)

While in the following passage Horn speaks of Tieck's novel *Abdallah* only, Carlyle applies this criticism to all of his novels:

Horn	*Carlyle*
Immature in most parts, it reveals throughout a tragic mood, ... in which several gloomy 'questions addressed to Fate' are brought up. (*Umrisse*, 105)[34]	Still regarded as immature products of his genius ... A gloomy tragic spirit is said to reign throughout all of them ... in wrapt earnestness 'interrogating Fate.' (*German Romance I*, 257)

The statements below give at least a hint that the phrasing and content are not Carlyle's own. The first pertains to Tieck's play *Blaubart*, the other to his novel *Franz Sternbald*:

Horn	*Carlyle*
Tieck presents here on a gay ground highly tragic characters. (*Umrisse*, 110)[35]	... 'a group of earnest figures, painted on a laughing ground.' (*German Romance I*, 265)

Here and there a voice might be heard that it was permissible to arraign this novel beside *Wilhelm Meister* ... However, the calm clarity of Goethe's style is nowhere achieved, but merely imitated with visible laboriousness. (ibid., 115–16)[36]	As a critic tells us, 'here and there a low voice might be even heard, voting that this novel equalled *Wilhelm Meister*; the peaceful clearness of which it, however, nowise attained, but only with visible effort, strove to imitate.' (ibid., 262)

In light of these passages it appears that Leopold's view, expressed in *Religiöse Wurzel* (68), that Carlyle verified every quote he used from his German sources is untenable.

The most significant passages in Horn's literary handbooks pertain to his use of 'das ewige Nein und das ewige Ja,' terms we encounter in Book II of *Sartor* as 'the Everlasting No' and 'the Everlasting Yea.'[37] Leopold found three examples of this phrase, one in the *Umrisse*, two more in the *Poesie* (volumes 2 and 3) (see *Religiöse Wurzel*, 55–6). They should, however, be considered in context to clarify their meaning more fully.

The first passage, from the *Umrisse* (198), mentions both phrases in connection with August Apel's novella *Der Freischütz*, used by Karl Maria von Weber as the basis of his Romantic opera of the same title. Horn feels that not every writer can make supernatural forces, such as the devil, come alive in fiction: 'The father of lies is not easy to portray, and he who does not carry the eternal Yes in his heart should carefully avoid the presentation of the eternal No.'[38] The second passage occurs in his discussion of the poet Johann Christian Günther, who, according to Horn, cannot experience the eternal Yes because of his inborn cynicism, which prevents him from adding the perception of supernatural vistas to his talent: 'Only he who bears the eternal Yes in his breast can conceive and visualize the negating spirit (compare Goethe's Faust), and only he who is capable of the most profound philosophical and pure religious seriousness can express true humour and serene wit.'[39] The third passage relates to the eternal Yes only, in regard to Klopstock's insufficient command of those sublime powers that should be part of the poet's insight into divine manifestations in this world: 'But he does not always find that complete sense of contentment, that eternal and blessed Yes.'[40] In his elaboration of this point Horn insists that, because of this inability, the character of Satan in the *Messias* is a failure, as the negative principle can be rendered only if the positive one is understood.

In addition to these three passages, a remarkable paragraph dealing with the notion of the devil appears in *Poesie* (vol. 4) that apparently escaped Leopold's notice when perusing it (*Religiöse Wurzel*, 67). Its significance lies in the description of the 'ewige Nein' as a spiritual state of being, a concept that matches Carlyle's. Under the heading 'Harmless reflections on the devil and how poets treat him,' Horn offers the following observations, linking them to the fact that, in German literature, the devil is always rendered as basically stupid:

> ... ignorant in the profoundest sense of the word he necessarily *had* to become, because the eternal No in which he reigns, stands in the most obvious contrast to all wisdom. I deliberately use the general vague phrase, 'reigns,' because a precise word like 'is' or 'lives' is totally unsuitable for him ... this would necessitate a Creative Yes in the opposition to which he alone can exist. On account of this continuous battling, he reveals a *Scheinleben* which, for him who does not carry the Eternal Blessed Yes in his own breast, appears from afar as the semblance of true life. The Devil not only fights this Yes in God and Man, but contends for his own No, as if it were the only wisdom.[41]

It becomes apparent from the context of the fourth passage that 'das ewige Nein' and 'das ewige Ja' are mental states of being, the one crushing, the other elevating man's spiritual existence. A continuous battle is being waged by the 'No state,' represented by the devil, against the 'creative Yes,' which lives in God and – by way of the Divine Idea, one could imagine – in man. This presentation matches Carlyle's rendering in *Sartor*. Teufelsdröckh too is assailed by the state of the 'Everlasting No' against which man, aware of his divine origin, voices a solemn declaration of defiance: 'Thus had the EVERLASTING NO (*das ewige Nein*) pealed authoritatively through all the recesses of my Being, of my ME; and then was it that my whole ME stood up, in native God-created majesty, and with emphasis recorded its Protest' (*Sartor*, 167).

Whatever our judgment on the effectiveness of Horn's formulation may be, it can hardly be shrugged off as inessential.

Part One

FICTIONAL TECHNIQUES AND DEVICES IN GERMAN SOURCES

(Sartor Resartus)

> 'I never cease to thank Heaven for such men as Richter, Schiller, Goethe. The latter especially was my evangelist.'
>
> Carlyle

TWO

Eccentric Originals and Their Editors

> For the commerce in material things has paved roads for commerce in things spiritual, and a true thought, or a noble creation, passes lightly to us from the remotest countries, provided only our minds be open to receive it.
>
> (Carlyle, 'State of German Literature')

Early German Originals

Eccentric originals date back to the pre-Romantic era when, under the all-pervading influence of Laurence Sterne's *Life and Opinions of Tristram Shandy* (1760), they became increasingly popular in eighteenth-century German fiction. Such personalities, called *Sonderlinge*, were at first conceived in the rationalistic tradition of the *Aufklärung*, and developed along the lines of the *Tristram Shandy* hobby-horse model. They frequently manifested their odd bent and whimsical humour by presenting opinions and tastes that deviated from the norm of humanity, resulting in voluntary isolation from an alien social environment. More often than not, they were of the scholarly type tinted with religious dissent or, better, an individualized application of Christian principles.

We meet with just such a product of the Age of Reason in Friedrich Nicolai's novel *Leben und Meinungen des Herrn Magister Sebaldus Nothanker* (1773–6). The title already indicates the model, transplanted into a German milieu. In keeping with Sterne's method, Magister Nothanker's personality is predominantly determined by a single characteristic: for him the world consists in speculative thought. Modest, sober, and sombre, he cherishes his own ideas above everything else, and does not change them to please anybody. Otherwise he bears the way of the world with humorous stoicism. The objective correlative to this attitude is his scholarly work on the biblical Apocalypse, which he tries in vain to get published. Nicolai's didactic intent is to present the only sane human being in a world of perverted values. Well aware that the times are topsy-turvy, he nevertheless does not give up his obstinate search for truth, living up to his name of 'Nothanker,' an anchor, or a kind of life-buoy, for those in need. In this perseverance he slightly resembles Teufelsdröckh, although he is by no means a Romantic personality.

Another enlightened version of Sterne's characterization is found in Theodor Hippel's *Lebensläufe nach aufsteigender Linie* (1778–81), where a further step is taken in the direction of emotional enfranchisement in the outgoing personality of a parson, a fiery and militant spirit. In spite of his scholarly habits, he despises intellectual snobbery and looks to Nature as the true university of man. The stress on action is very pronounced in this unusual member of the Protestant clergy, who insists that activity must be the end result of knowledge. Although no proof exists that Carlyle read these two novels, they are indicative of the didactic type of Sterne imitations in German literature, prior to Jean Paul's presentation of the same.[1]

Without Sterne, it must be stated, there would be no Jean Paulian humour, but it is only fair to add that the latter's characters are not mere stereotypes of those of his great model, whose *Tristram Shandy* he admits to having read more than forty times in his youth. The questions arise whether Carlyle could not have derived the personality of Teufelsdröckh directly from Sterne or if there are aspects of this character that Sterne alone could not have supplied? The answer may be found in the following observations.

Sterne, while introducing his unique mixture of sentiment and subjective humour into literature, is given to characterization from the outside. His method of heaping trait upon trait – in keeping with associationalist psychology – results in external character peculiarities that reveal themselves in behaviour. For our purposes, two types emerge, each equipped with a different set of hobby-horse relationships, which take on the form of a ridiculous ruling passion.

Shandy Senior is a theorizer of the truest water, subtle reasoning being his only approach to any given problem. This single-mindedness makes him not only a pedant but also a rational fanatic, a frame of mind that hardly can be said to mirror Teufelsdröckh's mental make-up. One might recall the episode, for example, when Tristram is wounded by a window-pane in a precarious spot. Mr Shandy, instead of applying an ointment, thumbs through a work on circumcision, finding comfort in its contents. It is impossible to think of Teufelsdröckh reacting in this manner under similar circumstances.

Uncle Toby, in contrast, belongs to the family of idyllic personalities that Jean Paul found so attractive. He remains the eternal child, unable to detect other people's shrewdness and insincerity. The 'angelic side' of Teufelsdröckh may show a remote affinity, but lack of knowledge of evil is not one of his characteristics.

In these representative types it seems hardly possible to recognize an obvious similarity with Carlyle's German savant. To add further dimensions to the humorous character was Jean Paul's achievement, who was also the first among his contemporaries to explore the nature of humour theoretically.

Jean Paul's Theory of Humour

Jean Paul's pronouncements on the humorous character are laid down in his *Vorschule der Ästhetik*, a work that Carlyle praised and frequently quoted.[2] In comparing him with other humorists, he finds Jean Paul superior to all: 'There is none that in depth, copiousness and intensity of humour can be compared with Jean Paul' (*Essays I*, 'Jean Paul Friedrich Richter,' 18). He gives a definition of this humour that indicates a vast range of humorous associations with the world, its creatures, and indeed, the universe at large: 'The essence of humour is sensibility; warm, tender fellow-feeling with all forms of existence' (ibid., 16), mentions its 'inverse sublimity' (ibid., 17), and lastly adds the following penetrative observation: 'It may be extravagant and even absurd: but still on the whole, the core and life of it are genuine, subtle, spiritual' (ibid., 18). He clearly perceives that Jean Paul's uniqueness consists in giving his humour a metaphysical turn. All these dimensions, including the spiritual element, Carlyle will include in the humorous chiaroscuro of his own Teufelsdröckh.

Before I elaborate a few highlights that might have had a bearing on an author in search of a character, Jean Paul's concept of literature must be briefly stated. Of crucial importance is his demand that the poet should relate life on earth to transcendental reality. The poet must turn to the divine flower-clock, instead to the iron wheels and cogs of the historical and secular clock (*Ästhetik*, V, 39). If the flower-clock represents eternal time, it follows that the writer must relate his work to infinity. It will not do, Jean Paul insists, to see in the universe nothing but man's market-place and, in the history of eternity, merely a town chronicle. In keeping with this approach, he demands that the writer place the sense of wonder directly into the soul of the character.

All of Jean Paul's characters possess this sense of wonder to a high degree. It is, indeed, the prerequisite for the high-minded man (*der hohe Mensch*), who can rise above the earth and trivial matters in contemplation of God. Whether this is done within the humorous-idyllic framework of a Wuz or a Fixlein, or with dualistic implications, as in Siebenkäs or Schoppe, depends on the set of circumstances in which these characters find themselves. A general guide, regarding three ways of life, resulting in three different personalities, Jean Paul provides in his preface to *Quintus Fixlein*:

> The first, rather an elevated road, is this: To soar away so far above the clouds of life, that you see the whole external world, with its wolf-dens, charnel-houses and thunder-rods, lying far down beneath you, shrunk into a little child's garden. The second is: Simply to sink down into this little garden; and there to nestle yourself so snugly, so homewise, in some furrow, that in looking out from your warm lark-nest, you likewise can discern no wolf-dens, charnel-houses or thunder-rods, but only blades and ears, every one of which, for the nest-bird is a tree, and a sun-screen and a rain-screen. The third, finally, which I look upon as the hardest and cunningest, is that of alternating between the other two. (*German Romance II*, 193–4)[3]

Jean Paul generally prefers the third way, 'the hardest and the cunningest,' for his own originals. For, in this alternating pattern of life, vacillating between reality and eternity, humorous elements are best brought out by way of contrast. Humour, enhancing the transcendental message, is symbolized by the gold ring: 'Humour is the ring of gold which is being worn in order to prevent the diamond ring from slipping off unnoticed' (*Ästhetik*, V, 21).[4] There are further detailed suggestions as to how the humorous-real and the sublime must be juxtaposed to be effective. The hero must, above all, be in a deeper sense symbolic of man, a simultaneous representation of Adam in his unfallen and fallen state. Part of the method used to create this 'symbolical individuality' is individualization by personal traits, down to the slightest details (ibid., 221).

In this connection Jean Paul remarks on the significance of names, humorous or otherwise, as an aid in characterization: 'Printed names are ... an indelible characteristic of every person' (ibid., 474).[5] They are important in establishing 'the devilish or angelic character ... in a way as only constellations of the zodiac can, such as Virgo, Leo, Scorpio, and Aquarius' (ibid., 475).[6]

He also suggests choosing a middle-aged man for a hero, one 'who lives in the far horizon mist of the past, where the heavens and the earth have merged one into another' (ibid., 233). This metaphor refers undoubtedly to a mixture of natural and supernatural experiences in such a man's life. His symbolical individuality should not be presented as extant from the cradle but should come forth in a grown man. Only later, he feels, should a few relics of childhood lore be added, significant not in themselves, but as expressive of the person the reader has now got to know. Brushing aside plot as unimportant, Jean Paul places emphasis on the character himself and the revelation of his soul. He is also aware of the importance of speech for purposes of characterization. Most effective are the seemingly serious tongue-in-cheek pronouncements.

Such partly general, partly specific comments would have been of interest to one himself in the birth throes of character creation. As Jean Paul demands, every utterance of Teufelsdröckh is timed by the 'eternal flower-clock' and linked to the faculty of perceiving the wonderful, most effectively stated in his disgust for machinery as wonder-destroying. Furthermore, Teufelsdröckh not only fits into Jean Paul's scheme of the alternating type of personality but may be considered a paradigm of the relationship between the natural and the supernatural. In him the sublime and the humorous-idyllic enter into a unique fusion. Finite aspects of life are presented in the Weissnichtwo setting, infinity in the watch-tower musings, where Teufelsdröckh contemplates 'this riddle of existence' and 'could clasp the whole Universe into his bosom' (*Sartor*, 32).

This humorous juxtaposition is not only applied to Teufelsdröckh's natural-supernaturalism but also developed regarding aspects of his work on clothes, made up of 'boundless, almost formless contents, a very Sea of Thought; neither calm nor clear, if you will; yet wherein the toughest pearl-diver may dive to his utmost depth, and return not only with sea-wreck but with true orients' (ibid., 10).

Teufelsdröckh is also a 'symbolical individuality,' as Jean Paul terms it. His mysterious parentage underscores the symbolism, as does his name, very pertinent to Jean Paul's 'angelic-devilish' suggestions: 'Gleams of an ethereal love burst forth from him,' but also 'a bitter sardonic humour ... that you look on him almost with a shudder, as on some incarnate Mephistopheles' (ibid., 32). As to his eyes, 'those lights that sparkle in it, may indeed be reflexes of the heavenly Stars, but perhaps also glances from the region of Nether Fire!' (ibid.).

Jean Paul remarks that, while the English have a strange preference for the hangman, the Germans are attached to the devil. Carlyle even incorporates the devil into his eccentric character's name. Much scholarly speculation has surrounded the name 'Diogenes Teufelsdröckh,' and the most awkward derivations have been suggested. Diogenes the Cynic, living in his tub, abstaining from the pleasures of the world, had been popular in German literature since the Renaissance. Ridiculing him as a philosopher who lives by his theory, esteeming him as an honest seeker for truth, Jean Paul refers to him more than thirty times in his works, with regard either to the Cynic's tub or to the lantern with which he sets out in broad daylight in search of an honest man. In this sense Jarno in *Wilhelm Meisters Wanderjahre* calls Wilhelm a second Diogenes in danger of letting his lamp go out in daylight.[7] It seems senseless to dissect the name further, beyond the slight suggestion contained in the chapter 'Genesis' in which the bearer of the name asks himself if it is to be thought of as foreshadowing his destiny (*Sartor*, 86). Teufelsdröckh may here simply be thinking of the search for philosophical truth, or he may have the 'God-born' meaning in mind. It is unlikely that Carlyle derived his initial knowledge of Diogenes from German sources as the story told by Laertius in *Lives of the Philosophers* was known to him (ibid., 255).

'Teufelsdröckh' has, of course, never been used as a surname in German, as Diogenes himself knows, having in vain searched all name catalogues and militia-rolls – the source in which Jean Paul found most of his humorous and eccentric names. In its 'dreck' form, which Carlyle used first (the 'dröckh' change being an afterthought), it designated an antispasmodic medicinal remedy, the Latin name of which is *asafoetida*, also used as an aphrodisiac. Carlyle may have come across it in Luther[8] and Goethe,[9] but mainly in Jean Paul, who uses it not once, as G.B. Tennyson reports, but seven times.[10] The usage Carlyle probably had in mind is given in *Schmelzles Reise*, where Schmelzle mentions a *Teufelsferment*, translated by Carlyle as 'Devil's Ferment,' so powerful that it could blow up the whole world. This thought bothers Schmelzle, who complains that this notion is forever 'fermenting in his head' (*German Romance II*, 191). Carlyle connects it with Jean Paul's many references to fermenting, i.e., *Gärung*, a word he introduces into *Sartor* particularly with regard to the activity of the Time-spirit: 'Oh, under that hideous coverlet of vapours, and putrefactions, and unimaginable gases, what a Fermenting-vat lies simmering and hid!' (*Sartor*, 22). *Teufelsdreck* is for Carlyle an agent, in the nature of yeast that makes the bread rise. Man is to be roused from comfortable slumbers, to hear the message contained in the clothes philosophy.

The change to Teufels*dröckh* was possibly an abortive attempt to make the name sound more 'altdeutsch' or 'Lutherdeutsch,' where Carlyle had read 'schröcklich' instead of modern German 'schrecklich,' and on the basis of this analogy changed 'dreck' into 'dröckh.' The last mystery to be solved consists in the added 'h' at the end of this name. Jean Paul, in the *Das Leben Fibels, Die Unsichtbare Loge*, and *Siebenkäs*, refers several times to a scholar by the name of Joh. Matth. Schröckh (1733–1808), the author of *Universal World History*. It seems quite likely that there is a connection between 'dröckh' and 'Schröckh.'[11]

E.T.A. Hoffmann also refers to *asafoetida*, but throughout by its Latin name. It stands for a flavour of devilish witticism that results in a certain tastiness and spiciness in literature.

Although Teufelsdröckh is hardly a man one would expect to meet in the street, he is nevertheless brought down to earth by several highly individualized traits, as Jean Paul demands. Details of his evenings spent in the 'Grüne Gans' come to mind, the devotion he receives from such different personalities as Lieschen and Hofrath Heuschrecke, and his inimitable laugh in the company of his poetical friend Jean Paul in person. Further in keeping with suggestions contained in the *Ästhetik* is the autobiographical account, rendered by a middle-aged man who embellishes it with his own reflections. Above all, the transcendental message is tempered with humour as part of the personality of the scholarly prophet who pronounces it. Were we to take it straight without the dash of the ridiculous, it would not be half as effective.

Besides the theoretical discussions on the original character in Jean Paul's *Ästhetik*, its presentation in his works confirms the theory of juxtaposition. In such personalities as Wuz, Fixlein, and Fibel, reality is adorned and transformed by the infinity of the imagination. In this frame of mind schoolmaster Wuz considers his humble closet as 'cut out or built into the immense dome of the universe ... so warm, so snug, so well' (*Unsichtbare Loge*, I, 424–5).[12] Fixlein, the poor teacher at a *Gymnasium*, can travel with ease back into his childhood the moment he opens his toy-chest. It is this unbroken continuity with the 'Golden Age' that finally saves his life, threatened by superstition in a moment of crisis. Fibel, another quiet individual, spends the last years of his life in a setting of comfortable seclusion in a wood among birds and squirrels to whom he plays on his organ: 'And in the morning and at nightfall, beginning and end, the colourful portals of Time and Eternity stood open facing each other' (*Leben Fibels*, VI, 546).[13] All these idyllic personalities can, at any time, in a playful mood alternate between the two levels of their existence, the natural and the supernatural.

But there are others. Armenadvokat Siebenkäs, whose name gives the novel its title, is an eccentric personality lacking the mental simplicity of the purely idyllic originals. He can therefore reflect on his own position in the form of dualistic humour, centring on the gap between idealization and reality. The world of reality acts as a disturbing factor in the development of his faculties. The milieu of the *Kleinstadt* is no longer idyllic. Poverty and debt are constant companions, as is a wife ill-suited to his needs. But Siebenkäs manages to rise above this level, securing for himself an amount of freedom from accident in a philosophical sense: 'Nothing evokes more humour ... than to coat one's inside with philosophy, similar to a Diogenes tub, against all external damage'[14] (*Siebenkäs*, II, 216–17). Investigating man's notions of happiness rather more closely, he finds them pettish, and also realizes that in order to preserve inner freedom it must constantly be rediscovered in a world in which man is imprisoned by circumstances.

Siebenkäs's relationship to Nature is important as it affects his ability to recover from his day-to-day problems. Only under the wide skies do his cares vanish, and he feels reunited with transcendental reality, which is so much part of his inner life. In Nature he feels the strength of faith in a Heavenly Father, whose visible manifestation she is, in the sense of a 'Garment of God' to which Teufelsdröckh also aspires.

As far as social ties are concerned, these are not very strong, leading to an element of revolt in Siebenkäs's reactions. He does not fall in line with any particular social set; he is not a status-seeker, but a keen observer of the estates and their social prejudices. As defence counsel of the poor he belongs to the small-town intelligentsia, but just as much to the poor for whose rights he stands up. We are in this instance strongly reminded of Teufelsdröckh, who quaffs his tumbler of Gukguk, proposing a toast to 'The Cause of the Poor, in Heaven's name and ——'s' (*Sartor*, 15). Although one could speak of a similarity of disposition between Siebenkäs and Teufelsdröckh, the former does not share Teufelsdröckh's aloofness. There is, rather, a deep sense of involvement in life mainly through experiences in love and the suffering it brings.

Wellek, in *Confrontations* (77), has drawn attention to librarian

Schoppe in Jean Paul's *Titan* as a possible prototype for Teufelsdröckh; however, he fails to bring any proof of this likeness, which is added here. Wishing to change the social texture, Schoppe revolts against any inhibitions imposed on him by society, and expresses this dissatisfaction by declaring war on all traditional concepts. His satirical criticism is indeed biting, but lacks Teufelsdröckh's constructive metaphysical approach. Schoppe is a totally negative intellect. At first humorous in his attacks on the philistine cult of utility in the Germans, the tone gradually darkens. There is an ever-increasing sense of isolation, until Schoppe looks down 'high and dry from his Berghorn' (*Titan*, III, 692). Schoppe is also a representative of Fichte's Idealism, though he misinterprets it. Conceiving it as expressing a complete solipsism, he is driven by the notion of the *Ich* into persecution mania. The *Ich* produces in his deranged mentality a double from whose stranglehold he tries to escape. This *persona*, 'der Ich,' supervises Schoppe in all his movements. No longer able to relate the Finite and the Infinite to each other in a harmonious fashion, this personality with great tragic potentialities breaks down. The same can hardly be said of Teufelsdröckh, who interprets reality according to his idealistic vision in a meaningful manner and, above all, takes a lively interest in questions of the day, eager to help solve them in his own way. Because of this basic difference one can hardly speak, as Wellek does, of 'the inner homogeneousness of the two men' (77).

It is an altogether different matter with airsailor Giannozzo of the 'Komische Anhang' to the *Titan*. Of all Jean Paul's heroes he is most obviously oriented towards transcendental values. The air is his true sphere, and when he descends to earth it is as a guest. All events that take place in this lower sphere he judges from his elevated vantage point. Jean Paul describes him as 'the impetuous, unrestrained Giannozzo ... embittered to the utmost by the civil exchange of lies and malice ... has fled the stifling air of deep prisons and streets to seek the mountain air'[15] (ibid., 905). He calls his own century one without intelligence or religion, where people chase with the eagerness of ratcatchers after 'Brotstudien, Brotschreiberei, Brotleben' (ibid., 929). Teufelsdröckh too deplores 'bread studies' and the lack of study of Self, and also meets the *Wiener Schub*, the 'Offscourings of Vienna' as Carlyle translates them, which Giannozzo sights from above. The detached evaluation of life on earth undertaken from his gondola has much in common with Teufelsdröckh's watch-tower pronouncements.

It is clear from Jean Paul's prototypes, if we may call them so, that Teufelsdröckh is most related to them in as much as he too lives on both the natural and the supernatural level. Reality does not stifle the inner vision. With Siebenkäs, and perhaps Schoppe, he shares keenness of intellect and metaphysical insights, although the former do not feel the urge to convey this awareness of the spiritual essence of life to mankind.

E.T.A. Hoffmann's Eccentrics and Tieck's 'Der Gelehrte'

The tendency towards splitting the self, which Jean Paul had shown in connection with Schoppe, is much more pronounced in E.T.A. Hoffmann's eccentrics. The clash between the *Ich* and the *Nicht-Ich* cannot be resolved, but grows into an insoluble conflict. To many of the artist personalities Hoffmann deals with, earthly existence is no longer a valid manifestation of the divine, as it stands between man and the *Urheimat*, the spiritual world. Man is an eternal wanderer between the two, a role not of his own choosing, but of necessity. The result is a tragic situation, a kind of limbo, through which Teufelsdröckh, who calls himself the 'Wanderer,' confined to 'this paltry little Dog-cage of an Earth' (*Sartor*, 182), also passes. An awareness of man's limitations saddens the heart of the clothes-philosopher: '*Ach Gott*, when I gazed into these Stars, have they not looked down on me as if with pity, from their serene spaces; like Eyes glistening with heavenly tears over the little lot of man! ... Too-heavy-laden Teufelsdröckh!' (ibid.).

This is not the happy mood of a Wuz, dreaming joyous dreams of the transparent glass ball of an Earth, spinning along to the music of the spheres, but rather the heavy gloom in which the musician Kreisler finds himself in his dark hours of despair when he vainly strives to bring forth his artistic visions into a dark, inimical world. Enthusiasm transports him above the earthly regions and keeps him there as long as the inspiration lasts; all the greater is the sense of loss after it vanishes. Kreisler shares with Teufelsdröckh 'satanic' laughter, bordering on insanity: '"That's too bad – that's too bad," Kreisler cried, while starting to burst into a crazy laugh that the walls resounded' (*Kater Murr*, IX, 38).[16] This behaviour, if not the implication, is reminiscent of Teufelsdröckh's roar of laughter 'loud, long-continuing, uncontrollable,' which makes the Editor fear that 'all was not right' (*Sartor*, 33).

Often Hoffmann's characters make an effort to escape these tensions by entering into a world of illusions, bordering on madness. Thus the musician in the tale 'Ritter Gluck' believes himself to be Gluck the composer, long dead at the time of the story. This musician develops a metaphysics of art expressed in symbols of life, which are all but crazy notions. He sees life as a broad highway where mostly exoterics, unconcerned with artistic creation, amble along. Only a few enter into the land of dreams and visions.

In 'Rat Krespel,' the *Sonderling* is in the beginning described with jovial humour. We hear of his strange habits, and his house designed without windows and doors – symbolic of the isolation of the artist – which were later haphazardly installed. There he lives 'like an anchorite with his old housekeeper in a dark house' ('Rat Krespel,' *Werke*, V, 77).[17] This is Krespel's official front, as seen from the outside by the superficial observer. Carlyle also employs this method when, in the opening parts of *Sartor*, he gives the reader an opportunity to feel superior to Teufelsdröckh through the latter's unsophisticated behaviour, as yet unaware of the face behind the mask of grotesque humour.

Strange Professor X. in 'Die Automate' is a mechanics genius, who devises the speaking Turk, a machine giving extraordinarily performances in clairvoyance. The reader first meets him in his mask and is ready to pronounce him a crackpot: 'clad in the old-Frankish fashion, a man of an alert appearance, whose small grey eyes cast a piercing glance, and whose sarcastic smile was hardly to be called attractive' ('Die Automate', *Werke*, VI, 91).[18] Behind this 'world of appearance' lies the professor's true self: he is an ardent scholar and a seeker of the springs of Nature. His absurdity is a deliberate camouflage, designed to hide a soul too easily wounded.

Particularly noticeable are parallels to Teufelsdröckh's living habits on the attic floor of the Wahngasse, symbolically called 'the pinnacle of Weissnichtwo' and 'the speculum or watchtower' (*Sartor*, 20), whence he overlooks the streets of the city and, at the same time, life on earth, as it is lived on the level of reality.[19] In one of the last of Hoffmann's tales, 'Des Vetters Eckfenster,' the cousin, an invalid, lives high up in a tiny room from where he is able to overlook the goings-on in the market-place: 'This market-place is ever a true image of changing life. Lively activity, the need of the moment, drove these crowds of people here; in a few moments everything will again be desolate, the voices confused in a chaotic din, ebbed off, and every deserted spot will proclaim "it was" with ghastly intensity.'[20]

Teufelsdröckh muses in the same vein when looking down at the Weissnichtwo market-place, where he 'might see the whole life-circulation of the considerable City; the streets and lanes of which, with all their doing and driving (*Thun und Treiben*), were for the most part visible there' (*Sartor*, 20). The theme of eternal change is also sounded: 'That living flood, pouring through these streets, of all qualities and ages, knowest thou whence it is coming, whither it is going? *Aus der Ewigkeit zu der Ewigkeit hin*' (ibid., 21). Carlyle goes beyond Hoffmann's reflections by imposing the clothes philosophy on these fleeting aspects of life: 'These are Apparitions: what else? Are they not Souls rendered visible: in Bodies, that took shape and will lose it, melting into air?' (ibid.).

Another such episode is rendered in Hoffmann's 'Der Deï von Elba in Paris.' In this tale the warder of the church steeple lives in his lonely abode with his servant, Lene, who, having attended his needs for twenty-five years, can also take over his chores in case of his death. Here the warder renders an account of the awakening city: 'From its deep abyss all sorts of ugly, dirty-grey exhalations rose up towards me. When they conglomerated above the knob on top of the steeple and joined the dainty golden morning clouds ... I could see the people below in the streets swarming, hustling, driving.'[21]

This passage is followed by a night scene from the same perspective: 'My steeple threw a long, black, giant-shadow across the market-place and across the houses, where the lights were shining all the brighter from the windows. In spite of it being long past midnight, gay company was still to be heard everywhere; glasses resounded, adding to the confused noise of loud conversation.'[22]

In both passages a mood is captured that Carlyle is well able to render; for example, 'these fringes of lamplight, struggling up through smoke and thousandfold exhalation' (*Sartor*, 22) and 'gay mansions, with supper-rooms and dancing-rooms, are full of light and music and high-swelling hearts' (ibid., 23).

Teufelsdröckh's physical appearance may also be connected with E.T.A. Hoffmann. In his preface to *German Romance*, introducing the story 'The Golden Pot,' Carlyle describes the author's 'tiny stature' as 'little and incredibly brisk' (*German Romance II*, 5). This description falls into line with that of Teufelsdröckh as the 'little Sage' (*Sartor*, 26) and a 'little figure ... in loose, ill-brushed threadbare habiliments' (ibid., 16). Teufelsdröckh's small stature is once more stressed in a comparison with Jean Paul himself. It sounds like a slip of the tongue when Jean Paul and Teufelsdröckh are referred to as 'the large-bodied poet and the small' (ibid., 33), as the latter is a scholar and not a poet. Did Carlyle think of Hoffmann here, who, as he points out in the preface to 'The Golden Pot' (*German Romance II*, 12–13), had visited Jean Paul while staying in Bamberg? As the frontispiece for *German Romance II* he chose an etching of tiny Hoffmann sprawling in an easy chair with a long tobacco pipe and an intimated studio background.

In the same preface, Carlyle lovingly dwells on the description of Hoffmann's performance in the wine-house 'Lutter und Wegner,' where he used to meet friends and strangers in what might be called 'Mermaid Sessions': 'Strangers who came to Berlin went to see him in the tavern; the tavern was his study, and his pulpit, and his throne: here his wit flashed and flamed like an *Aurora Borealis*; and the table was forever in a roar; and thus amid tobacco-smoke and over coarse earthly liquor, was Hoffmann wasting faculties which might have seasoned the nectar of the gods' (*German Romance II*, 15). Teufelsdröckh's similar performances in 'Zur Grünen Gans' are too well known to have to be cited, taking place in a setting 'where all the Virtuosity' and nearly all the Intellect of the place assembled of an evening' (*Sartor*, 15). In spite of what Carlyle's brother Alex contributed to the scene, it is hardly believable that Carlyle worked without a literary model, in this case Hitzig's account of Hoffmann's life, which Carlyle paraphrases and quotes in his prefatory comments on 'The Golden Pot.'

A last source that may have contributed to Carlyle's overall concept of a German scholar is Tieck's story 'Der Gelehrte.' This work, which Horn reviews most favourably in his *Poesie und Beredsamkeit* (IV, 230–7), introduces as its hero a scholar who comes, as far as his living habits are concerned, closest to Teufelsdröckh. He is described as an intellectual, a classical scholar of some stature, who has completely retired into the loneliness of his *Studierstube*, where he lives a secluded life surrounded by his books. His hatred of noise had led him to sell his own house, situated adjacent to a smithy. The family of his landlord, the councillor, considers him to be a ghost or a fool, except their daughter Lenchen, who admires the withdrawn bachelor. In this case there is a final return to normal life for the *Sonderling* type in the form of marriage with a congenial wife.

The interest focuses on the setting of the story, which enhances the myth of the scholar as a peculiar and superior personality. When Gertrud, the aged female servant, permits Lenchen, during the owner's absence, to sneak up to the *Gelehrtenstube*, we see the scholar's quarters through the eyes of a young girl, to whom it seems a paradise of 'otherworldliness,' expressive of values totally different from those to which she has so far been exposed in her own home. A sacred mystery surrounds the place, which only the initiated can perceive and value. Aspects of his personality remain strange to the common mind, represented by Gertrud: 'Who can say what he puts together in his head from all this heathenish stuff, for such a classical scholar is no better than a heathen, my child. He never goes to church, because he can't stand the organ he says ... Yes, Lenchen, it makes me thoughtful and sad because I'm so fond of the master.'[23]

Essentially new seems to be the fact that a scholar serves as a true model for a novel-hero.

Sauerteig's Relationship to German Originals

A word remains to be said about Gottfried Sauerteig, the less illustrious German eccentric, and much less colourful colleague of Teufelsdröckh. He is a voice rather than a distinct personality, which goes to show how much Jean Paul's demand for the 'minutest individualization' of the eccentric character contributes to Teufelsdröckh's success. Sauerteig too acts as a ferment, in the sense in which Jean Paul employs the word 'fermenting,' or *Gärung*. It effects the finer nature of man in the same fashion in which 'one needs more *yeast* and *leaven* in order to make a fine dough rise' (*Jubelsenior*, IV, 472).[24] More a literary critic than a metaphysician and prophet, Sauerteig, equipped with his book *Aesthetische Springwurzeln*, shows some affinity with Friedrich Schlegel. This *persona* employs a magical picklock to open intellectual doors that otherwise would remain closed. Carlyle comments in some detail on the function of this 'start-root' in his *Unfinished History of German Literature*, where it plays an important part in one of the tales he relates, called 'The Enchanted Kaiser': 'This invaluable root, or fibre, for it is of the smallest dimensions, can no more be dispensed with in Treasure-digging than *Wünschelruthe* (Divining-rod), and may perhaps be as old as it, that is, older than Tacitus' day. For if the rod by its trembling point out where the Treasure is, the *Springwurzel* must start all locks and bolts, natural or preternatural, that secure it there' (ibid., 43, fn.).

With regard to questions of aesthetics, Sauerteig is well able to handle his magical instrument, but Carlyle himself, taking the role of the editor in his essay 'Biography,' pretends not to approve of it wholeheartedly: 'The Professor and Doctor is not a man whom we can praise without reservation; neither shall we say that his *Springwurzeln* (a sort of magical picklocks, as he affectedly names them) are adequate to "start" every *bolt* that locks up an aesthetic mystery: nevertheless, in his crabbed, one-sided way, he sometimes hits masses of the truth' (*Essays III*, 49).

While Carlyle only once revives Teufelsdröckh in *Past and Present* – he otherwise seems to have got lost for good on the London old-clothes market – Sauerteig insists on coming back with a controversial opinion, as late as *The History of Frederick the Great* (II, 120).

In *Past and Present* all three commentators – Dryasdust, Sauerteig, and Teufelsdröckh – appear, each of them with a different function to fulfil, of which only the last two concern us here. Sauerteig is clearly the man of the day, concentrating on metaphysical aspects of life but without the magnificent style that enhances Teufelsdröckh's pronouncements in *Sartor*. The topics are the same: concepts of Nature, the idea of reverence, fashionable wits and their worship – all echoes of German sources, or what Carlyle would have his readers believe can be gleaned from them. In the same work Teufelsdröckh, introduced as 'a distinguished man ... who thus writes to me what in these days he notes from the Wahngasse of Weissnichtwo, where our London fashions seem to be in full vogue' (*Past and Present*, Bk. III, 215), waxes wordy on democracy under the guise of the clothes philosophy – not a very impressive performance, seemingly coming from a tired man. The eccentric original, initially developed with so much vigour and conviction from traits suggested by Carlyle's German readings, has become a shadow of itself.

The Editor in Goethe, Jean Paul, E.T.A. Hoffmann, and Hauff

Carlyle's literary technique of using the editor as narrator in *Sartor* has been little discussed in connection with German sources. If mentioned at all, it has been attributed in a vague way to the influence of Jean Paul, without a detailed investigation of such works as could have served Carlyle as models. It is quite likely that, in presenting a German professor's work, Carlyle would have wished to employ new literary devices he had come across in his readings to render foreign thought more effectively with an appropriate flavour.

Jean Paul is by no means the only German Romantic writer who used this method. Carlyle had met with the intervening editor in his translation of Goethe's *Wilhelm Meisters Wanderjahre*,[25] where, in a section titled 'A Word from the Editor,' he is introduced very late in the book, obviously as an afterthought, to explain certain deficiencies in the joining of parts: 'We find ourselves in more than one way impeded; at this or that place, threatened with one obstruction or another. For we have to solve the uncertain problem of selecting from those most multifarious papers, what is worthiest and most important, so that it be grateful to thinking and cultivated minds' (*Wilhelm Meister II*, 300).

At this point the editor does not have to fill in a continuous story line. A sorting job has to be done, a selection must be made from among a variety of papers, e.g., sketches, narratives, poems, statistics, and technical subjects. He complains mainly about confusion: 'Now here are the Journals more or less complete, lying before us; sometimes communicable without scruples, sometimes ... seemingly unfit for insertion ... So likewise we fall in with little anecdotes, destitute of connection, difficult to arrange under heads; some of them, when closely examined, not altogether unobjectionable' (ibid., 301).

An editorial passage in *Sartor* (193) comes close to this rather restrained complaint: 'Without pretending to comment on which strange utterances, the Editor will only remark, that there lies beside them much of a still more questionable character; unsuited to the general apprehension; nay wherein he himself does not see his way.'

A feeling of genuine frustration is much more pronounced in Carlyle's English editor who, besides having to cope with the task of bringing some coherence into utter biographical confusion, has to extract philosophical notions from a foreign language. After the arrival of the bulky material from Hofrat Heuschrecke, he finds himself confronted with 'a Metaphysico-theological Disquisition, "Detached Thoughts on the Steam-engine," or, "The continued Possibility of Prophecy" ... On certain sheets stand Dreams, authentic or not ... Anecdotes, oftenest without date of place or time, fly loosely on separate slips, like Sibylline leaves. Interspersed also are long purely Autobiographical delineations ... In all Bags the same imbroglio' (*Sartor*, 78).

This description goes beyond Goethe in its fantastic disorder; a humorous note prevails, lacking in Goethe's editorial perplexity, which does not disclose much of the editor's personality by way of his reactions. Only occasionally he adds a comment of his own.

On the whole Carlyle's English editor shares with Goethe's counterpart the desire to remain behind the scenes: 'Who or what such Editor may be, must remain conjectural, and even insignificant' (ibid., 13). However, he has taken it upon himself to introduce his readers to a strange mode of thought cleared from prejudice, in order to 'evolve printed Creation out of a German printed and written Chaos' (ibid., 80). For this very reason his editorial comment is much more searching, and includes opposition to opinions held by the author, Teufelsdröckh himself, the man of genius: 'Such passages fill us, who love the man and partly esteem him, with mixed feelings' (ibid., 45). An added feature is that his reaction is primarily that of an Englishman who takes pride in his native traditions and institutions, prepared to take a stand, if needs be, to defend them against a foreigner: 'the Editor thinks it needful to give warning: namely, that he is animated with a true though perhaps a feeble attachment to the Institutions of our Ancestors; and minded to defend these, according to ability, at all hazards' (ibid., 13).

Readers acquainted with Jean Paul's writings will have noticed the Jean Paulian note in the *Sartor* passage quoted above, referring to the imbroglio among the papers. It seems safe to say that Carlyle, in following some of Jean Paul's editorial suggestions, expanded what he had initially learned from Goethe in the use of this device. Jean Paul's editor, besides being a collector and an interpreter, is much more of a mediator between the story and the reader. A personal relationship is established that expresses itself in a humorous vein.

In *Schmelzles Reise nach Flätz,* which Carlyle translated, the editor introduces himself by way of a mystification. He will not disclose how army-chaplain Schmelzle's self-revealing portrait has fallen into his hands. He had written down his own thoughts and digressions on a separate sheet, referring back to the proper pages of the manuscript; but, as he had omitted to insert the corresponding numbers in the text, he had confused the printer, who simply set them down in footnote form under the text in an incongruous fashion.[26]

While in this little work editorial comment plays a subordinate role, in Carlyle's second translation from Jean Paul, the *Das Leben des Quintus Fixlein,* editor and author become one. Documents of an extraordinary kind are being presented in this life of a schoolmaster. They consist of scraps of paper on which Fixlein has sketched his early past, containing acts and plays of his childhood which he used to file in chronological order in the drawers of his child's desk. The editor, who calls his chapters 'letter-boxes,' explains his unmethodical grab-bag procedure: 'I will now clutch blindfold into his days, and bring out one of them: one smiles and sends forth its perfumes like another' (*German Romance II,* 214).[27]

Although involuntarily, the English editor in *Sartor* must also resort to such means with regard to the content of the paper bags and their enigmatic fragments.

In Jean Paul's *Leben Fibels,* the method of conveying the biographical materials is even more remarkable. The editor, who has bought Fibel's life story from a book-auctioneer, unfortunately finds only a few pages within the covers, the rest having been sold for scrap paper. He therefore encourages the inhabitants of the place to return to him their wrapping papers, in order that he may piece Fibel's biography together from such remnants or flying leaves. The chapters of the patched-up book are accordingly named 'Pepper-bags,' 'Bodice Patterns,' and 'Thread-winders.'

The method employed by Jean Paul in the *Titan* actually comes closest to Carlyle's. The editor receives the material, as in *Sartor*, in sturdy paper bags on mail days, which he calls his biographical timber, and further data from Hofrath Hafenreffer, a counterpart to Hofrath Heuschrecke, who produces the paper bags full of notes marked with the signs of the zodiac.[28]

The conveyance chosen in Jean Paul's *Hesperus* is most amusing: a dog carries the biographical documents in a small pumpkin tied to his collar. For a period of forty-five 'Dogpost-days,' the animal swims through a lake in order to reach the editor's dwelling-place on an island. The pumpkin contains letters written in an unknown hand, imploring and finally demanding from the editor that a biography be written from these data. He takes on the assignment because he 'seldom denies anything crazy' (*Hesperus*, I, 509). On the forty-fourth Dogpost-day, the dog stays away and the story must needs come to an end, although the characters are still alive and continue to enact their part of the story.

Teufelsdröckh is also very much alive while his book is being edited, and the reader frequently, if sparingly, gets news regarding his whereabouts from the editor. In the beginning he has mysteriously disappeared from Weissnichtwo; towards the end, he shows up in London. The conclusion of the book – which is unsatisfactory when judged in terms of fiction – may have sprung from Carlyle's wish to leave himself some room to manoeuvre, in case the work would be a success, as he anticipated. In the course of a continuation he might have planned to unravel Teufelsdröckh's parentage, besides discussing social philosophy such as St Simonian beliefs.

While in these examples the conveyance of the biographical material is akin to that described in *Sartor*, more specific similarities are to be found in Jean Paul's youthful work *Auswahl aus des Teufels Papieren* (Berend Edn. I, 292) and *Maria Wuz* (*Werke*, I, 422). In the former work the reader is introduced to the Jewish scrap dealer Mendel, who gives a lively account of this troubles concerning the death of scholar Hasius, his debtor, who left him nothing but paper in lieu of payment. As Mendel cannot sell it wholesale, he decides to have the manuscript printed in an effort to recover his loss. When the printer remarks that the scathing satire could only have been written by the devil, Mendel takes this comment literally, and imagines the devil to have slipped into Hasius's body at night to perform this task. Worried about the reputation of such a book, he asks the editor to keep strict silence (*Stillschweigen*) on the whole matter. According to this fiction, the devil is shown to have acted as a subeditor, revising Hasius's observations on man and the world in a brilliant satirical vein, a truly 'devilish mood.' It is therefore significant when, in the denouement, Satan divests himself of his clothes, and old Adam appears underneath.

This sense of mystification is also present in *Sartor*, where the Editor, it may be remembered, refers to Teufelsdröckh's satirical observations as 'his half-devilish way' to 'deceptively *in*lock both Editor and Hofrath' (*Sartor*, 202-3).

In *Maria Wuz*, Jean Paul employs an editorial technique I would like to call one of conscious dissociation. In this idyllic description of one who finds contentment in a restricted existence, the editor does not wish to be identified with the schoolmaster. Wuz might as well live on another planet, for his joys are such as the reader can never experience to the same degree. Lacking his childlike naïveté, we partly pity, partly admire him for displaying qualities we ourselves have lost in what is usually called the battle of life. This technique, which Jean Paul deliberately employs, is an effective means to set off the uniqueness of a strange being.

Carlyle's Editor shares this basic approach with Jean Paul. Teufelsdröckh is also an original, although he has little in common with simple Wuz. He remains an enigma to ordinary humanity, what the Editor calls 'a quite new human Individuality, an almost unexampled personal character' (ibid., 10). The Editor has access to certain facets of this personality, but he cannot fathom it, just as Jean Paul cannot penetrate into the recesses of Wuz's nature.

Editors also appear in several of E.T.A. Hoffmann's novels. In the *Elixiere des Teufels*, the subtitle already evinces editorial activity: 'Posthumous Papers by Brother Medardus, a Capucine.' The Editor receives them from the Prior of the Monastery who had held them in safekeeping in the archives: 'After I diligently studied the papers of the Capuchin brother Medardus – a hard task on account of the small, illegible monkish handwriting of the departed – it appeared to me as if what we usually call dream or imagination could be the symbolical perception of the secret thread which winds itself through our lifestory.'[29]

Except for this symbolical hint, the reader is left on his own to unravel this thread. However, towards the end of the book the Editor inserts a 'Parchment of the old Painter,' which partly solves the unexplained riddles regarding Medardus's ancestors.

In *Lebensansichten des Katers Murr*, the editorial method is much more refined. Through an initial confusion, conductor Kreisler's biography has been printed together with the cat's life story that gives the novel its title. The literary efforts of the scholarly cat have been written down on the back of proofsheets (*Makulaturblätter*) belonging to Kreisler's book, which the compositor took to be emendations and additions by Kreisler himself. As a result, the publication presents Kreisler's life interrupted by Murr's views on mice and men.

With regard to Kreisler's part, the Editor tells the reader that he was fortunate enough to strike up an acquaintance with 'the little Privy Councillor,' who stands in the same relationship to Kreisler as Hofrath Heuschrecke does to Teufelsdröckh, and is otherwise just as unimportant for the further development of the story: 'For the Editor of these pages it is the most fortunate event in the world that he got an account of the remarkable conversation which took place between Kreisler and the little Privy Councillor, red hot, so to speak. Thus he was able to bring before your eyes, dear reader, at least a few episodes concerning the early youth of this extraordinary man, whose biography he felt under a compulsion to write down.'[30]

The similarity with Carlyle's technique is obvious. In both cases a mediator produces biographical facts, however unsatisfactory in their enigmatic profusion, while the Editor is in despair about the nature of the notes received. Kreisler's biographer comments in the following vein: 'The biographer is once more upset about the abruptness of the information received, wherefrom he has to piece together the present story.'[31]

As far as Murr's observations on life are concerned, the editor's comment is humorous throughout. In every aspect of his writings, Murr reveals himself as a potential Philistine, full of pretensions and prejudices that are striking in the cat-context. This work by Hoffmann seems particularly important because Carlyle also employs the term *Maculatur-Blätter* in parentheses, translating it as 'waste printed-sheets' (*Sartor*, 278).

A last editorial extravaganza is invented by Wilhelm Hauff (a protégé of Franz Horn) in his *Memoiren des Satan* which relates to the German Satanic School in a striking fashion.[32] In this case the devil's manuscript, written in cipher, has to be prepared for publication; Satan provides the key. The Editor, who had previously tried his hand at poetry, now serves the cause of literature on a lower level, 'translating immortal works of foreign literature for our dear German public,'[33] just as Carlyle's counterpart translates Teufelsdröckh's work for the benefit of the English. Satan, who calls himself Herr von Natas ('Satan' spelled backwards), comments on his studies at various German universities where he received a PHD by writing a dissertation entitled 'De rebus diabolicus.' His witty observations are interrupted and elaborated upon by the Editor. The decoding job is not a difficult task, but the manuscript is in unbelievable disorder, as Satan did not start at the beginning and cannot express himself well enough in the German idiom. In order to make reading easier, the Editor outlines the content of the memoirs in the form of headlines: 'In addition, consider the chaos in which he presents everything! Others (I, the editor, for example) would at least have begun with a baptismal certificate – not an easy thing for the devil to provide, – but with an event related to some form of chronology. I have thumbed through the manuscript, (not daring to read it before each page has at least been consecrated).'[34]

In substance the editorial method as applied in *Sartor* is very effective because of a fusion of various aspects contained in Carlyle's German models. The Editor helps the reader to understand an unfamiliar way of looking at Nature in a supernatural manner, and prepares him for a better understanding of the Philosophy of Clothes by way of selections put together with an amount of shrewdness. He also counterbalances Teufelsdröckh's exuberance with a more sober approach, making his ideas more acceptable to English readers. In addition, he has a pronounced national character, with a pinch of cant, and does not always take the German professor seriously. The issues at stake are much more involved than in his literary models, going far beyond satire and idyll, which merely form part of the pattern in which the whole is cast.

THREE

The Idylls of Teufelsdröckh

'Still Eden! green flower-chequered chiaroscuro!'

(Jean Paul, *Quintus Fixlein*)

Youth at Entepfuhl and *Wahrheit aus Jean Pauls Leben*

The placing of Teufelsdröckh's autobiographic material in the centre of *Sartor* brings back to mind Jean Paul's request that, in order to be effective, relics of childhood and youth should be introduced at a time when the reader can relate them in a significant way to the mature personality already presented.

This demand is fully met in *Sartor* in the chapter entitled 'Idyllic,' where the Editor searches for biographical material when this extraordinary personality has been firmly established in the reader's mind as the originator of the clothes philosophy and a man of some renown. Preconditioned in this manner, he will interpret the biographical facts in the light of what he already knows. Episodes insignificant in themselves, such as Gneschen contemplating the eternity of the Kuhbach, are now, for the reader, indicative of Teufelsdröckh the Thinker. According to this image he will constantly find and match up signs emblematic of future developments. This is Carlyle's deliberate intention: after having familiarized himself with Teufelsdröckh's view of the world, the reader is now to be let in on how he arrived at it. Obviously such a technique aids greatly in the interpretation of a biography 'philosophico-poetically written' (*Sartor*, 75).

If this biographical approach appears to be most effective with regard to such aims, the idyllic-romantic setting, comprising youth at Entepfuhl, schooldays, and first love, recommends itself as a favourable climate for the original to develop his peculiar bent.

Jean Paul comments in his *Ästhetik* on the value inherent in the idyllic genre, as the most suitable setting for childhood and youth, defining it as 'the full happiness of seclusion' (V, 258). In this period of life, he claims, when wishing and longing are the predominant moods, the child is naturally disposed to enter into the Romantic land. However, he denies that this is simply a Golden Age vision, as it leads on 'a long hard ladder of thorns past the rosebush and the first soft thorns, finally up to a few roses.'[1]

This formula is also applicable to Teufelsdröckh's youthful experiences, where a few Scotch thistles are added for contrast's sake before the curtain rushes down, over both poetic idylls and love romance, with a Jean Paulian metaphor, never to be raised again.[2] From then on the philosophical part of the biography takes over, and Teufelsdröckh enters the speculative dream-grottoes of the mind.

Besides these general tendencies, which may be considered coincidental by those unfamiliar with Carlyle's German background reading, there are definite points of resemblance in form and structure between *Sartor* and Jean Paul's own autobiographical account. This unfinished work, dealing with the author's youth up to his twentieth year, published in three small volumes, Carlyle undertook to review in his second Richter essay of 1830 (*Essays II*, 96–159), at a time when plans for Teufelsdröckh's personality were already shaping up in his mind.

Carlyle speaks of these recollections of childhood and youth, known to him under the title *Wahrheit aus Jean Pauls Leben*,[3] as 'almost celestial,' likely a reference to its singular emphasis on supernatural aspects. At the same time Carlyle repeats Jean Paul's warning to the reader 'not to believe that there were no sour days, no chidings and the like' (*Essays II*, 'Jean Paul Again,' 110), showing the need to include a 'few soft thorns' to avoid sentimentality. Third, he comments on the spirit of genial humour in which Jean Paul appoints himself professor of his own history, delivering lectures on the autobiographical subject.

Such observations are not unrelated to Teufelsdröckh's idylls: in the account of his youth, transcendental 'glimpses' are provided, while rougher aspects of the youthful sage's path are not smoothed over; a kind of second self in the person of the Editor adds a humorous note. As far as plot structure is concerned, it does not contain any amount of realistic action, but is built around emotional insights and the tensions developed through them. In other words, a highlighting of life from a subjective point of view is attempted, resulting in a very specific relationship between man and a supernatural world that projects itself into the world of reality.

For Jean Paul, awareness of self is central to any intuitive insight, described in the following passage, translated by Carlyle: 'Never shall I forget the inward occurrence, till now narrated to no mortal, when I witnessed the birth of my Self-consciousness, of which I can still give the place and time. One forenoon, I was standing, a very young child, in the outer door, and looking leftward at the stack of the fuelwood, – when all at once the internal vision, "I am a ME (ich bin ein Ich),' came like a flash from heaven before me, and in gleaming light ever afterwards continued: then had my Me, for the first time, seen itself and forever'[4] (*Essays II*, 'Jean Paul Again,' 111).

Teufelsdröckh's concern with self: 'Who am I; what is this ME?' (*Sartor*, 53) occurs early in the book, as it is one of the key questions that open up the clothes philosophy. His autobiographical contemplations, comparable to Jean Paul's observations quoted above, centre on time and eternity: 'It struck me much, as I sat by the Kuhbach, one silent noontide, and watched it flowing, gurgling, to think how this same streamlet had flowed and gurgled, through all changes of weather and of fortune, from beyond the earliest date of history' (ibid., 102).

In the one case a world opens up within; in the other an individual life expands into what seems to a twelve-year-old an eternity of time. The Editor points out future implications: 'In which little thought, as in a little fountain, may there not lie the beginning of those well-nigh unutterable meditations on the grandeur and mystery of TIME, and its relation to ETERNITY, which play such a part in this Philosophy of Clothes?' (ibid., 103).

In the first lecture Jean Paul, the assumed professor of self-history, turns to the life story of his grandparents while he himself still slumbers in the cradle: 'But for now may the hero and object of these historical lectures lie and sleep in his cradle and at his mother's breast unobserved, as this one long morning sleep of life is not as yet of general world-historical interest.'[5]

Teufelsdröckh's biography opens similarly, to give the real professor a chance to contemplate the nature of sleep and waking: 'Sleep on, thou fair Child, for thy long rough journey is at hand! A little while, and thou too shalt sleep no more, but thy very dreams shall be mimic battles' (*Sartor*, 90).

The parents Jean Paul introduces are pious and poor. This stress on want and poverty runs through the whole autobiographical account, imprinting itself on Carlyle's mind. He not only translates the following passage in his 'Jean Paul Friedrich Richter Again,' but also refers to it in his *Reminiscences* (vol. I, 199):

'In my Historical Lectures', says Paul, 'the business of Hungering will in truth more and more make its appearance, – with the hero it rises to a great height ... nevertheless, I cannot help saying to Poverty: Welcome! so thou come not at quite too late a time! Wealth bears heavier on talent than Poverty ... When among the flames of youth ... the oil of Riches is also poured in, – little will remain of the Phoenix but his ashes ... The poor Historical Professor, in this place, would not, for much money, have had much money in his youth. (*Essays II*, 'Jean Paul Again,' 122)[6]

Gneschen also experiences care in the 'Idyllic' chapter: 'Nevertheless, I were but a vain dreamer to say, that even then my felicity was perfect. I had, once for all, come down from Heaven into the Earth. Among the rainbow colours that glowed on my horizon, lay even in childhood a dark ring of Care, as yet no thicker than a thread' (*Sartor*, 97).

In the first lecture, Jean Paul furthermore speaks of the distinct impression he retained of a young student who used to carry him around as a child, uttering the wish that this same person might read these lines: 'could it be possible that he might still be alive, in his high sixties and as a seasoned scholar would see these lectures in print, and then recall a small professor ... ach Gott, if this could be and he would write, or the elderly man were to visit the old one!'[7]

Carlyle has the Editor indulge in the same kind of wishful thinking with regard to Teufelsdröckh's mysterious father: 'Nay, since Books, like invisible scouts, permeate the whole habitable globe ... may not some Copy find out even the mysterious basket-bearing Stranger, who in a state of extreme senility perhaps still exists; and gently even force him to disclose himself; to claim openly a son, in whom any father may feel pride?' (*Sartor*, 89).

In the second lecture, under the heading 'Dorfidyllen,' Jean Paul brings reminiscences of life in his native Joditz, which in their mood and setting find a literary counterpart in Carlyle's chapter 'Idyllic,' describing life in Entepfuhl.[8] However much Carlyle may have incorporated his own remembrances of Ecclefechan into this chapter, he did not write it without a literary model of the kind Jean Paul was able to provide, in keeping with his desire to adhere to a truly German setting. In Joditz, a village cut in half by a little brook of 'Kuhbach' proportions, Jean Paul starts his schooldays, already in trousers, primer in hand, 'on the cover of which was imprinted in true gilt-letters (and rightly so), the content of the first page.'[9] It can hardly be called a coincidence that Teufelsdröckh also refers to such gilt letters in a rhetorical question: 'what matters it whether such Alphabet be in large gilt letters or in small ungilt ones, so you have an eye to read it?' (*Sartor*, 97). Both boys experience joy and pride at this moment and make speedy progress, under the guidance of 'the emaciated, consumptive, but alert school-master' (*Selberlebensbeschreibung*, VI, 1052) and a 'downbent, brokenhearted, underfoot martyr' (*Sartor*, 101), respectively.

Besides the philosophical inclination, a poetic talent lies latent in Jean Paul as well as in Teufelsdröckh. The Professor of Self-History advises his readers that 'in the future cultural history of our hero it may be doubtful, if he will be more naturally disposed towards philosophy or poetry.'[10] The poetic sensitivity expresses itself in an undetermined longing experienced in Nature: 'He still remembers of a summer-day, when returning towards two o'clock, he overlooked the sunny hues on the hillocks and the rippling waves of the cornfields and the fleeting shadows of the clouds; an unexperienced, undefinable longing overcame him ... Ach, it was the whole man, desirous of heavenly goods inherent in life, lying as yet unheeded and colourless in the deep wide darkness of the heart.'[11]

Teufelsdröckh, 'an incipient Philosopher and Poet in the abstract' (*Sartor*, 100), also shows 'symptoms of a spirit singularly open, thoughtful, almost poetical' (ibid., 102). Symptomatic is his supper on the orchard wall: 'On fine evenings I was wont to carry-forth my supper ... and eat it out-of-doors. On the coping of the Orchard-wall, which I could reach by climbing ... my porringer was placed: there, many a sunset, have I, looking at distant western Mountains, consumed, not without relish, my evening meal. Those hues of gold and azure, that hush of World's expectation as Day died, were still a Hebrew Speech for me; nevertheless I was looking at the fair illuminated Letters, and had an eye for their gilding' (ibid., 92–3).

As far as the intrusion of the world is concerned, the *Jahrmarkt* and annual cattle-fair are, for both youths, at the centre of idyllic pleasures. While Jean Paul describes the bustle in terms of music played by the band, young Teufelsdröckh feasts his eyes on the colourful hurly-burly, presided over by a Merry-Andrew.

Interest in animal life manifests itself soon in both boys, particularly in the episodes dealing with swallows. While Jean Paul envies them their secluded happiness in a quiet nook, young Gneschen observes their activity and seemingly ceaseless toil –

Jean Paul	*Carlyle*
The young swallows he called happy because they could sit so snugly in their built-in nests during the night. (*Selberlebensbeschreibung*, VI, 1081)[12]	Why mention our Swallows ... snug-lodged in our Cottage Lobby? ... there they built, and caught flies, and twittered, and bred. (*Sartor*, 96)

The tone darkens when entrance into active life by way of removal to the city, for purposes of higher education, takes place. Jean Paul shows dissatisfaction with the educational methods employed at the *Gymnasium*: 'Such is man in all professions and all offices; he does not care to change slavish machines into free spirits thus to reveal their creative, ruling, and productive powers. On the contrary, they wish to show it in reverse by hooking up the next mental super-machine to another intermediate machine, and attach this finally to the last one ... All this linking up is done by the *same* machine-supervisor. God the image of freedom, only wants to raise free spirits; the Devil, the image of bondage, only wants to raise his own likeness.'[13] The role of the Devil as a master-mind in league with machinery and bondage fits some pronouncements made on the subject by Teufelsdröckh, who by no means lingers lovingly over his academic training: 'We find, moreover, that his Greek and Latin were "mechanically" taught; Hebrew scarce even mechanically' (*Sartor*, 104).

Here end the major parallels regarding the idyllic mood of the whole, the nature of the incidents narrated, and the kind of observations made. Whereas Jean Paul's autobiography leads up to the *Gymnasium* at Schwarzenbach only, Teufelsdröckh continues with a full description of university life, friendship, and the love-triangle plot. That both autobiographies have much in common becomes increasingly clear when the tone of Carlyle's own *Reminiscences* is compared to that of Teufelsdröckh's idylls. In the former the softening poetic glow is absent. Instead, a harsh, rugged, and rather depressing note is struck, which would not enable the reader to recognize in the one the supposed prototype of the other.

Teufelsdröckh's Romance and Jean Paul's Concept of Love

Besides the influence on the 'Idylls,' Jean Paul's *Liebeserlebnis* can be traced in Teufelsdröckh's romance with Blumine, who owes more than her name to Jean Paul.[14] The love relationship is characterized by anticipation rather than fulfilment. This is typical of Jean Paul's descriptions of love sentiments. They always have an ethereal quality about them, expressed by the word *Seelenfreundschaft*. Unsensuous in substance, the love union is a melting together of souls, not of bodies. A touch, a kiss, constitutes the utmost in physical contact, not from a sense of excessive prudishness, but on account of the transcending nature of the emotion. In spite of this lack of sensuous reality, Jean Paul is able to convey a prolonged mood of enchantment, often using nature settings to suggest the dream-world atmosphere that is simultaneously rapturous and sublime.

The influence of such love relationships on Jean Paul's heroes is a far-reaching one. Space and time are lost in an all-embracing sentiment where ecstatic moments count more than a whole lifetime. This disposition is a prerequisite for the effectiveness of Jean Paul's emotional experiences, which are prominent in the lives of his idealistically inclined lovers. However, this readiness to see a whole universe in what constitutes only a part of man's existence can lead to fearful disillusionment and utter despair. The Jean Paulian lover is frequently heading for this kind of reaction. In youth untouched by the material world, he slowly, sometimes never, learns its ways. Usually a poet in disguise, high-strung and overly sensitive, he constantly attempts to impose his vision of other-worldliness onto ordinary life, and onto the woman he loves, ready to admire but not to desire her.

Carlyle considers Jean Paul's heroines a success. He speaks of them as 'white, half-angelic creatures, meek, still, long-suffering, high-minded, of tenderest affections, and hearts crushed, yet uncomplaining' (*Essays I*, 'Jean Paul Richter,' 21). In this connection aspects of Blumine come to mind. She is 'a magic vision, for him inaccessible, almost without reality' (*Sartor*, 138). A few examples from the range of Jean Paul's lovers will illuminate this perspective.

Gustav of *Die Unsichtbare Loge* is a youth who has been raised in a subterranean vault, in order to be removed from negative influences that might impede his development. As a result, he never feels quite at home in this world, but remains a product of the *Grotto*. His Christian spirituality is able to rise above earthly concerns. Considered a weakling by his father, who notices his weepings, he is nicknamed 'the weeping soldier' by the old officer. A youthful personality of the finest fibre, he shares the sensitivity of young Teufelsdröckh' who is also named 'the Tearful' (*Sartor*, 104) by his school-fellows.

Gustav's love for Beata shows itself in an ever-increasing rapture, resulting in a vision of a lovers' Elysium. By way of the landscape, the reader participates in this trance-like state: 'A rainbow of suns, joined into a string of pearls, was set around the earth and circled around it ... groves and alleys formed of giant flowers, as tall as trees, zigzagged in veiled shapes across the meadow ... like a happy blush the evening dusk undulated between shadowy shores ... Gustav sensed this to be the evening of eternity, and eternal bliss.'[15]

Landscape also has a role to play in the developing affection between Teufelsdröckh and Blumine. Admittedly, Carlyle is more down to earth, less symbolical, and not as daring as Jean Paul in the poetic associations, but quite as serene. Here the *Waldschloss* glitters in the western sunbeams like an Eldorado: 'from the wide-opened doors, fair outlook over blossom and bush, over grove and velvet green, stretching, undulating onwards to the remote Mountain peaks: so bright, so mild, and everywhere the melody of birds and happy creatures' (*Sartor*, 137).

The kiss as a symbol of soul-union is expressed in similar images in each case. Gustav and Beata experience it in this manner: 'Then it arrived, the unearthly moment, which had dropped earthwards through a thousand heavens, the moment when the human heart rises to its highest love, beating for two souls and two worlds ... kindred souls flared up like two tall flames into a single one.'[16]

Quintus Fixlein, in Carlyle's translation, bends over Thiennette's 'pale angelic face, the lips of which he timidly pressed but did not kiss, till all-powerful love ... drew the two closer together, and their two souls, like two tears, melted into one' (*German Romance II, 'Quintus Fixlein,'* 253).[17]

Teufelsdröckh's embrace and kiss bear the additional agony of a bitter-sweet parting forever: 'their lips were joined, their two souls, like two dew-drops, rushed into one, – for the first time, and for the last![18] Only on the basis of an analysis of Jean Paul's *Liebeserlebnis* can it be claimed that the inspiration and foundation of these lines stem from Jean Paul's initial formulation.

Carlyle is also fond of expressing love relationships in a cosmic or otherworldly setting, as Jean Paul is in the habit of doing: 'It was appointed ... that the high celestial orbit of Blumine should intersect the low sublunary one of our Forlorn ... the upper Sphere of Light was come down into this nether sphere of Shadows' (*Sartor*, 136). A seductive element is completely absent in Teufelsdröckh's vision of Blumine. She shares with all the 'Queen's of this Earth,' not only many-coloured angel plummage, but the following angelic traits: 'all of air they were, all Soul and Form; so lovely, like mysterious priestesses, in whose hand was the invisible Jacob's-ladder, whereby man might mount into very Heaven' (ibid., 133).

Such traits are not only in keeping with Jean Paul's descriptions but also with his theory regarding emotions, as laid down in the *Ästhetik*, where he claims that 'the greatest objection *against* the description of sensuous love is not a moral but a poetical one.'[19]

Another example is young Albano of *Der Titan*, who, storming through the park, wrapped up in love visions of Liane, does not think of her immediate physical presence, but, employing the Jacob's ladder, used by Carlyle in the above quotation, jumps off into empyrean spheres: 'Finally alert he jumped off the top rung of his Jacob's-ladder with all his senses alert into the uncovered, living heavens; a shining mountain peak, encircled by colourful cup-shaped flower petals, received him and rocked him under the stars.'[20]

Liane remains a distant figure, the centre of an emotional dream world. This feature is stressed by her blindness. Expressive of angelic sainthood, this flower virgin, called a *schöne Seele* by Jean Paul, burns up all selfish emotions in Albano. He becomes a giving lover, tender and protective towards the weak. In this novel Liane's mother interferes with the love affair in the same manner in which Blumine's aunt does. After Liane's death Albano is driven by the spectre of agony to a life of travel in which Nature descriptions matching his mood are reminiscent of those of Teufelsdröckh in *Sartor*.

In *Flegeljahre*, Wina stands for the image of the flower-goddess, an epithet Teufelsdröckh also uses for Blumine (*Sartor*, 135). Jean Paul has the admiring Walt give a closer description of the immediate impression Wina makes on him: 'I see a human flower, which blooms without consciousness ... because she is Love herself, and seeks love, she attracts all life ... He stepped into the light-flooded room, still drunk with dreams; half-blinded he looked at the white slender Wina with the light white hat, looking like a flower-goddess.'[21]

Carlyle's favourite novel was Jean Paul's *Hesperus*, a copy of which he owned. In both Richter essays he particularly mentions its lofty notions on love and quotes from 'Extraleaves' and Preface (I, 9; II, 135). The quintessence of Viktor and Klothilde's relationship is 'a friendship which does not fetter two souls with earthy, metal and soiled bonds, but with spiritual ones which weave this world to another and man to God' (*Hesperus*, I, 535).[22] The description of the garden party in the same novel shows similarities with the 'Aesthetic Tea' session in *Sartor*. The tea-drinking circle in Jean Paul's grotto is enlivened by Viktor's readings from his diary (*Hesperus*, I, 705), while Teufelsdröckh's brilliant conversational powers lead on to transcendental themes (*Sartor*, 140). But while Jean Paul lets emotions flow freely and exuberant fancies take over, extravagance is checked by Carlyle and rendered in mellow half-tones: 'And yet as the light grew more aërial on the mountain-tops, and the shadows fell longer over the valley, some faint tone of sadness may have breathed through the heart; and, in whispers more or less audible, reminded every one that as this bright day was drawing towards its close, so likewise must the Day of Man's Existence decline into dust and darkness' (ibid., 141).

As such passages show, Carlyle makes Teufelsdröckh much more aware of the limitations of the love ecstasy. Heaven is there, but the joy is a transitory one. Accordingly, love does not have as permanent an impact on Teufelsdröckh. While Victor thinks of his beloved Klothilde long after she is dead, and his emotions for her still indirectly guide his life, Teufelsdröckh's love life remains a closed book after his first disappointment. He keeps eternal silence on the matter and views women from that point on as 'Pieces of Art ... [he] has lost thought of purchasing' (ibid., 135). The whole affair is tinted, if not dyed, with a goodly portion of 'sulphurous Humour' (ibid., 134). The voyage into dreamland is compared with navigation in unknown seas, where the solitary rover will be detained on a Calypso-Island that 'falsifies and oversets his whole reckoning' (ibid., 132). We are further given to understand that the earth holds more Blumines 'resigned to wed some richer' (ibid., 144). The ironic overtones of Teufelsdröckh's reflections of love are alien to Jean Paul. In spite of what Siebenkäs experiences in marriage in the way of 'thornpieces,' he forgets them when he meets his ideal woman, Natalie. There may be humorous passages on love in Jean Paul, but he does take love seriously. It always stretches out filaments towards the supernatural.

Kater Murr and *Peter Lebrecht* as Influences on Carlyle's Love Image

Teufelsdröckh's love for Blumine ends in disillusionment, and we ask ourselves why fulfilment was denied him. In many German romantic writers, most pronounced in E.T.A. Hoffmann perhaps, the very fact of non-fulfilment proves to be a valuable incentive for the artist. Not having to accommodate itself to the practical problems of daily living, love is allowed to remain in the supernatural sphere, whence it came. Love and the beloved become an ever-present ideal, untarnished by being lowered to the more pedestrian planes of life. Inspiring but not interfering with the artist's calling, they aid the creative effort.

Hoffmann goes even further by demanding that the artist should voluntarily renounce, before the ideal is defaced by contact with the real. The beloved may otherwise become a hindrance for the artist, dragging him down to the trivial level of everyday existence. The symbol of 'heavenly love' is the Naphtha-flame, which never dies: 'When at last will the destroying fire in your breast turn into a pure Naphtha-flame, nourished by the deepest awareness of art?' Master Abraham in *Kater Murr*[23] asks conductor Kreisler, who is passionately in love with Julia. The abbot, in whom Kreisler also confides, elaborates on the necessity of renunciation in love: 'If you renounce you save yourself from destruction; never, never can nor will you participate in the imagined happiness of earthly love.'[24]

In *Sartor*, the love relationship does not affect art directly. Blumine does not act as an inspiration for Teufelsdröckh, but the practical benefits of the one-sided soul communion are the same as in the case of Hoffmann's artist, for whom the beloved must remain a vision: Teufelsdröckh is free to turn to his vocation as a man of letters, which, after a period of search and frustration, he finds mapped out for him. After the Blumine episode, the Editor assures us, Teufelsdröckh 'would never wed ... never even flirt' (*Sartor*, 135).

Carlyle may have looked to other German sources as well to describe additional episodes from Teufelsdröckh's life story in keeping with the German decor he had chosen. Tieck's novel *Peter Lebrecht* may have proved helpful, particularly as far as plot mechanics are concerned.

The story pattern of the remarkable youth Peter Lebrecht, who as a person has little in common with Teufelsdröckh, strikes one as similar to that adopted in *Sartor*. Lebrecht is also raised in a small village in the same idyllic setting; however, that milieu is scarcely elaborated: 'When at first my thoughts awoke, I found myself in a little house of a village. I still remember very well the willowtree that stood in front of the door, and the sunbeams playing on its branches. A swarthy man, whom I called Father, and a very friendly woman, whom I called Mother, were my daily society.'[25]

Like Teufelsdröckh, he is told by his mother that she and his father are merely foster-parents, and that for various reasons his true parents must remain unnamed. The news is broached with the same laconic terseness in both accounts:

Tieck	*Carlyle*
For my mother told me that she and my father were not my *true* but merely *foster-parents,* and that the	It only concerns us to add, that now was the time when Mother Gretchen revealed to her foster-son that he

name of my natural father could not be given for a variety of reasons. (*Peter Lebrecht*, I, 80)[26]	was not at all of this kindred. (*Sartor*, 107)

Lebrecht is being acquainted with this significant fact prior to leaving for the *Gymnasium*, Teufelsdröckh before entering university.

Eventually Lebrecht does receive more information about his father, who was formerly a nobleman and has now taken holy orders. There is reason to believe that Teufelsdröckh's father is also not a rustic personality. The stranger who brings the green-veiled basket full of Teufelsdröckh to the Futterals speaks in a rather high-flown manner about the 'invaluable loan' (*Sartor*, 84), withdraws gracefully, salutes gravely, and drives off in a coach-and-four.

Young Lebrecht has, in the meantime, become a private tutor to the two sons of a high official, an occupation well known to Teufelsdröckh as well. There he gets involved in a romance with Louise, who shows signs that she is not indifferent to Lebrecht's attentions, although she is considered to be as good as engaged to a young nobleman, Herr von Bärenklau, who shows some resemblance to Towgood. Lebrecht is, at first, ignorant of this connection between the two, until the mistress of the house reminds him of his position and bids him abstain from his infatuation, as the planned marriage would be most advantageous for her young ward. The high official, in contrast, encourages Lebrecht to continue his wooing and even procures a position for him to give the forthcoming marriage financial backing. On arrival of the wedding guests, the groom finds himself without his bride, as von Bärenklau has eloped with Louise.

In this novel the triangle of Lebrecht, Louise, and von Bärenklau parallels that of Teufelsdröckh, Blumine, and Towgood. Teufelsdröckh also reacts with surprise when suddenly the 'gay Barouche' (*Sartor*, 151) appears, carrying the newlyweds past the unhappy wanderer. He is obviously unaware of the fact that a relationship of sorts must have existed between Blumine and Towgood, and that it was the reason why Teufelsdröckh and his beloved 'were to meet no more' (ibid., 145).

In appearance both Louise and Blumine belong to the same 'angelic' female type. Louise's whole bearing 'showed indescribable gentleness, bordering on the melancholy. Every word she said, sounded like music to my ears.'[27] In spite of blushes and slight tremors, however, these ladies are quite capable of standing their ground when it comes to making a decision.

Criticism of the nobility, centring in *Sartor* on the epitaph of Count

Zähdarm and side glances at Towgood's insufficient training for any position of responsibility, is, in Tieck's novel, connected with von Bärenklau. His arrogance is singled out as his most obnoxious trait. He confronts his rival and lectures him on his social position: 'Who are you? What good fortune do you possess that you could offer her? You are Herr Lebrecht and nothing more, and the dividends you could claim from your love would be poor indeed.'[28] The Editor in *Sartor* uses similar arguments in criticizing Teufelsdröckh's love mania in retrospect: 'Thou foolish "absolved Auscultator," before whom lies no prospect of capital, will any yet known "religion of young hearts" keep the human kitchen warm?' (*Sartor*, 144).

While Teufelsdröckh wins over Blumine by way of philosophical dispute, Lebrecht finds favour with Louise by reciting poetry that is not even his own: 'many self-evident things we repeated a thousand times over, without ever attempting to explain poetic phrases which were obvious nonsense. The conversation of two lovers is like a melody on an Aeolian harp – always the same sounds without rhyme nor rhythm, but nevertheless pleasing to the ear in their monotony when heard in a beautiful landscape.'[29]

This quotation is not given for similarity of content with any meeting between Teufelsdröckh and Blumine, but for the ironic tone in which the love scene is rendered.

This same type of slight ridicule is also adopted by Carlyle. After a description in the Jean Paulian mood, 'amid lambent glances, laughter, tears, and often with the inarticulate mystic speech of Music' (*Sartor*, 143), this conclusion is drawn by the Editor: 'Our readers have witnessed the origin of this Love-mania, and with what royal splendour it waxes, and rises' (ibid., 144). This splitting up of the reaction into two voices – one emotionally involved in the romance, the other reporting on it in the manner of an outsider – increases the complexity. The following thought association, which likens Teufelsdröckh to a balloon, once more states his case in a satirical vein: 'We view, with a lively pleasure, the gay silk Montgolfier start from the ground, and shoot upwards, cleaving the liquid deeps, till it dwindle to a luminous star: but what is there to look longer on, when once, by natural elasticity, or accident of fire, it has exploded? ... Suffice it to know that Teufelsdröckh rose into the highest regions of the Empyrean, by a natural parabolic track, and returned thence in a quick perpendicular one' (ibid., 144–5).

Tieck uses the same metaphor with a slight variation, leaving out the explosion of the balloon, in keeping with his less emphatic style:

'Once the lover has entered into the realm of poetry, it is impossible to drag him into the prose of common life. He is like a Montgolfier that got off its moorings, having torn the securing ropes; patiently the audience must wait below until the light air gradually evaporates, and by itself it falls back onto the ground.'[30]

Lebrecht's first reaction after Louise's elopement is one of 'gloomy, dark indifference,' even in wording, not unlike Teufelsdröckh's experiences in his 'Wanderings and Sorrowings' (*Sartor*, 146). He has lost his ability to orient himself in life and, by travelling far and wide, seeks refuge in Nature. His observations on Nature are, however, not in any way comparable to the philosophically tinted landscapes opening up into eternity that Teufelsdröckh unrolls before his readers, in order to prepare them for the spiritual autobiography that is about to unfold.

FOUR

Spiritual Autobiographies, German Style

> The ground upon which I assume the existence of something beyond myself, does not lie outside of myself, but within me.
>
> (Fichte, *Bestimmung des Menschen*)

Self-Revelation in the Protestant Tradition

However much has been written about the Calvinist subpattern in the central chapters of Book II of *Sartor*, little probing has been done into literary forms of spiritual self-relevation that stand in the German Protestant tradition.[1] It should not be forgotten that, at the time of his acquaintanceship with German influences, Carlyle had found Calvinist religious faith unsatisfactory. This explains his eagerness to focus on manifestations of a faith less narrow and more sophisticated as far as insights into man's soul were concerned. In this regard, the common Protestant religious backgrounds of much that Carlyle admired in German literature needs to be considered, as it too contributes models that illuminate the autobiographical aspects of his work.

The emergence of the spiritual autobiography in Germany is intimately connected with the Pietist movement, which arose within the Lutheran Church towards the end of the seventeenth and continued well into the eighteenth century. Its primary aim was to reinstate the Christian faith in the hearts of men, whence it was felt it had been ousted. What was needed, Jakob Böhme (1575–1624), the theosophic mystic, and later Phillip Jakob Spener (1635–1705), 'the Father of Pietism,' claimed, was a return to devout Christianity from the aberrations of dogmatic legalism that imperilled Christian freedom. The Collegia Pietatis therefore demanded the fashioning of a new type of Christianity, with faith as its soul. This was the aim of the Böhmische Brüdergemeinde (Moravian Brethren), organized in 1722 by Count Zinzendorf.

The Pietists maintained that, in order to become a new man, a rebirth (*Wiedergeburt*) had to take place, based on examination of conscience. Soul-searching was central to this new approach and included training of the will, to direct it with all intensity towards spiritual salvation. Sensitive observation of self was often accompanied by agonies of doubt and despair prior to repentance of sin, as the turning-point towards the New Life. Although at first rather pitiful attempts at gaining psychological insights in this manner were being made, self-reflection did eventually result in a form of literary autobiographical self-analysis.

What are these Christian autobiographies all about? At first sight there emerges from them an often unsuccessful attempt to relate insignificant events of everyday life to the will of God. In most cases pathetic rather than inspiring, these documents of inner struggle stress man's readiness to take on responsibilities in this world as a servant of God. To aid the divine will to manifest itself, to bring it into harmony with man's own, is the central theme. In this spirit, experiences of the life of the soul are being faithfully, sometimes pedantically, recorded, and interpreted in a religious sense. Usually a sudden consciousness of sinfulness strikes the writer, followed by absolute faith in divine grace. A good example of the tension arising from the wretchedness of sin and the desire for perfection is the eighteenth-century autobiography of Johann Jakob Moser (1701–85).

The result of this soul-searching varies: sometimes an elation at the ideal of election is all too obvious, leading to what modern psychology would label superiority complexes; sometimes the sense of obligation to the divine will releases the best qualities inherent in the individual. In the latter, a type of vision emerges, accurately reflecting the mental make-up of the personality struggling for inner clarity, the aim of which is God. 'Love not pleasure, love God' is a command writ large in many of these documents. Men like Philipp Jakob Spener (1635–1705) already fervently try in this world to live up to the ideals of Pietism. It is in this manner that these early spiritual autobiographies are always related to some form of Christian metaphysics.

It is hardly surprising that the idea of a spiritual journey, comes to the fore in these efforts of the individual soul to reach out for moral perfection in ordinary life. Count Zinzendorf's diary, for example, is subtitled 'Reihenfolge meiner Wanderschaft.' Others compare their attempts, in the best Protestant tradition, to struggles, as, after the Reformation, Luther's spiritual wrestlings for the New Faith were commonly stressed. A soul that undertook such travels had first to show the ability to grasp a truer notion of eternity by looking into itself. For only in the individual self the powers lay dormant that could penetrate into the world of the spirit. In man the finite and the infinite met; he could elevate himself towards the supernatural only by way of the inner light.

This ideal was not achieved without an amount of training in self-observation. For this very reason August Hermann Francke (1663–1727), founder of the famous orphanage in Leipzig, encouraged his pupils to write 'Diaries of the Soul,' he himself leaving a most memorable document of this kind called 'Selbstzeugnisse,' full of darkest despair and inner struggles with a cold, indifferent heart, finally touched by divine grace. Thus doubts are destroyed and strength is gathered to achieve great and lasting activities for the benefit of mankind. For, according to Protestant traditions, not to live in cloistered virtue but to prove oneself in actual life is the way that leads to the kingdom of God.

It was also Francke who noticed a certain pattern underlying his own and other self-observations. Three basic stages are distinguished:

1 / Worldly life (*Weltleben*)
2 / Perturbation (*Aufschreckung*)
3 / Insight (*Erleuchtung*)

Known as the 'Halle System of Conversion' it is mentioned in Goethe's 'Bekenntnisse einer schönen Seele.'

It should be noted that nowhere in these autobiographical accounts would we read of intellectualized religious experiences. From Francke to Zinzendorf, emotional consent, in the form of faith, is central to this type of conversion, as is a sudden realization of the individual's responsibilities in active life. In the light of these German Protestant autobiographical traditions, Teufelsdröckh's spiritual experiences no longer appear uniquely 'Calvinist.'

'Die schöne Seele' in *Wilhelm Meisters Lehrjahre*

To come closer to a realization of the springs of one's being, and then proceed to action in the direction towards which these insights lead, is one of the important messages contained in *Wilhelm Meister*. It lies at the core of the 'Bekenntnisse einer schönen Seele,' Goethe's poetical rendering of Fräulein von Klettenberg's Pietistical writings, which he incorporated with emendations into the sixth book of *Wilhelm Meisters Lehrjahre*.[2]

Although this book furnishes a remarkable example of autobiographical soul-searching, the method of confession is also employed in other parts of Goethe's novel as an indirect means to test applicants who wish to join the *Turmgesellschaft*. In connection with the rolls exhibited in the initiation room, Jarno tells Wilhelm, who also becomes a member, that they are a form of self-revelation, giving the society valuable clues regarding the personality of the writer. Apprentices and Masters are chosen on the basis of these autobiographies, favouring those individuals who feel intensely and confess sincerely. Nobody is advanced to the rank of Master who does not clearly recognize the purpose he was born for, and is determined to proceed along his way (*Wilhelm Meister II*, 129). In this connection it is interesting to recall that Goethe's name in Freemasonry circles was 'Meister.'

The search for spiritual communion between the Soul and the Invisible, as the 'Schöne Seele' calls God, takes its course in an individualized manner and is not directed by a conventional belief in valid norms. Such norms are indeed questioned and, in part, even resisted. The inner voice aids the soul in uncovering the laws of its own being and gives it strength to follow them, despite disapproval and censure by society at large. True values are discovered by intuitive insights, in contrast to mere appearance or *Schein*. Once a reorientation has taken place, all subsequent actions in this world are guided solely by these inner laws.

This is in brief the nature of the spiritual development that takes place within the life-pattern of the 'Schöne Seele.' Born into an upper-class family with court connections, the young girl does not have to struggle with poverty, but with bad health. As she is confined to bed by illness for many months, the introspective tendency is increased in a personality whose response to life is an emotional one. Not only does the child converse with the Invisible Power, but the longing for God, dimly felt, increases by involuntary isolation.

After this initial stage of response to the supernatural, she enters into a period of dissipation in social activities after regaining her health, a time when 'feelings towards the Invisible were almost totally extinguished'[3] (*Meister I*, 403). In looking back at these years of estrangement from God, the 'Schöne Seele' considers them to have been the emptiest in her life: 'I have lived away in mere corporeal cheerfulness; I never took myself to task, I never prayed, I never thought about myself or God'[4] (ibid.). Complications arising out of her love affair with Narziss, as well as his illness subsequent to a duel, awaken a desire to turn to God with her troubles: 'Him I had quite forgotten those four wild years; I now again began to think of him occasionally; but our acquaintance had grown cool; they were visits of mere ceremony these; and as, moreover, in waiting on him, I used to dress in fine apparel, to set before him self-complacently my virtue, honour and superiorities to others, he did not seem to notice me, or know me in that finery' (ibid., 409–10).[5]

A period of disbelief on rational grounds is indicated by Narziss's lending his bride literature of the Enlightenment, presenting a case against religious faith by way of discursive reasoning: 'He often gave me writings which opposed with light and heavy weapons, all that can be called connection with the Invisible' (ibid., 413).[6] The 'Schöne Seele' faithfully reads these, but neither gains nor loses anything after having done so.

The theme of dearth is skilfully brought in at this point, not of little consequence as a symbol of impending change: 'Our spring was over. The summer came and all grew drier and more earnest' (ibid., 415).[7] It is brought about by a sudden rebirth of spiritual needs. Probing into her own soul she realizes that her interrupted relationship to the Invisible must be reinstated. Employment with unworthy things detracts from this communion: 'Yet by what means could I help myself or extricate my mind from the calls of a world where everything was either cold indifference or hot insanity' (ibid., 416).[8]

Hand in hand with the decision to renounce society once and for all, and to follow the dictates of her innermost feelings, goes an ever-clearer awareness 'that there are loftier emotions, which afford us a contentment such as it is vain to seek in the amusements of the world; and that in these higher joys, there is also kept a secret treasure for strengthening the spirit in misfortune' (ibid., 417).[9] The 'Schöne Seele' feels trapped and is unable to draw the consequences from these insights: 'I was hemmed in by a ring drawn round me' (ibid., 416).[10] Struggles ensue, particularly as the decision to follow her own conscience in matters of religious belief includes giving up Narziss, who is not ready to grant concessions on this point. The necessity to expand into hitherto unexperienced realms leads to a clean break with the past. The symbol for this is the shattered glass bell: 'But at last, when after many thousand struggles, and thoughts continually renewed, I began to cast a steady eye upon the bond ... I at once perceived it to be only a glass bell, which shut me up in the exhausted airless space:

One bold stroke to break the bell in pieces, and thou art delivered!' (ibid., 418).[11]

Renewed faith in God's presence is the final outcome: 'I was not without God in the world. He was near to me, I was before him. This is what, with a diligent avoidance of all theological systematic terms, I can with the greatest truth declare' (ibid., 427).[12]

In the stage of inner fulfilment by faith, the transcendental vision of life is reached. The 'Schöne Seele' is now capable of looking at human society at large with a certain detachment, beholding 'the tumult, off my watchtower, from afar' (ibid., 431) and at the same time to reach out for the supernatural: 'Shortly I became convinced that my soul had acquired a power of soaring upwards, which was altogether new to it' (ibid., 434).[13]

Spiritual emblems of the Herrnhuter community aid in this attempt. She also finds impressive the bold figurative style in which Zinzendorf speaks of mighty truths.

In the wake of the conversion, Nature also takes on a deeper meaning as manifestation of the divine: 'How gladly did I now see God in nature, when I bore him with such certainty in my heart! How interesting to me was his handiwork' (ibid., 455).[14]

Constant commitments regarding care for others in need and sickness further stress activity in life, a duty that must not be shunned as part of the Protestant tradition of obligation to the living. It is carried out in spite of the canoness's own precarious constitution. When finally the death of her father results in greater freedom of movement for her, she has learned the need for voluntary restriction of liberty: 'The invaluable happiness of liberty consisted, not in doing what one pleases ... but what one regards as right and proper' (ibid., 453).[15]

Associations widen. Having used up all her spiritual strength in 'striving exclusively after the one thing needful' (ibid., 443),[16] the values contained in art have been neglected by the 'Schöne Seele.' A meeting with her uncle, a great art lover, leads to a discovery of the connectedness between the divine, the beautiful, and the good in man: ' "If we can conceive it possible," he once observed, "that the Creator of the world himself assumed the form of his creature, and lived in that manner for a time upon earth, this creature must appear to us of infinite perfection, because susceptible of such a combination with its Maker. Hence, in our idea of man there can be no inconsistency with our idea of God" ' (ibid.).[17]

These aesthetic extensions of thought, although no longer a part of the actual conversion, left their mark on Carlyle with regard to his notions of the sanctity of the human form, confirmed by his readings of Novalis. Initially, however, it is through Goethe that Carlyle was able to find a place for art in his concept of spiritual life. For it is man, as an artist, who creates 'some form, the pattern of which originates in his spirit' (ibid., 444).[18]

While the 'Schöne Seele' further refines her spiritual nature, already looking upon the body as 'a foreign substance, a garment [which] will fall to pieces like a vesture' (ibid., 454),[19] the book ends on a strong note of action, handed down to the reader by way of the physician's advice: 'To be active is the primary vocation of man' (ibid., 455).[20]

From this interpretative sketch it becomes clear that the 'Bekenntnisse' contain leading themes that were subsequently developed by Carlyle in Teufelsdröckh's autobiography, even if all individual phases cannot be paralleled. In *Sartor,* as there, we find initially a close intuitive relationship with the Infinite or Invisible in the seclusion of childhood, however different in detail. There follows a period of estrangement from God, introducing Unbelief. Typically enough, this period of doubt is largely expanded in Teufelsdröckh's account, while it is only intimated in that of the 'Schöne Seele.' Ensuing spiritual struggle, leading to a crisis, is resolved by the strength of renewed faith in the divine presence of a personal God. Again, Carlyle's emphasis is different. Spiritual suffering is intensified in *Sartor,* subdued in Goethe's rendering of the 'Bekenntnisse.' Both conversions are very singular experiences, deviating from the prescribed pattern of Christian conversions in general. This deviation has been noticed mainly by Harrold in the case of *Sartor,* but has not been related to the account given in Goethe's work.[21] The result for both participants is a deep sense of inner freedom, a new attitude to Nature as an expression of the divine, and a general direction of thought towards the transcendental. A number of similarities can be noted: the reference to the watchtower, the concept of happiness as not consisting in doing as one likes, the body as a garment, the importance of emblems, and the seeds of the gospel of work.

The various spiritual stages are, of course, seen through different temperaments and described in different styles. Teufelsdröckh's metaphors are bold, his style is dynamic and exaggerated, his formulations are forceful and vivid. The stage of doubt is prolonged, the shadows of despair deepened. That 'transient knitting of these shaggy brows' and 'mad fermentation' (148) add so much more immediacy to his spiritual experiences that the harmonious and balanced account of the

'Schöne Seele' appears rather mild and quiet in tone next to so much furor and vehemence.

Faust's Struggle with Doubt and Despair

Although, with a view to examining the development of the spiritual autobiography, 'Bekenntnisse' has been dealt with first in this chapter, it does not represent the primary impact of Goethe's work on Carlyle. Prior to any influences derived from *Wilhelm Meister* – both the *Apprenticeship* and the *Travels* – Faust's struggle with doubt and despair deeply impressed itself on a mind that was experiencing a similar conflict. Indeed, the form this doubt takes in the 'Everlasting No' is related to characteristics that both Faust and Mephistopheles possess in Goethe's drama.

Carlyle had no need to be introduced to the problem of doubt by any German writer, as it was part of his own mental disposition. What he stood in need of was an acknowledgment of this state as peculiar also to other searching minds, as well as a resolution of the conflict, showing that a way out of this state of spiritual torment was possible. He therefore read Goethe's *Faust* primarily with his own case-history in mind; later, in a state of regained health, he could look back on and describe his experience of *Faust* in a symbolical manner, elevating it onto a plane of universality where it was applicable to all men in a state of growth.

The impact of Goethe's *Faust*, containing a dramatized treatment of what Carlyle considered to be spiritual problems close to his own heart, made itself felt at a time when the message contained in *Wilhelm Meister*, reported in a style full of calm depth and mellow serenity, had not as yet reached him. In his early essay of 1822, 'Faustus: From the German of Goethe,'[22] the interpretation of the drama from a purely moral angle is remarkable, as is the biographical relationship he draws between Goethe's life and his own.

Besides being emblematic of human life at the universal level, *Faust* is expressive of Goethe's own early woes and doubts, darkness and despondency, suffered during his passage from youth to settled manhood. Carlyle links the struggle to himself, expressing the thought that Goethe understood his own aberrations. With these objects fixed in his mind, he concentrates in his criticism exclusively on the characterization of Faust and Mephistopheles. While the former is drawn towards order, represented by God and the concept of cosmos, the latter stands for the principle of disorder and chaos. In this manner, Carlyle sees these figures as 'discordant but strangely related to each other' ('Faustus,' 260). This formula is simplified but appropriate, so that he employs it again in *Past and Present,* describing Abbot Sampson as 'the Missionary of Order; he is the servant not of the Devil and Chaos, but of God and the Universe' (*Past and Present,* II, 92).

Faust is largely characterized as presented in the opening scenes in his Gothic chamber, where from a search for truth 'his mind has returned back more faint and full of doubt' ('Faustus,' 254). In a state of mental convulsion, Faust admits 'that day or night his anguish never ceases; that existence is a burden to him; and death his only hope' (ibid., 257). This is merely a part truth as far as Goethe's meaning goes. Faust is admittedly in a state of hopelessness, but for reasons Carlyle does not take into consideration. His frustrations spring from the realization that knowledge does not take him any closer to his most fervent wish, his overruling desire, to comprehend the springs of Nature. Moral anguish does not enter into the picture until he begins his tragic involvement with life. Faust's *Leitmotif* at this stage is *Wissensdrang* (thirst for knowledge), which in no way despises intellectual means, however much he questions the usefulness of the mind as an ultimate instrument for probing into Nature's secrets.

Of this Renaissance spirit, we hear nothing. For Carlyle, Faust is a soul-searcher, without any of his Titanism: 'It is to the character of Faust, however, as displayed in the opening scenes of the play, that we turn for the highest proof of Goethe's genius. They give us the most vivid picture we have ever seen of a species of mental convulsion, at once in the extreme degree moving and difficult to paint ... It is the destruction of a noble spirit by the force of its own thoughts; a suicide of the mind, far more tragical than that of the body ... when his earthly hopes are all blasted, no moral consolation is in store for him' (ibid., 266). Faust's sin consists, for Carlyle, in his doubting the existence of Providence and the foundation of moral distinctions.

The same lack of complexity, although less obvious, is visible in the delineation of the character of Mephistopheles, defined as 'a moral, not a physical devil,' resembling some 'French *philosophe* of the last century' (ibid., 253). Such a trait means for Carlyle 'the perfection of the intellectual faculties with a total absence of the moral' (ibid., 259). His presence acts 'like a moral Harmattan, the mortifying wind of the desert, under which every green thing is parched and dies' (ibid., 260).

In subsequent discussions this characterization of protagonist and antagonist becomes fuller but does not broaden to include other aspects. Having once wrongly linked Goethe's portrayal of doubt and despair to the author's struggles as an individual, and to his own in a moral sense, Carlyle continues to use this approach also in the essay 'Goethe' that prefaces his translation of *Wilhelm Meister.* Contending that the contest between the good and the bad principle in human nature should be the indirect subject-matter of all true poetry, he praises *Faust* as successfully depicting the 'struggle of Man's Soul against Ignorance, Sin and Suffering' (*Wilhelm Meister* I, 19). A foreshadowing of Teufelsdröckh is indicated when the work is described as delineating 'the fate of human enthusiasm struggling against doubts and errors from within, against scepticism, contempt and selfishness from without' (ibid., 4–5). Carlyle also related himself to Faust, whose curse he mentions as emblematic of his previous state of mind in his correspondence with Goethe.[23]

More searching comments are contained in Carlyle's essay 'Goethe's *Helena,*' reviewing Goethe's initial continuation of *Faust* I in the *Helena*-act, now a part of *Faust* II. Faust is here identified with the image of man: 'The Soul of Man still fights with the dark influences of Ignorance, Misery and Sin; still lacerates itself, like a captive bird, against the iron limits which Necessity has drawn around it; still follows False Shows, seeking peace and good on paths where no peace or good is to be found' (*Essays I,* 155).

In addition, a most extraordinary Faust story is being invented by Carlyle, one that shows some affinity with Teufelsdröckh-in-the making, and might as well be a description of the latter's personality: 'If Mephistopheles represent the spirit of Denial, Faust may represent that of Inquiry and Endeavour: the two are by necessity in conflict; the light and the darkness of man's life and mind ... with a whirlwind impetuosity he rushes forth over the Universe to grasp all excellence; his heart yearns towards the infinite and the invisible ... Confiding in his feeling of himself, he has started with the tacit persuasion that he must be *happy*' (ibid., 158).

Here, we feel, themes are crowding to the fore that clarify Carlyle's view of life rather than Faust's. But this is not all. To our astonishment we read that Faust had not spent his youth and manhood, as others did, 'in the sunny, crowded paths of profit, or among the rosy bowers of pleasure, but darkly and alone in the search of Truth.' Should it, Carlyle asks the reader, after having virtually invented Faust's past life, 'end in the pale shadow of Doubt?' (*Essays,* ibid., 159).

It has already been said in connection with Carlyle's first essay on

Faust that the protagonist's despair in Goethe's work was caused by a feeling of incapability to come closer to the *Urgrund* of things, the spirit of Nature itself. The desire for personal happiness with which Carlyle invests him is completely absent from the thoughts of Faust, who wants to experience the emotions of *all* mankind. Details of Faust's imagined youth are pure invention. His sufferings do not spring from the fact that 'he is still a stranger to that law of self-denial, by which alone man's narrow destiny may become an infinitude within itself' (ibid., 161). What actually happened was that Carlyle had linked up Faust 'the son of Light and Free-will' (ibid.) with the solution given in *Wilhelm Meisters Wanderjahre*. This was the solution of renunciation that he himself was to apply to his own hero Teufelsdröckh, who as a personality shows affinities with Carlyle's version of Faust.

He continues to treat Faust's predicament with great sympathy, claiming that he cannot be regarded as wicked, but merely as misguided and miserable: 'For how many living hearts, even now imprisoned in the perplexities of Doubt, do these wild piercing tones of Faust, his withering agonies and fiery desperation "speak the word they have long been waiting to hear!" ' (*Essays I, 'Goethe's Helena,'* 162).

Mephistopheles is also rounded out more fully as a personality in 'Goethe's *Helena*. He is described as 'a cultivated personage, and acquainted with the modern sciences' (ibid., 156). Carlyle takes obvious pleasure in adding contemporary colouring to the portrait of the Denier, who works with an 'attorney intellect: it can contradict, but cannot affirm ... he combines perfect Understanding with perfect Selfishness of logical Life with moral Death' (ibid., 157–8). Undoubtedly, Mephistopheles is, for Carlyle, a Utilitarian who represents the Son of Night in modern dress.

These expanded characterizations of Faust and Mephistopheles did have an indirect effect on the emergence of Teufelsdröckh's personality as drawn in the 'Everlasting No.' He himself alludes to Faust when recalling his state of deadly isolation: 'Some comfort it would have been, could I, like a Faust, have fancied myself tempted and tormented of the Devil' (*Sartor*, 164). In spite of these resonances one could hardly call *Sartor* a 'Victorian Faust,'[24] as Faust's problems do not, first and foremost, lie where Carlyle sees them. To him Faust's struggle is a purely spiritual one, because the germ of such an interpretation lay in Carlyle's own mind long before he came into contact with Goethe's drama. He chose to read *Faust* in this light, giving the work a totally subjective interpretation that fitted it better into his scheme of things.

Carlyle sees embodied in Faust the eternal human situation of all who 'have dared to say No and cannot yet say Yea; but feel that in the No they dwell as in a Golgotha, where life enters not, where peace is not appointed them' (*Essays III*, 'Characteristics', 31). In search of affirmation and the philosophical elaboration of the problem of Doubt and Despair, we turn to Fichte.

Doubt Removed by Faith in Fichte's *Bestimmung des Menschen*

No systematic comparison has yet been undertaken of Fichte's *Die Bestimmung des Menschen* (*The Vocation of Man*) with Carlyle's *Sartor* to show the applicability of philosophical thought in Fichte's popular work to the central chapters of Teufelsdröckh's spiritual autobiography. Scholarly interest has focused exclusively on Fichte's *Über das Wesen des Gelehrten* (*Nature of the Scholar*), which Carlyle acknowledged as a source (*Essays I*, 'State of German Literature,' 60; *Heroes*, 156–7). This neglect is all the more surprising as there are more aspects of Fichte's philosophy contained in *Sartor* than *Über das Wesen* can supply: References to the 'Divine Me,' the 'Celestial Me,' and the 'Self' are certainly not elaborated in *Über das Wesen*, a work that is primarily concerned with the ethics of the teaching profession and the manifestation of the 'Divine Idea.'

Where then was Carlyle to turn in his effort to clarify the position of Transcendentalism on such questions? Jean Paul and Novalis, both basically Transcendentalists, would prove helpful in the poetical elaboration of ideas, but could hardly be considered philosophers in their own right. Carlyle's aversion to purely technical philosophical inquiry ruled out the highly abstract theorems of the *Wissenschaftslehre*, while *Die Bestimmung*, with its concrete illustrations of much of Fichte's thought, must have recommended itself for such a study. Whereas no external proof exists that Carlyle read *Die Bestimmung*, he employs especially in his essay on Novalis – phrases and definitions he can have found nowhere but in the above work.[25]

Already in the opening chapters of *Sartor*, the nature of the 'Divine Me,' the *Über-Ich*, is being referred to 'whereby he is revealed to his like, and dwells with them in UNION and DIVISION' (*Sartor*, 65). Nobody unacquainted with the ability of the *Über-Ich* to split itself up into so many personal *Ich* could have set down this remark full of transcendental implications.

It is, however, in the central chapters of Book II 'The Everlasting No,' 'Centre of Indifference,' and 'The Everlasting Yea,' containing Teufelsdröckh's spiritual biography, that the closet affinity of *Sartor* with *Die Bestimmung* is reached, for here Carlyle considers even more directly such notions as the *Ich*, its consciousness, the realization of Self in activity, and the *Nicht-Ich*, all dealt with at length and in a popular form in *Die Bestimmung*. As the philosophical implications are in Carlyle merely suggested rather than consecutively developed – enriched and, at the same time, obscured by symbols – *Die Bestimmung* provides the systematic derivation of thought which Carlyle leaves out. This failure to give an insight into the working of Teufelsdröckh's mind in the labours of spiritual crisis is especially evident after the defiance of the Everlasting No. The reader does not find out how the new state of consciousness is reached. Carlyle merely shows Teufelsdröckh's application of the new belief in freedom, gained in the fire-baptism of the Rue Saint-Thomas de l'Enfer. However, Fichte's *persona*, the reflecting *Ich* of *Die Bestimmung*, henceforth to be called the 'Ego,' supplies some of the missing links. Both the 'Ego' and Teufelsdröckh may be analysed in their own right as fictitious personalities who, besides bearing some traits of their authors, stand for a good deal more of universal significance.[26]

Fichte leads the 'Ego' through three successive stages of development. These lend the book its structural pattern and correspond loosely with Carlyle's chapters in the following manner:

Fichte	*Carlyle*
Book I. Doubt	'The Everlasting No'
Book II. Knowledge	'Centre of Indifference'
Book III. Faith	'The Everlasting Yea'

The fact that philosophy finds its last truths revealed in Faith calls for an explanation: for Fichte the free choice of a philosophical system bears the mark of an ethical-religious act, based on faith. This attitude to philosophy as expressing a *Weltanschauung* related to the personality of the holder is explained in the *First Introduction to the Wissenschaftslehre*: 'What kind of a philosophy a person chooses depends on what kind of a man he is; for a philosophical system is not a dead piece of chattel which you can pick up and dispose of according to whim, but it is spiritualized through the soul of the person who holds it' (*Werke* I, 434).[27]

Delivered at first in monologue, and later in dialogue form, the reflections presented in *Die Bestimmung* read like a spiritual autobiography. The opening situation shows the 'Ego' musing on the question

'What am I, and what is my vocation?' This question is voiced by a mind convinced of the logic of philosophical Determinism, and answered by a reference to the validity of sense experience: 'I have put faith only in the concurrent testimony of my senses, only in repeated and unvarying experience; what I have beheld I have touched – what I have touched, I have analyzed' (*Werke* II, 169; Smith, I, 323).[28]

Equipped with this empirical approach, the 'Ego' begins by examining Nature, of which it believes itself to be a part. Not only does the 'Ego' find that every form of existence, be it plant, animal, or man, is determined by all other phenomena, but it begins to realize that for this very reason any sense of freedom is merely an illusion: 'I myself with all that I call mine am a link in this chain of the stern necessity of Nature' (*Werke* II, 179; Smith, 334).[29]

Admitting to itself that this system is satisfactory for understanding, the 'Ego' immediately encounters doubts regarding its truth. The reason for such doubts is found in this system's utter neglect of emotional and moral values, which violates the Ego's deepest intuitions and wishes. Furthermore, if Nature acts within man, he cannot be held responsible for becoming anything but what Nature determined him to become. Man, in spite of his own striving, cannot produce the smallest change. Fichte's 'Ego' is not prepared to have its sense of freedom explained away by philosophy. It is to much aware of its own will, its innate desire to love; but the question still remains open: 'Am I free and independent? or am I nothing in myself, and merely the manifestation of a foreign power?' (*Werke* II, 195; Smith, 351).[30]

All through Book I, an intense emotional involvement, a spiritual distress, caused by the opposition of the system of logic to the desires of the heart, is evident. With a sure sense of the dramatic, Fichte develops the dualism between Freedom and Necessity: 'The system of freedom satisfies my heart; the opposite system destroys and annihilates it. To stand cold and unmoved amid the current of events, a passive mirror of fleeting phenomena – this existence is insupportable to me. I scorn and curse it, I want to love, want to lose myself in sympathy, be joyful and sad' (*Werke* II, 196; Smith, 351).[31]

This state of doubt becomes unbearable to the 'Ego': 'What power can deliver me from it? What power can deliver me from myself?' (*Werke* II, 198; Smith, 354).[32] Thus the first book ends on a note of indecision and despair.

This pervasive general tenor of despair in Fichte's Book I also forms part of the emotional distress of Carlyle's 'Everlasting No.' In the preceding chapters, this mood had been carefully built up. Even as early as the 'Idylls' of Teufelsdröckh we hear of 'the ring of Necessity whereby we are all begirt' (*Sartor*, 97) with which Free Will often comes into painful collision. Later, at the university stage of his education, his 'whole Universe, physical and spiritual was as yet a machine' (ibid., 133), while, in the 'Sorrows of Teufelsdröckh,' 'Life has become wholly a dark labyrinth; wherein, through long years, our Friend, flying from spectres, has to stumble about at random' (ibid., 152).

The last quotation strongly suggests Fichte's phrasing at the opening of Book II of *Die Bestimmung*: 'I sought but stumbled ever deeper into the labyrinth' (*Werke*, II, 199; Smith, 355).[33] The state of mental depression in Teufelsdröckh is not primarily caused by Blumine's marriage but rather by the impact of a general mechanistic philosophy: 'To me the Universe was all void of Life, of Purpose, of Volition, even of Hostility: it was one huge, dead, immeasurable Steam-engine, rolling on, in its dead indifference' (*Sartor*, 164).

This extended description evokes the empirically conceived world that Fichte's 'Ego' had found lacking in emotional values. The reaction of both protagonists in this spiritual drama is the same. Teufelsdröckh's 'continual, indefinite, pining fear' (ibid., 166) recalls the Ego's 'anguish and fear gnawing at my vitals' (*Werke*, II, 199; Smith, 355).[34] Carlyle adds loss of religious belief, which means loss of everything. Without a moral purpose, striving for virtue appears to be a meaningless exertion, for the 'Ego' as well as for Teufelsdröckh:

Fichte	*Carlyle*
I blush for what I know to be the best in my nature – for the sake of which alone I would exist – as for a ridiculous folly. What is most sacred to me has become a prey to scorn. (*Werke*, II, 196; Smith, 352)[35]	Is the heroic inspiration we name Virtue but some Passion, some bubble of the blood, bubbling in the direction others *profit* by? (*Sartor*, 160)

Up to this point parallels with regard to the development of lines of thought are visible. Doubt and despair in Fichte's 'Ego' are based on the logically convincing but emotionally unsatisfactory solutions of philosophical Determinism. The distress of Carlyle's Teufelsdröckh is caused by a mechanical interpretation of life inherent in philosophical Materialism. Both protagonists feel keenly the loss of moral values. In Fichte's 'Ego' an inner voice claims freedom to be no mere illusion; in Teufelsdröckh the concept of duty still lingers on: 'Thus, in spite of all

Motive-grinders ... was the Infinite nature of Duty still dimly present to me' (*Sartor*, 162).

Here parallels end. While Fichte, in Book II, by way of transcendental criticism lays the foundation for a new conception of the universe, leading out of the maze of Doubt to 'Faith,' Teufelsdröckh shakes off fear by boldly asserting that he is free. It is left to the reader to find out from hints that he assailed and defied the Everlasting No with weapons of sceptical Idealism, when he affirmed: '*I* am not thine, but Free, and forever hate thee!' (ibid., 168). The temper of misery is changed, the new 'Child of Freedom' feels strong, like 'a spirit, almost a god' (ibid., 167). Besides defiance and indignation we hear of a ME writ large: 'Thus had the EVERLASTING NO (*das ewige Nein*) pealed authoritatively through all the recesses of my Being, of my ME; and then was it that my whole ME stood up, in native God-created majesty, and with emphasis recorded its Protest' (ibid.)

Even here we are still not enlightened as to how it all came about. What Carlyle omits is contained in the most theoretical of the three books of *Die Bestimmung*, entitled 'Knowledge.' While in *Sartor* we are confronted with a personification of the spirit of denial in the form of a Mephistophelian devil, Fichte states in transcendental terms the reasons for his belief that man is not part of Nature, but above it, a God-created Me. From these explanations we can gather that the 'Divine' or 'Eternal Me' resists the onslaught of the Everlasting No. This 'Me,' which is part of the eternal will, defies Naturalism or Materialism in the 'Everlasting No' chapter. The spiritual rebirth is an awareness of the powers of the 'Me' to defy the 'Not-Me,' or *Nicht-Ich*. We therefore turn to Fichte's Book II in the hope that it will supply philosophical reasoning where Carlyle, stating the *effects* of the awakening only, remains obscure.

Fichte's 'Knowledge' provides the middle stage between Doubt and Faith, on the way from negation to affirmation. Its contents offer philosophical criticism, based on the *Wissenschaftslehre*. Fichte takes a considerable risk in attempting to crowd these involved deductions into fifty pages. We are not surprised, therefore, at the *deus ex machina* appearance of a Spirit, who guides the reasoning 'Ego,' by way of skilful questioning towards his conclusions.

In the ensuing dialogue, the deterministic philosophy is invalidated step by step, and the fallacy underlying it is revealed. Having started from the wrong assumption, that philosophy begins with the unity of being, the 'Ego' is now being shown that it begins with the unity of consciousness: 'In all perceptions you perceive in the first place only your own condition' (*Werke*, II, 201; Smith, 358).[36] The 'Ego' realizes that it can feel only its own state, when touching a so-called object; that colours, sounds, and textures are its own affections. The same holds good for spatial forms, which are not experienced by the senses but are the outcome of the constructive activity of the completing power of the mind. All attributes of 'objects' are derived from the internal state of the 'Ego.' This was the message Carlyle had attempted to convey in his essay 'Novalis,' ending his explanation with the tree-passage, used as a valid illustration of the existence of 'objects' in the mind only (*Essays II*, 25). Fichte's Spirit summarizes his conclusions for the benefit of the 'Ego' as much as for the reader: 'You perceive then that all knowledge is merely a knowledge of yourself; that your consciousness never goes beyond yourself; and that what you assume to be a consciousness of the object, is nothing but a consciousness of your own supposition of an object, which, according to an inward law of your thought, you make necessarily simultaneously with the sensation itself' (*Werke*, II, 222; Smith, 378).[37]

The Spirit then proceeds to do away with the object notion altogether, replacing it with the *Nicht-Ich*, or 'Not-Me,' which we shall follow as far as is necessary for an application to Carlyle's use of the term. With the definition of the *Ich* and the *Nicht-Ich*, the question must be asked: 'Since the thing cannot know itself, how can a knowledge of it arise? – How can a consciousness of the thing arise in me?' (*Werke*, II, 225; Smith, 381).[38] What, we may add, is the connection between the *Ich* and the *Nicht-Ich*, the object of knowledge?

According to Fichte there is no need for such a link, except in the consciousness of the *Ich*, which has knowledge of the *Nicht-Ich*. This consciousness was born when subject and object emerged from the *Ur-Ich*, in which they were originally one. The *Ur-Ich*, also termed the 'Divine Me,' split itself in a creative act into other finite *Ichs*. By way of its origin, the *Ich* is subject and object, the *Nicht-Ich*, as a mere reproduction of the self, no more than appearance, or *Erscheinung*. For, if subject and object fall together in the *Ur-Ich*, there is no such thing as a *Ding an sich*.

The final result of this philosophical reasoning, which overreaches Kant, who had let the *Ding an sich* stand as a cause for thought, holds out a solution for the problems of both the 'Ego' and Teufelsdröckh. If, as the Spirit claims, the *Nicht-Ich* is nothing but a power outside of me arising from my own consciousness, the particular and manifold manifestations of the external world must arise in the same way. It follows that the phenomenal world is merely an *Abbild*, and the pictures we fear are only of our own mind's making: 'And with this insight, mortal, be free, and forever released from the fear which has degraded and tormented you! You will no longer tremble at a necessity which exists only in your own thought; no longer fear to be crushed by things which are the product of your own mind ... As long as you could believe that a system of things, such as you have described, really existed independently of you, and that you yourself may be but a link in this chain, such a fear was well grounded ... It was from this fear that I wished to set you free' (*Werke*, II, 240; Smith, 397).[39]

Here we catch up with Teufelsdröckh at the stage when he defies the Everlasting No, and shakes base fear away from him forever. A power inside him, the *Ur-Ich*, or eternal Will, asserts itself as standing above Nature. He has discovered his true self, or 'Divine Me,' in its 'God-created majesty' (*Sartor*, 167).

Thus the 'Ego' and Teufelsdröckh are delivered from fear of 'iron necessity' – Fichte's term (*Werke*, II, 239) – but at the cost of annihilation of all existence. Only shadows of reality remain, as the 'Ego' reproachfully tells the Spirit: 'I might be content that this material world beyond me should vanish into a mere picture, or be dissolved into a shadow; I do not cling to it – but according to your precious reasoning, I myself disappear no less than it' (*Werke*, II, 241; Smith, 398).[40] This idea of the material world as a realm of shadows is later associated with pictures and dreams in Fichte's work in the same way that Carlyle uses these images, not only in the central chapters, but at the beginning of *Sartor* (54). Fichte's formulations are less striking than Carlyle's but convey the same notions on the nature of reality: 'There is nothing enduring, either out of me, or in me, but only ceaseless change ... pictures which float past ... I myself am one of these pictures ... All reality is transformed into a strange dream' (*Werke*, II, 245; Smith, 402).[41]

Before the Spirit vanishes, he gives the disheartened 'Ego' the advice to seek out reality behind appearances, not, however, by way of knowledge: 'The reality, in which you did formerly believe – a material world existing independently of you, of which you fear to become the slave – has vanished ... You now seek something real lying beyond appearances ... But in vain would you labour to create this reality by means of your knowledge; or to embrace it by your understanding. If you have no organ by which to apprehend it, you will never find it' (*Werke*, II, 246–7; Smith, 404).[42]

With error having been destroyed but truth not as yet established, the 'Ego' finds itself in the same position as Teufelsdröckh in the 'Centre of Indifference,' where, with his newly gained freedom, he is now clutching 'round him outwardly on the NOT-ME' (*Sartor*, 170), casting his satirical eye over the wide panorama of the earth, which is still 'a Dog-cage' (ibid., 182). While in Fichte's 'Knowledge' the *Nicht-Ich*, or 'Not-Me,' had been philosophically defined, Teufelsdröckh tests it in practice. It becomes a kind of arena in which the newly discovered *Ich*, or 'Me,' realizes its potentialities, for positive teachings have not yet emerged. He is beginning to become active as a 'spectre-fighting man' (ibid., 170), observing man in general working on the *Nicht-Ich*, and manipulating Nature. This work is carried out on a large scale by tradition: 'Of man's Activity and Attainment the chief results are aeriform, mystic, and preserved in Tradition only' (ibid., 171). Some gains emerge from this changed attitude to life: 'Wretchedness was still wretched; but I could now partly see through it, and despise it. Which highest mortal, in this inane Existence, had I not found a Shadow-hunter, or Shadow-hunted; and, when I looked through his brave garnitures, miserable enough?' (ibid., 182).

From such Fichtean musings we gather that his practical experience of the 'Not-Me' gave Teufelsdröckh a broader scope and deeper insights than the 'Ego' could ever hope to receive from a purely theoretical investigation. Teufelsdröckh's bonds are indeed loosening, although he has not yet entered into any creative activity as the ultimate means for expressing his 'Me.'

Book III of *Die Bestimmung* has been called Fichte's 'Critique of Practical Reason,' in so far as he here attempts to state a *Lebensphilosophie*, true to his observation that once found, Truth must be applied to life. Fichte here sets down his own system of ethical Idealism and formulates a transcendental vocation for man, based on Faith as the crowning glory of all philosophical inquiry.

The Spirit, before departing, had given the distressed 'Ego' new hope by indicating that man possessed a faculty with which to apprehend truth, that is, a reality beyond the world of pictures. At the same time, the Spirit makes it quite clear that this organ is not knowledge, under which term Fichte understands the perception of scientific fact and of physical phenomena.

Fichte's position concerning the value of knowledge must here be briefly restated, if the dominant role of the Will in his system of values is to be rightly understood. Just as the popular exposition of philosophical knowledge was employed as a means to an end – to cast a bridge from Doubt to Faith – knowledge is justified only with regard to its function within the moral order, permitting man a fuller performance of his duty. The fact that the Will has complete priority over knowledge has been overlooked by critics like M. Storrs, who is intent on proving Fichte's *Ich* to represent intellect alone (*The Relation*, part II, 53ff.). According to Fichte's opinion as stated in *Die Bestimmung*, man is to develop all his faculties and gain knowledge, 'only with the purpose of preparing thereby within me a larger field and wider sphere of duty ... I ought to exercise my powers and capacities in every possible way – but only in order to render myself a more serviceable and fitting instrument of duty' (*Werke*, II, 310; Smith, 469).[43]

The new organ to which the Spirit had indirectly referred at the end of Book II, as a means of comprehending spiritual reality, is Faith: 'I have found the means by which to apprehend this reality. Knowledge is not this means ... every knowledge presupposes something higher ... It is Faith' (*Werke*, II, 253; Smith, 411).[44] Faith does not stand for any individual opinion, but for transcendental reason in its fullest meaning, connected with the Will and resulting in action: 'Not merely to *know*, but according to your knowledge *to act*, is your vocation: thus it is loudly proclaimed in my innermost soul ... Not for idle contemplation and consideration of yourself, no, for action you are here. Your action, and your action alone, determines your worth' (*Werke*, II, 249; Smith, 401).[45]

Faith is connected in this passage with an inner voice that leads away from mere presentation and cognition 'to something that is greater and higher than all knowledge, and that contains within itself the end and object of all knowledge' (*Werke*, II, 249; Smith, 406).[46] Where does this voice come from, which is so closely connected with an urge for independent action in man? Must it be obeyed? The 'Ego' decides to trust this voice with Faith which alone can interpret it correctly. This is done because the 'Ego' wills it, not because it must.

From the above it follows that Fichte, starting out from the desire for action as an inborn urge in man, relates it to the Will, a faculty superior to knowledge, by way of Faith. Faith leads to voluntary obedience to the inner voice or conscience, with the aid of which man is able to perceive truth. Conscience functions as a mediator between the eternal Will and the act, in accordance with the dictates of the moral law: 'The voice of conscience, which imposes on each his particular duty, is the light-beam on which we come forth from the infinite' (*Werke*, II, 299; Smith, 458).[47]

Man's ability to receive by way of conscience intimations of the moral law is peculiar to his intermediary position between two orders, in both of which he partakes: 'This then is my whole sublime vocation, my true nature. I am a member of two orders: the one purely spiritual, in which I rule by my Will alone; the other sensuous in which I operate by my deed ... The former alone gives it significance, purpose, and value' (*Werke*, II, 288–9; Smith, 447–8).[48]

Without reference to the existence of these two orders, Fichte's idea of renunciation can hardly be understood, for it is precisely the decision of the Will to dedicate life to the higher order, represented by the eternal will of God. The ability in man to make this decision in favour of the moral order frees him from the bonds of Necessity and helps establish a higher form of life, even within the natural order.

But there is another aspect to this as well: the Spirit had demonstrated in Book II that the phenomenal world had no independent existence and no validity. The 'Ego' now realizes that, in the light of a higher second order, the world of the *Nicht-Ich*, or 'Not Me,' reveals its true function, that is to stimulate the *Ich* into action. Here is man's theatre, here he must realize his ideals, conveyed to him from transcendental reality to which he also belongs. In this sense Fichte maintains: 'My world is the object and sphere of my duties, and absolutely nothing more' (*Werke*, II, 261; Smith, 419).[49] This insight rules out an evaluation of men as 'well-fitted cogs in the machine' (*Werke*, II, 281). What Nature has lost of its Goethean splendour, the Universe has gained in Fichte's eyes: 'The universe appears before my eyes clothed in a more glorious form. The dead inert mass has vanished and in its place there flows onward an eternal stream of life, of power, and of action.' (*Werke*, II, 315; Smith, 474–5).[50] Many references in *Sartor* echo this line of thought.

From this point onwards moral Idealism turns to mystical religion. In prophetic language there follows an invocation to the living Will, not known by name, not to be encompassed in narrow definitions. Death is considered as a form of higher life that, concealed up to then from the natural eye, is now made visible: 'Did no reasonable being who had once beheld the light of this world ever die, there would be no ground to wait for a new heaven and a new earth' (*Werke*, II, 318; Smith, 477).[51]

Turning from Fichte to Carlyle's 'Everlasting Yea,' one might say that he captured the contents of Fichte's Book III, 'Faith,' in a single sentence of the first paragraph: 'Our Life is compassed round with Necessity, yet is the meaning of Life itself no other than Freedom, than Voluntary Force' (*Sartor*, 183). In this sentence, freedom under the moral law, necessity, and the power of the Will – all terms of paramount importance in *Die Bestimmung* – are fused together to state the theme of Teufelsdröckh's further contemplations. Throughout the chapter, transcendental terms, which may well have been adopted from *Die*

Bestimmung, are set in a fictional background. After Teufelsdröckh's healing sleep, for example, he awakens to a new Heaven and a new Earth, pronouncing the annihilation of self as the first moral act. A transcendental world begins to emerge from behind the veil of appearances, foreshadows and foresplendours of Truth, and faith in the God-like nature of the universe, which had also to the 'Ego' appeared in 'a more glorious form.'[52] A further step in the direction of compassion and love for mankind is also made, which Fichte emphasizes in the sermon-like last part of 'Faith.' The strict command 'Love not Pleasure; love God' (*Sartor*, 192), in which the 'Everlasting Yea' is rooted, is a clear call to duty with transcendental implications of a striving towards the divine. The further reference to Fichte's *Wissenschaftslehre* as applied Christianity stresses once more belief in conduct: 'But indeed Conviction, were it never so excellent, is worthless till it convert itself into Conduct' (ibid, 195).

On the whole it is hard to discern in the 'Everlasting Yea' any element that stems from a particular author, as all are fused together in such a way that they are hardly identifiable. This pertains particularly to Carlyle's statements on action and duty, such as '*Do the duty which lies nearest thee*' (ibid., 196). Although a translation from *Wilhelm Meisters Lehrjahre*, it shows overtones of Fichte's ideas on duty in the context of 'this poor, miserable, hampered, despicable Actual, wherein thou even now standest' (ibid.).

It nevertheless seems plausible that Fichte's *Die Bestimmung* served as a philosophical backbone for the intellectual elements in the central chapters of Book II of *Sartor*. Focusing on the individual and his personal vocation, it was singularly well suited to Carlyle's needs. Here he found outlined stages of a mental development he could well apply to Teufelsdröckh's spiritual crisis. For Teufelsdröckh is an individualist; the problems he wishes to solve in the central chapters of his autobiography are his own. Carlyle may have felt attracted to *Die Bestimmung* by its non-technical, popular treatment of philosophical issues. From whatever source he received his introduction to notions such as the 'Me' acting in accordance with the moral law in the world of the 'Not-Me,' they are Fichte's terms, employed in *Sartor* in very much the same way Fichte used them in *Die Bestimmung*. The similarity in application of transcendental terminology therefore also makes it likely that this source exerted an influence on Carlyle. The fact that Carlyle never cited *Die Bestimmung* may be explained by his habit, as Harrold describes it, 'of acknowledging only those sources which he either translated or closely paraphrased.'[53]

Neither can a similarity of form be overlooked. Both works are essentially philosophical monologues, if we for a moment disregard the fictional element in *Sartor*. In Fichte's work the soliloquy turns for the length of Book II into a dialogue between the Spirit and the 'Ego,' before returning to the previous form in Book III. Teufelsdröckh's utterances also have the quality of monologues, in so far as they are direct reflections or aphorisms from the depth of his paper bags. The division into three central chapters is roughly equivalent to the three-book division in *Die Bestimmung*.

There are, of course, differences. Defiance is more pronounced in Carlyle, Fichte does not stray from the intellectual level, although emotion is not totally absent. Carlyle's solution is closer to revelation, Fichte's to systematic thought. Carlyle avoids rational explanations, while Fichte devotes a whole book to philosophical criticism of the problem.

But the line of thought expressed in the course of the spiritual awakening the protagonists undergo suggests a significant parallel. The 'Ego' and Teufelsdröckh experience greater spiritual maturity as a result of their wrestlings with philosophical problems, caused by their rejection of a deterministic and materialistic concept of the universe. Both pass through stages of doubt and despair before reaching a solution in Faith, guided by the dictates of conscience, in harmony with the eternal Will. Both acknowledge the existence of two orders – one of mere appearance, the other of transcendental reality. Central to both Fichte and Carlyle is above all the emphasis on a dynamic moral principle that demands moral action.

Part Two

LEADING THEMES
(Sartor Resartus, Heroes, Past and Present)

'The Progressive Culture of the human race is the object of the Divine Idea, and of those in whom that Idea dwells.'

Fichte, *The Nature of the Scholar*

FIVE

A German Philosophy of Clothes

'Kleider machen Leute' (Clothes make the man)

(German proverb)

Supernatural Garments

In spite of Swift's initial influence on Carlyle's philosophy of clothes, by way of the germane passage in the *Tale of a Tub* likening the universe to 'a large suit of clothes, which invests everything,'[1] *Sartor* goes far beyond this source, where the notion is merely developed along orthodox religious lines in a strictly satirical context. Carlyle seems to have been aware of this restricted application of the clothes philosophy by Swift, whose humour he finds lacking with regard to a more meaningful interpretation of life.[2] What Carlyle was after – heightened symbolical meaning and added metaphysical depth – he associated with German literature, if we interpret correctly the English editor's complaint regarding the 'total want of a Philosophy of Clothes' in his own country and his designation of it as 'a foreign suggestion' (*Sartor*, 8).

Teufelsdröckh is, in this respect, obviously indebted to Goethe, for immediately after having translated the speech of the Earth-Spirit from *Faust*, centering on the loom of time where the garment of God is being woven, he links his own philosophy to it: 'It was in some such mood, when wearied and fordone with these high speculations, that I first came upon the question of Clothes' (*Sartor*, 56). Was Carlyle indeed 'endlessly indebted to Goethe in the business?' (*Reminiscences*, I, 288).

Of the emblematic quality of Goethe's works, Carlyle was at all times very much aware. In his copious criticism he refers to him as 'a singularly emblematic intellect' (*Essays I*, 'Goethe,' 244), who, by way of this rare faculty, fashions a new form of spirituality.

This process of 'bodying forth the form of things unseen' (ibid.) lies at the very core of the clothes philosophy, and it is therefore to Goethe that Carlyle initially turns for his ability to see life in 'bright aërial emblematic glimpses' (ibid., 162). The vivid image of the weaver's shuttle rattling back and forth in time, fashioning the divine vestures, obviously left a lasting impression on Carlyle, as the most perfect emblem for notions of his own, as yet unexpressed but not uncontemplated.[3] Here finite symbols stood for infinity and were hallowed by the deeper meaning they rendered up to those who could read them. Readily Carlyle seized upon this idea for the supernatural aspects of his clothes philosophy and employed it not with regard to Nature alone, but respecting the emblematic quality of life itself. This symbolic expansion is also Goethe's message, in the *Chorus Mysticus* at the end of *Faust*: 'All transitory things are merely symbols.'[4]

Carlyle's indebtedness to Goethe for the garment of God concept has been generally acknowledged by scholars. Attention has also been drawn to Carlyle's translation of the key lines by L. Metzger.[5] Goethe's 'Und wirke der Gottheit lebendiges Kleid,' which shows the Earth-Spirit simply weaving the living garment of God, is rendered by Carlyle in a more explicit fashion: 'And weave for God the Garment thou seest Him by' (*Sartor*, 55). Carlyle loses in poetic quality what he gains in emphasis: that which reveals God, the reader surmises, is not simply alive but also good. Interestingly enough, however, Carlyle dismisses his own translation when applying the line to Teufelsdröckh's autobiography, returning to Goethe's more effective rendering: 'Or what is Nature? Ha! why do I not name thee GOD? Art not thou the "Living Garment of God"? O Heavens, is it, in very deed, HE then, that ever speaks through thee; that lives and loves in thee, that lives and loves in me?' (ibid., 188).

This passage, Goethean in concept and written in the *Werther* style,[6] has never really been explained in context; such explanation would help to clarify Carlyle's so-called ambiguous relationship to Nature. In this most quoted passage from the 'Everlasting Yea,' Teufelsdröckh is a character in a fictional setting, not someone making philosophical statements per se, a fact that has been obscured by thought-hunting. The whole tone of his utterance shows that he is in a state of rapture, full of delirious joy. This state must be understood as springing from the final solution of the previous opposition in his own mind between a mechanistic concept and an organic view of the universe. Is Nature living and divine or dead and demoniacal? The decision he must and does make is in favour of the former. The 'living garment' expresses this choice, and is, in this context, much more than a phrase or 'a mere figure of speech' Carlyle picked up.'[7]

There is a difference, however, between the immediate reaction of the youthful Teufelsdröckh and the general philosophical attitude of Teufelsdröckh the mature man, who accepts a variety of truths about Nature and life. This becomes clear from the reservation with which he introduces Goethe's Earth-Spirit lyric, by first making a reference to 'Nature, with its thousandfold production and destruction' (*Sartor*, 55). In contrast to his youthful enthusiasm displayed in the early jottings, Teufelsdröckh in his later years is well aware of the obscuring tendencies of Nature, or, to employ another clothes metaphor, 'Nature's veil.' The man who writes his clothes volume is no longer twenty-one; his concept of Nature is more diversified.

Both ideas, that of Nature as the Garment of God and Nature as a Veil, are also found side by side in Goethe's works. Carlyle would have come across the latter in *Faust I*: 'Mysterious even in broad daylight, Nature retains her veil. What she does not wish to reveal to your spirit, you can never wrench from her with levers and with screws.'[8] Nature remains an enigma, an unsolved mystery to man. While Goethe is basically making an anti-Baconian statement, and is not passing judgment on Nature for any delusive quality, Carlyle adds an element of distrust.

A good illustration of Carlyle's view, thus far seemingly unnoticed, is a passage from *Faust* he misquotes with a significant amendment. In the Conservation on Religion, taking place between Gretchen and himself, Faust explains his relationship to God in the famous words: 'Feeling is all, Name is sound and smoke obscuring the splendour of Heaven'[9] Carlyle changes 'Name is sound and smoke' to 'Nature is sound and smoke' when quoting the passage,[10] expressing the thought that Nature acts as a kind of smoke-screen, obscuring man's vision. The same phrasing is used by Carlyle in his essay 'Novalis,' (*Essays II*, 28) which in context clearly shows that the substitution of 'Nature' for 'Name' was not accidental: 'Not only has the unseen world a reality, but the only reality: the rest being not metaphorically, but literally and in scientific strictness, "a show"; in the words of the Poet, "Schall and Rauch umnebelnd Himmels Gluth," Sound and Smoke overclouding the Splendour of Heaven' (ibid.).

In continuing to trace the supernatural application of the philosophy of clothes, it is evident that Carlyle also included the human body within its range. Are there any implications in his sources that contributed to the idea of building analogically to the Nature-garment of God, the body-garment of the soul?

It is possible that Carlyle found in Goethe's 'Bekenntnisse einer schönen Seele' the nucleus of such a garment symbol (*Wilhelm Meister*, I, 454).

There the thought is expressed that the vesture-body veils the soul of man, obscures the true self, which can emerge only when the garment dissolves. This is, of course, basically a Platonic concept, but it is doubtful if Carlyle went to Plato to seek it out. In Carlyle's view, man too is drawn into the emblematic cycle, and if the analogy is correct, it follows that the divine spirit must shine through the garment of flesh: 'Deep-hidden is he under that strange Garment; amid Souls and Colours and Forms, as it were, swathed-in, and inextricably overshrouded: yet it is sky-woven and worthy of a God' (*Sartor*, 65). This passage shows man's emblematic nature in a somewhat diffused light, as if the divine element manifests itself in spite of itself. Overlaid with other elements, it appears shrouded, until 'his earthly Vesture falls away, and soon even to Sense becomes a vanished Shadow' (ibid., 266). From these examples it appears that Goethe's influence on Carlyle, regarding supernatural aspects of the clothes philosophy, cannot be restricted to the Earth-Spirit passage in *Faust I*. Around such germs of thought, influences gleaned from other readings would cluster, gaining in substance by way of association.

Carlyle also attempted, and partially succeeded in, pressing the 'Divine Idea' into the service of the clothes philosophy. Doing so, however, required modifications.

Fichte's view of Nature, as laid down in *Über das Wesen des Gelehrten*, clashed with the God-like aspect Carlyle had found emphasized in Goethe, but it harmonized with Carlyle's remnants of Calvinism. Fichte regarded Nature, or the *Sinnenwelt* as he somewhat disparagingly calls it, in a philosophical sense as a *Nicht-Ich* – a practice ground for the *Ich* to develop its active powers and test its strength. As a *Nicht-Ich*, Nature was inferior to man: not acting but being acted upon, she must be shaped and formed by him to become 'more human'; not having a will of her own, she was unable to participate in moral values. In addition, Fichte suggested that negative forces were a part of Nature, at least in latent form. For these reasons he expressly warns his students, in *Über das Wesen*, not to fall victim to the Nature myth, a warning uttered with all too obvious side glances at Schelling (*Works* VI, 363).

In an attempt to adjust his concept of Nature to accommodate both Goethe's and Fichte's point of view, Carlyle did not always achieve a seamless fusion. In *Sartor*, the two stand side by side. Within the fictional setting they are explained as stages of a youthful and a mature opinion. Outside the autobiographical chapters they appear to be, more or less, unrelated to each other. While the interpretation of Nature as divine still predominates, overtones of Fichte's attitude are clearly discernible. A cautious note is struck by a reference to Nature as 'good, but ... not the best' (*Sartor*, 59). Nature, the Time-vesture of God, 'reveals Him to the wise, hides Him from the foolish' (ibid., 264). Was Nature, in this sense, 'but a garment,' merely the show of things?

This ambiguity reappears. In later works, where the clothes philosophy is abandoned, a darker interpretation of Nature prevails throughout. In *Past and Present*, Carlyle chooses the dualistic image of the Sphinx to underscore this aspect: 'Nature, like the Sphinx, is all womanly celestial loveliness and tenderness; the face and bosom of a goddess, but ending in claws and the body of a lioness. There is in her a celestial beauty, – which means celestial order, pliancy to wisdom; but there is also darkness, a ferocity, fatality, which are infernal. She is a goddess, but one not yet disimprisoned' (*Past and Present*, Bk I, ii, 7).

The notion that Nature has to be set free, that it must be made more human in Fichte's sense, is here strongly pronounced. In the earlier *On Heroes* Carlyle even speaks, at the height of his worship for heroic men, of 'the dark hostile powers of Nature' (*Heroes*, 17), giving the hero plenty of scope to make her both moral and human.

Besides these difficulties arising out of a varied concept of Nature, Carlyle had to invent a suitable symbolic vesture for the 'Divine Idea.' In 'State of German Literature,' he introduces Fichte's notion together with a symbol to clothe it in: 'According to Fichte, there is a 'Divine Idea' pervading the visible Universe: which visible Universe is indeed but its symbol and sensible manifestation ... To the mass of men this 'Divine Idea' of the world lies hidden: yet to discern it, to seize it, and live wholly in it, is the condition of all genuine virtue, knowledge, freedom' (*Essays I*, 58).

The reference to the universe as the symbol of the 'Divine Idea' is clearly Carlyle's ingenious addition. As far as Fichte is concerned it reveals itself in Man, as its active tool. Neither does Fichte make any pronouncements regarding the role of the universe as a symbol for the Divine Idea.[11]

In such wide and commodious vestments as the Universe, or 'All Appearance,' man could also be accommodated: 'The Universe is but one vast Symbol of God; nay if thou wilt have it, what is man himself but a Symbol of God' (*Sartor*, 220).

Besides investing the 'Divine Idea' with a variety of clothes symbols, Carlyle offers another solution by looking through all clothes, including those of Nature, at the 'Divine Idea' itself. This perspective is achieved by Teufelsdröckh, who 'looked fixedly on Existence, till, one after the other, its earthly hulls and garnitures have all melted away' (ibid., 255). In this manner the Divine Idea is the highest fulfilment of the clothes philosophy but at the same time leads to its destruction. Any suit of clothes is, in the supernatural sense, 'put on [only] for a season, and to be laid off' (ibid., 74). Clothes are an aid for those who have not yet fully learned to see, but an obstruction for others, who have had their eyes opened.

Phosphoros, a dark symbolic figure in Zacharias Werner's *Die Söhne des Thals*, which Carlyle reviewed in his 'Life and Writings of Werner,' is identified by him as 'an emblem of the spiritual essence of man and an emblem of his history' (*Essays I*, 113). Only Carlyle's already awakened interest in the clothes philosophy can explain his preoccupation with this allegorical episode. Calling it a 'strange phantasmagoria,' he promises his readers a little glimpse, which turns out to be a lengthy one: a four-page translation, faithfully rendered in poor verse that reads like a parody rather than an illumination of Werner's meaning. Prior to having given himself over to pride, Phosphoros had led a supernatural existence. After his fall, he is being punished by God in the following manner: he is being cast into a prison called Life, and given earth and water for a garment (*Essays I*, 109).

Hampered in his movements by the earthly garments, he can see only a reflection of the universe, where once he freely roamed, in a mirror that his compassionate sister places in front of him. When gazing into this glass, 'his earthly garments pressed him less' (*Essays I*, 'Life and Writings of Werner,' 110). Phosphoros is finally liberated by the Saviour of the Waters, obviously an allusion to Christ, rising from the Jordan. His garments are then washed; their stiffness vanishes, and they grow light and transparent. As the process of salvation proceeds, Phosphoros now experiences bliss:

His nature melted in the mighty All;
...
For Chains and Garment cumber'd him no more;
The Garment he had changed to royal purple,
And of his Chains were fashion'd glancing jewels. (ibid., 112)

There are more than a few complexities contained in this philosophy of clothes, Werner style, as might be expected from this expert in mystic and mystification. The earthly garment in Werner's vision stands between man and God, not merely in the form of a veil, but as an inhibiting factor that hems in the movements of Phosphoros-Man. All of this is, in a larger sense, 'time-vesture,' which obscures the substance of eternity, if man chooses to be oblivious to divine vision. Only if willing to believe can man wear the earthly garment, as a vesture of God. Werner greatly stresses the notion that imprisonment in life is the result of sin. This sin is Pride, not as Harrold believes, 'the sin of individuation.'[12]

This basically Christian version of the clothes philosophy implies that if man, with the aid of supernatural guidance, reads Nature correctly, his vision will be restored, and he will wear his garment as a symbol of his covenant with God. It is understandable that this reading of the God–Man relationship by way of the vestment of Nature appealed to Carlyle's outlook and religious temperament. In *Sartor*, too, revelation of the divine source of Nature depends on the right interpretation.

Natural Clothes

Besides considering the supernatural aspect of clothes as symbolizing the 'Garment of God,' Carlyle discusses clothes in a social context. For this view of clothes, Goethe furnishes the chief example, in an episode in *Wilhelm Meisters Wanderjahre.*

Wilhelm, who visits the Pedagogic Province in order to enrol his son Felix in that prestigious institution, notices that the pupils do not wear uniforms, but are dressed in a variety of clothes. He takes this up with the Overseer: 'The great variety of shape and colour in these children's clothes attracts my notice: and yet I do not only see all sorts of colours, but a few in all their shades, from the lightest to the deepest. At the same time I observe that by this no designation of degrees in age or merit can be intended; for the oldest and the youngest boys may be alike both in cut and colour' (*Meister*, II, 261).[13]

The Overseer, himself committed to silence, promises disclosure by the Elders of the Province. Eventually Wilhelm is let in on the secret: 'It will be explained, when I tell you, that by this means we endeavour to find out the children's several characters ... the pupils are permitted to select what colour they please and so likewise, within moderate limits, in regard to shape and cut. Their procedure in these matters, we accurately note; for by the colour we discover their turn of thinking; by the cut their turn of acting' (ibid., 267-7).[14]

Here the chosen garment is a true expression of the bearer, just as, on the metaphysical level, the Garment of God reveals the Deity itself. Because individually designed clothes aid the Elders in gaining valuable insights into the personality of each child, they are reluctant to introduce uniforms. Not without underlying humour, the Elder remarks that, by way of clothes, certain trends are invisibly regulated: 'We have had cases where the disposition of our children verged to generality; where one fashion threatened to extend over all ... We let our stores run out ... we introduce something new and attractive; by bright colours and short smart shape, we allure the lively; by drab shades, by commodious many-folded make, the thoughtful; and thus by degrees restore the equilibrium' (ibid., 277).[15]

In the *Sartor* chapter 'The World in Clothes,' these ideas on clothes are applied and partly expressed in Goethe's phrasing:[16] 'From the soberest drab to the high-flaming scarlet, spiritual idiosyncrasies unfold themselves in choice of Colour: if the Cut betoken Intellect and Talent, so does the Colour betoken Temper and Heart' (*Sartor*, 35).

It is not to be ruled out that Goethe also furnished the 'first rags,' that is, the use of clothes to hide man's hideousness and to support his vanity. In this connection clothes are often empty status symbols rather than tokens of true worth. In his youth, Goethe had written two carnival plays, treating on these aspects of life in a humorous fashion: *Das Jahrmarktsfest zu Plundersweilern* and *Pater Brey* (*Gedenkausgabe*, vol. 4, 160; 171). As an entry in his *Notebooks* (121) shows, Carlyle knew the former play and read it, possibly being attracted by its name, the word *Plunder* signifying rags, particularly old clothes. An old-clothes fair could be considered as a perfect locale for Teufelsdröckh's observations on the vanities of this world, revealing themselves symbolically in decaying clothes: 'Alas, move whithersoever you may, are not the tatters and rags of superannuated worn-out symbols (in this Ragfair of a World) dropping off everywhere, to hoodwink, to halter, to tether you ...?' (*Sartor*, 226). This same thought is stated in similar terms by the Editor as typical of Teufelsdröckh's outlook in general: 'Did we not hear him complain that the World was a "huge Ragfair" and the "rags and tatters of old Symbols" were raining-down everywhere ...?' (ibid., 235). In his essay 'Goethe,' Carlyle also mentions the 'rag-gathering age' (*Essays I*, 228), a reference he repeats in *Sartor* (253), in the 'Organic Filaments' chapter, where Goethe is set up as a prophet 'in these rag-gathering and rag-burning days.' The connection between rags and clothes is already established in the chapter on aprons (45), where we hear of 'Rags or Clothes-rubbish.'

Carlyle would also have come across a variety of thoughts on natural clothes in Jean Paul's works. His reading of Jean Paul was not limited to the humorous *Schmelzles Reise nach Flätz* and the idyllic *Quintus Fixlein*, although both also contributed to the philosophy of clothes. Fixlein muses on clothes: 'for him a garment was a sort of hollow half-man to whom only the nobler parts and the first principles were wanting; he honoured these wrappings and hulls of our interior' (*German Romance*, II, 202).[17] This remark reveals an awareness of the emptiness of clothes, as well as certain respect for their former significance. The same sentiments are expressed in *Sartor* (239): 'The gladder am I, on the other hand, to do reverence to those Shells and outer Husks of the Body, wherein no devilish passion any longer lodges, but only the pure emblem and effigies of Man: I mean, to Empty, or even to Cast Clothes.'

Comments on clothes, however, are particularly abundant in Jean Paul's youthful writings, a period he later termed his 'satirical vinegar factory.' Early works such as *Grönländische Prozesse* and *Aus des Teufels Papieren* are made up of a formless mass of satirical reflections under such headings as 'Clothes-press for Virtues and Vices,' 'Women and Dandies,' and 'The Third Adam,' to name just a few of the pertinent themes.

Carlyle mentions both pieces in his essay 'Jean Paul Friedrich Richter,' commenting on their keen wit and characterizing them as 'altogether indescribable performances' (*Essays I*, 6). The two passages cited below suggest that he studied both of these satirical sketches fairly carefully.

The first pertains to a remark Jean Paul makes on Boileau's unfortunate encounter with an aggressive turkey, an episode to which reference is also made in *Sartor*:

Jean Paul	*Carlyle*
Boileau's peck must be credited to the beak of a turkey ... [Fn. by Jean Paul :] According to *L'année litteraire*, Boileau was injured by this animal in a touchy spot; according to Helvetius his misogyny stemmed from this injury. (*Grönländische Prozesse*, I, 1, 186-7)[18]	By what strange chances do we live in History? Erostratus by a torch ... Boileau Despréaux (according to Helvetius) by the peck of a turkey. (*Sartor*, 50)

If this parallel might be considered coincidental, the phrasing of the following passage, dealing with the ear of Dionysius, shows further evidence of similarity, in the rendering of such phrases as 'tausendzüngiges Elend' as 'jarring hubbub' – a sound-painting of the noisy lament of misery:

Jean Paul	*Carlyle*
... the world expects that her great men, in spite of the many ears that have to close to many-tongued misery, keep open the ear of Dionysius to hear an indictment ... rather than a self-defence (*Aus des Teufels Papieren* I, 1, 1448)[19]	a Dionysius' Ear, where, in stifled jarring hubbub, we hear the indictment which Poverty and Vice bring against lazy Wealth ... (*Sartor,* 242)

The following fragment associates clothes with a distorted sense of values, in preference of external elegance: 'I know that the suit of honour has only been tailored to cover up lack of merit ... Fashions alone should be taken seriously, because folly is the tailor of Europe ... even proud philosophy in its cynic cloak must yield to the silk mantle ... the significance of most of the idols of good society lives on the surface, and therefore its external side is its best' (*Grönländische Prozesse,* I, 1, 99-100).[20]

This type of satire is carried over into Jean Paul's later works, where he opts for a broader appeal with wider social implications. The following elaboration of the martyrdom of the fashion-conscious dandy has much in common with the 'Dandiacal Body' chapter in *Sartor,* where Teufelsdröckh reflects on the whole Dandiacal Sect and, in particular, on the individual dandy as 'a witness and living Martyr to the eternal world of Clothes' (*Sartor,* 272):

The dandy can be assured of my whole compassion, even if I cannot help him. What has such a body done that each morning – in the courtroom this is the time of torture application – the barber tweaks his impeccable hair with glowing pincers ... that the cobbler fits his crippled feet with tight shoes, while the criminal investigator only maltreats healthy ones, by making them step into short Spanish boots ... He wears the thorny crown of hairpins, a sansculotte sceptre for shame and demands vinegar on his cross, in order to slim down his waistline ... he is an innocent martyr of elegance (*Putz*). (*Palingenesien Werke* IV, 780-1)[21]

In the *Kampanertal*, Jean Paul extends his copious use of clothes symbols to include aspects of religion. The novel, which deals mainly with the problem of the immortality of the soul, contains an 'Extra-harangue' in the form of descriptions of the woodcuts contained in a Protestant catechism. These were so poorly executed and so irrelevant to the religious content that Jean Paul invented a completely new story for them. Here his imagination knows no bounds with regard to the plot he invents for the pictures. Noteworthy with regard to Carlyle are his interpretations of the illustration of the third commandment. Under the title 'Parität der Religionen in der Kleidung', he discusses the clergyman's clothes, and in particular the question whether a Protestant divine or a Catholic priest is standing in the pulpit: 'The human upper part, full of the powers of the soul, which he dresses according to the Lutheran fashion ... while in the lower regions [covered by the pulpit] we can imagine room enough for the culotte and lower parts of the bishop, dressed up in a pallium' (*Kampanertal*, IV, 651).[22] In the continuation of the chapter, the discussion of the pallium is as significant for Jean Paul as are the episcopal aprons for Carlyle in the 'Aprons' chapter of *Sartor*, where he also uses the expression 'Overseer of Souls,' possibly a translation of Jean Paul's *Seelenhirt*.[23]

The fifth commandment is illustrated by a woodcut of Cain killing Abel which, according to Jean Paul's invented story, might as well be taken for a jealous husband hitting his wife's lover over the head with a guitar-case (*Futteral*)[24] – a feasible explanation in view of the shape of the club that Cain applies to Abel's head. The clothing of the two contenders is compared to the *gallus togatus* and the *gallus braccatus*: 'the long-chinned chap lies on the campbed of the earth as a sansculotte or *gallus togatus*; while the woodcutter and fighting-cock, clad as *gallus braccatus*, swings the implement of attack' (*Kampanertal*, IV, 660-1).[25] A footnote explains the meaning of the unusual terms: 'Gallia togata was the name of *that* part of Gallia whose population adopted the Roman toga; Gallia braccata the *trousered* one, which remained true to its old customs and pants' (ibid., 660, fn.).

In 'The World in Clothes' chapter of *Sartor*, we find, among other items in a long list of clothes, including Chinese silks, 'Afghaun' shawls, and Celtic philibegs, the *Gallia Braccata* (38) as part of a whole barrage of Jean Paul borrowings, all dealing with aspects of *Putz*, or decoration, a word Carlyle often adds in parentheses when dealing with clothes.

Carlyle also mentions Tieck's *Franz Sternbalds Wanderungen* in *German Romance I* (262) as the imaginative history of a student of painting. In it, the German painter Albrecht Dürer is made the mouthpiece of an artist's clothes philosophy. On the occasion of his visit to The Netherlands, the master-painter Lukas van Leyden, his host, brings up the topic, commenting on Dürer's habit of introducing modern garb into several of his pictures, even when dealing with ancient stories. His guest admits this and tells of his custom of inventing strange and fantastic clothing: 'I believe it to be a good idea, one I have always adhered to in the past, to use people's costumes in a physiognomical manner ... I must admit that I like to place an absurd hat on the head of a wild, bad rascal, and also add some other symbol to his external appearance' (*Franz Sternbald*, 775).[26]

Dürer then relates his reasons to the symbolic meaning of art in general, which he considers to be a token for our immortality, for a secret sign by way of which the eternal spirits recognize each other in a marvellous fashion. One is tempted to call this a philosophy of clothes, painter's version, which may indirectly have added to Carlyle's concepts.

The reflections on clothes contained in E.T.A. Hoffmann's works have partly sinister, partly magical implications. In the *Elixiere des Teufels*, the life-story of a monk – conceived along lines of M.G. Lewis's *The Monk*, but of greater artistic merit – the religious habit plays a decisive role. It is employed for purposes of treachery and deceit, as a cover-up for the love intrigues designed by Count Viktorin, carried on by Father Medardus, the last descendant of a sinful family. In contrast, the habit also stands for the deeply religious yearnings of Count Hermogen, who wears it out of inclination. This dual application of clothes imagery to represent the cloaking of crime and sin as well as the conspicuous emblem of virtue and true desire for an ascetic life is complex. However, Hoffmann uses clothes imagery to do more than evoke two extremes of human behaviour; Hermogen's aged teacher and adviser believes clothes to affect the actions of the bearer in a fateful manner:

> I beseech you, Hermogen, throw off this hateful garment. Believe me, a strange power lies in such external things. Do not take it ill if I ... remind you of actors, who often, once they have thrown themselves into a costume, feel stimulated by strange forces, and thus more readily act in character with the role they are representing ... Don't you think that if your step were no longer hemmed in by this long gown to solemn gravity, you would again walk at a quick pace, run and skip as you used to do? ... Off with this black garment that does not become you! (*Elixiere des Teufels*, II, 56-7).[27]

Medardus, having been led through pride, sensuality, and uncontrolled passion into sin, rids himself of his habit and orders a suit of civilian clothes, made by a tailor who considers himself to be an artist. This *Kostümkünstler* creates fantastic forms and figures in his clothes store, and fills them with a life of their own:

> You see the modern dandy in all possible variations, sometimes radiating confidence and boldness, sometimes wrapped up in himself, uncommunicative, naïvely flirting, ironical, witty, bad-tempered, melancholy, bizarre, in high spirits, dainty or forward. The youth who for the first time has a suit made without the restricting advice of his mother or tutor; the man of forty who uses powder on account of his white hair; the old man fond of a gay life; the scholar who has to move in society ... all these hang in my friend's store. (ibid., 92).[28]

This dealer in clothes is, of course, much more than a tailor in the literal sense. He is a creator, an artist who devises new personalities with the aid of garments.

The same aspect is emphasized in 'Prinzessin Brambilla,' a tale in the form of a *Märchen*, in which Hoffmann allegorizes his vision of art and its relation to life. Giglio the actor and his lover, the seamstress Giacinta, live on the level of reality *and* of art, by slipping into costumes the crazy tailor Signor Bescapi has designed. Their occupations further their readiness to believe in the world of illusion conjured up for them during the Roman Carnival, which for brief hours lets them forget their humdrum existence. Signor Bescapi is characterized as 'a tailor who wished to fill the phantastic garments he designed with phantastic people.'[29] Here an artist creates a world of his own, of which the garments of the imagination are the very symbols. In this way, the tailor-artist acts out the dreams of 'the great charlatan,' who is the initiator of it all. Whether Hoffmann here has the tailor-as-writer image in mind or refers to the artist in general is unclear, but the latter meaning would be more in line with his usual stress on artistic creativity. Many allusions to clothes are scattered throughout this *Märchen*. From the outset, metaphysical speculation sets the pace for the trend of thought that permeates the whole tale: 'In short, the spirit carries along the body like an uncomfortable garment, which is everywhere too wide, too long, too clumsy' (X, 40).

Natural clothes with broader implications for society as a whole also feature in Werner's drama *Söhne des Thals*. Adam of Valincourt, president and ancient sage of the secret union, attempts to convince the young Templar knight Robert d'Heredon that new social clothes must be tailored, as the old ones can no longer be mended: 'Do you want to tailor where you can create anew? Are tattered rags to be patched onto the torn garments of mankind, where man feels the vocation and the strength to make divine ones? Tell me, should he do so?' (*Söhne des Thals* II, 5, i).[30]

While the notion of social clothes is merely intimated by Werner, Carlyle considerably enlarges it, linking it to the question of Palingenesia, or Newbirth of Society, discussed in chapter 8.

Literary Clothes

Clothes-rags can, of course, also represent literature itself, both its valuable and its worthless manifestations. Jean Paul, for satirical purposes, puts his finger on the latter sore spot. The Devil is to be made responsible for much 'paperwork', tears rags to turn them into paper, and, in the person of the rag hacker, 'will not altogether be at rest,' as we are told in one of the footnotes in *Schmelzles Reise nach Flätz* (*Werke*, VI, 22, fn. 32; *German Romance*, II, 148). He is also in the literary business proper occupied in writing satires on man's stupidity and folly.

Carlyle's 'Prince of Time' also has his fingers in the literary pie – to be more specific, in British journalism. The history of British newspaper journalism, which Teufelsdröckh has been searching for in all Weissnichtwo libraries, is entitled *Satan's Invisible World Displayed* – although this turns out to be merely a blunder on the part of the German professor who has confused titles (*Sartor*, 45).

In Jean Paul as well as in Carlyle, the attitude to contemporary literature is quite negative. Jean Paul speaks ironically about the enrichment of German literature by way of the paper aprons of Parisian cooks in *Quintus Fixlein*, a passage which Carlyle applies to English conditions in the 'Aprons' chapter of *Sartor*:[31]

Jean Paul	*Carlyle*
It was also this respect for all waste-paper that inspired him with such esteem for the aprons of French cooks, which, it is well known, consist of printed paper; and he often wished some German would translate these aprons. Indeed, I am willing to believe that a good version of more than one of such paper aprons	I consider these printed Paper Aprons, worn by the Parisian Cooks, as a new vent, though a slight one, for Typography; therefore as an encouragement to modern Literature, and deserving of approval; nor is it without satisfaction that I hear of a celebrated London Firm having in view to introduce the

might contribute to elevate our Literature ... and serve her in place of a drivel-bib. (*Fixlein, German Romance*, II, 223)[32]

same fashion, with important extensions, in England. (*Sartor*, 44)

The figure of the Dandy is central to Jean Paul as an image of superficial judgment on books. He stands for the reader who does not desire to be illuminated by the content of a book, merely wishing to be entertained – in this being similar to a bat, who, fleeing the light of the candle, wants only to feed on the tallow (*Grönländische Prozesse* I, 1, 212). In one of his extra-harangues entitled 'Clothes Prescription for Books,' part of the *Komischer Anhang zum Titan*, Jean Paul introduces the Dandy once more in a context that forms an interesting parallel with Carlyle's application of the same: 'With regard to books, the clothes luxury is as evident as it is enormous. Religious devotional works, formerly gliding along in modest clerical robe and mourning cloak, now dress up like dandies in the English style, wear galoon trimmings and nevertheless speak of God.' (*Komischer Anhang zum Titan*, III, 989).[33]

References to the tailor appear as well: 'It would seem unnecessary to cut out paper-heroes with a pair of scissors if tailors were available who could cut true heroes out of cloth' (*Grönländische Prozesse*, I, 1, 202).[34] If a doubt lingers in the readers' mind that the tailor stands for the writer and the cloth for literature, it may be silenced by the following passage in which the identification is complete: 'Philosophy discovers, poetry beautifies the discovery; the one is Columbus, who discovers America, the other Vespucius Americus, who names it; one is the clothmaker, the other the tailor' (*Grönländische Prozesse*, I, 1, 102).[35]

These various passages introduce three important elements that Carlyle also employs: Dandies, Tailors, and the Cloth. What remains to be done is to integrate these symbols into the larger clothes concept. Carlyle takes this step; both Dandies and Tailors are, according to Teufelsdröckh, 'cloth-animals, creatures that live, move and have their being in Cloth' (*Sartor*, 271); but, while the Dandies display a stupid cult of self-worship under the canon of Bulwer's *Pelham*, the Tailors design new clothes and thus bring knowledge of the divine to man, clothed in the garment of language: 'What too are all Poets and moral Teachers, but a species of Metaphorical Tailors?' (ibid., 290). The image of the tailor-poet has here been expanded to include the moral teacher, who fuses poetry and philosophy together. This identification is reinforced in the reference to the greatest living Guild brother, Goethe.

The distinction between tailor-poets and dandy-novelists is an important aspect of the clothes philosophy, particularly as thoughts on this topic are among the last recorded utterances of Teufelsdröckh in *Sartor*. Carlyle himself identifies with the image of the lonely Taylor, whose signpost Teufelsdröckh notices on his wanderings through Edinburgh: 'I came upon a Signpost whereon ... stood painted the Effigies of a Pair of Leather Breeches, and between the knees these memorable words, SIC ITUR AD ASTRA' (*Sartor*, 291). Besides being a reference to the *Aeneid* and the Canongate armorial motto, *Sic itur ad astra* is the essence of the clothes philosophy. By way of relating the visible to the invisible, the transient to the eternal, one takes the path to the stars. Carlyle is obviously the tailor-writer 'sighing indeed in bonds, yet sighing towards deliverance, and prophetically appealing to a better day' (ibid.). This better day is the one dawning for society as the result of an application of the clothes philosophy, when mankind once more will follow intimations from above.

Franz Horn also uses references to clothes in order to illustrate trends in literature in his history of literature, *Poesie und Beredsamkeit der Deutschen*. Speaking of their significance, Horn sees in them a sign of social change, usually for the worse. In his chapter 'Bemerkung über die Mode', clothes become symbols of artificiality and general deterioration, ending in the following general reflection: 'The external garments in which we daily see ourselves and others are for the imagination, yes indeed, for the mind and the heart of greater importance than we are inclined to believe, as the usual histories of German education are completely silent on this point.'[36] He gives a detailed description of the clothes worn around the time of the Thirty Years War, which are symptomatic of a perverted taste that also manifests itself in literature.

In 'Literarische Moden,' Horn discusses Literary Fashions, pointing out that the Germans are inclined to worship new literary idols nearly every five years. He who arrived only yesterday on the literary market is considered nothing compared to the author who arrived today full of empty bathos, sham vigour, and ringing word jingles: 'In their heads and literature itself it looked much like the confusion in the pharmacy of Pater Brey' (*Poesie*, IV, 286). The reference is here to Goethe's carnival play in which a pedlar complains about the jumble in his medicine chest, where he also carries *Teufelsdreck* among his wares. The spirit of the whole discussion shows some similarity with Carlyle's *Sartor* chapter 'Dandiacal Bodies,' as far as point of attack and method of ridicule are concerned.

In Lecture 10 of *Über das Wesen des Gelehrten*, where Fichte discusses the problem of the writer and his claim to participation in the Divine Idea, he also uses a clothes reference. With regard to literary trends, he attacks the bad reading habits of his age: 'The new luxury from time to time demands new fashionable articles, because it is impossible to expect someone to read over again what he has read once already, or even to read what our predecessors read – just as it is considered improper to appear in the same garment several times in high society, or to dress according to the fashion of our grandparents' (*Fichte, Werke*, VI, 440).[37]

Carlyle's reading of German notions regarding clothes may well have provided a nucleus around which the cells of his fully developed thoughts on vestures in all their varied significance could cluster, grow, and diversify.

SIX

Renunciation as a Way of Life

> Our physical as well as our social life, customs, habits, worldly wisdom, philosophy, religion, indeed, many a chance happening, all cry out at us that we should renounce.
>
> (Goethe, *Dichtung und Wahrheit*).

Goethe: *Entsagen* and Its Relation to Action

In discussing Goethe's creed of *Entsagen*, as it is revealed in *Wilhelm Meisters Wanderjahre*, it should be kept in mind that renunciation does not precede but follows the call to action. Wilhelm, in the course of his development towards greater maturity, first decides to live an active life, before the meaning of *Entsagen* and its effect on right action become increasingly clear to him. For this reason, activity or *Tätigkeit*, as Goethe chooses to call it, must be examined first.

Tätigkeit, the foremost message of *Wilhelm Meisters Lehrjahre*, does different things to different people. For Wilhelm, *Tätigkeit* comes at the end of a period of trial and error spent in search of talents he does not really possess. In quitting the stage and joining the Society of the Tower, he embarks on true activity, for which his Indenture is the symbol. Thus, in relation to the central character, *Tätigkeit* receives its fullest treatment, as a solution offered Wilhelm in his ardent desire to lead a meaningful life. His false start, which had resulted in dissatisfaction and frustration, is related to the fact that Wilhelm had not as yet found himself. Misguided by a wrong estimation of his personality and his abilities, he 'sought for cultivation where it was not to be found,' and had fancied that he 'could form a talent without the smallest gift for it' (*Meister*, II, 74).[1]

This initially negative experience is, however, not considered to be time wasted. Only error could lead Wilhelm to a truer estimation of his own abilities and their consequent development in an activity more in keeping with them. The Abbé, spiritual leader of the Society of the Tower, insists on the necessity of error as part of the process leading to maturity. According to his principles, 'to guard from error is not the instructor's duty' (*Meister*, II, 74);[2] he should lead the erring pupil in such a way that insight is reached as a result of it. In this sense, error has a positive side to it and forms part of the learner's journey towards a goal. When Wilhelm mildly chides the Abbé for not having pointed out his errors to him sooner, their role within his development is clearly stated: 'He who only tastes his error, will long dwell in it, will take delight in it ... while he who drains it to the dregs will find it out' (ibid., II, 74).[3] Wilhelm is in the fortunate position to have avoided guilt during these abortive experiences, being in this respect better off than others: 'None of your follies wilt thou repent; none wilt thou wish to repeat; no luckier destiny can be allotted to man' (ibid., II, 75).[4] By way of action Wilhelm will now have to get better acquainted with himself, learn to forget himself in activity prescribed by duty and how to live for the sake of others.

Besides stating the value of error, the Abbé also defines the nature of *Tätigkeit* with regard to the individual: 'He maintained that with man the first and last consideration was activity and that we could not act on anything, without the proper gifts for it, without an instinct impelling us to it' (*Meister*, II, 100).[5]

This pronouncement relates *Tätigkeit* to talent and a calling, but it does not give guidance as to how true *Tätigkeit* is to be embarked upon. The 'Indenture' illuminates aspects of this question, as it pertains to both art and life. This document, handed to Wilhelm at a time when error has been recognized but right action has not as yet been undertaken, contains a variety of maxims, tailored to his particular needs. It becomes clear from these *sententiae* that action must be related to thought: 'To act is easy, to think is hard; to act according to our thought is troublesome' (*Meister*, II, 75).[6] The necessity of perseverance is indirectly stressed in the strange statement 'Every beginning is cheerful,' a reversal of the German proverbial saying 'Aller Anfang ist schwer' (Every beginning is hard). It seems to imply that initial drive helps overcome difficulties, but to carry any task to completion demands perpetual application, which can only be accomplished by a sense of duty. In the Indenture we also find references to words as being good but not the best; the importance of the spirit in which actions are carried out; the notion that only in wrong-doing are we conscious of our acts – precepts that Carlyle refers to, in one form or another, in his writings.

In the interpretation of these insights, Jarno comes to the assistance of a rather bewildered Wilhelm, who has been pronounced free and no longer an apprentice: 'Thy Apprenticeship is done; Nature has pronounced thee free' (*Meister*, II, 77).[7] Jarno not only explains that, through action alone, man can check and watch himself, but also remarks that 'there are few who at once have Thought and the capacity of Action. Thought expands, but lames; Action animates but narrows' (ibid., 29).[8] Man must, in other words, be on constant watch to balance action against thought so that neither lameness nor narrowness results.

These fine distinctions rule out pat solutions and bring into play a variety of qualities inherent in each individual. What applies in Wilhelm's case is, for example, not effective for Lothario, an outgoing and energetic personality who would therefore seek a different seedfield. For Lothario, the notion of an immediate and practical duty would be more appealing; for Wilhelm, an unfolding of inner capacities related to art and intellect would be desirable. Go-spirit, the symbol of America as the place where *Tätigkeit* could still be accomplished, has led Lothario into a different kind of error than Wilhelm had experienced in search of personal culture. He has missed out on the right perspective, overlooking vast possibilities for improvement on his own estates, right on his doorstep, where he might put his capabilities to good use. The recognition of this fact is the first move in the direction of right activity for him: 'In America, I fancied, I might accomplish something; overseas, I hoped to become useful and essential ... How differently do matters now appear! How precious, how important seems the duty which is nearest me, whatever it may be' (ibid., 11).[9] These contemplations lead to the insight that determines Lothario's future actions: 'I will return, and in my house, amid my fields, among my people, I will say: "Here or nowhere is America!" '[10] It follows that, if activity is a manifestation of self, 'to do the work that's nearest' means to do the work the particular individual is best suited for, rather than to do the work that is closest at hand.

Besides this essential aspect *Tätigkeit* as a solution to problems of personal fulfilment and maturity, there are others related to different characters. For the 'Schöne Seele,' *Tätigkeit* stands as an injunction at the end of her 'Bekenntnisse,' as a guideline. *Tätigkeit* is, in this case, the crowning glory of a regained awareness of spiritual self.[11]

But *Tätigkeit* is also a medicinal remedy, as in the case of the unfortunate harper, who suffers unbearable doubt and despair with regard to his own tragic past. His whole frame of mind, as described by the physician, comes close to that of Teufelsdröckh, in 'The Everlasting

No' although for other reasons: 'Wrapped up in himself, he has looked at nothing but his own hollow empty Me, which seemed to him like an immeasurable abyss. It was really touching when he spoke to us of this mournful state. "Before me," cried he, "I see nothing; behind me nothing but an endless night, in which I live in the most horrid solitude ... Yet here there is no height, no depth, no forwards, no backwards; no words can express this never-changing state ... No ray of Divinity illuminates this night' (*Meister*, II, 16).[12] To awaken the harper's activity is the means employed to cure his impending insanity.

The highest form of *Tätigkeit* is creative activity, discussed by the uncle of the 'Schöne Seele' in the 'Bekenntnisse.' In connection with the paintings exhibited in his picture gallery, he remarks on the ability of the artist to shape, from the huge quarry of life, a distinct form: 'Deep within us lies the creative force, which out of these can produce what they were meant to be; and which leaves us neither sleep nor rest, till in one way or another ... that same has been produced' (*Meister*, I, 444).[13]

A final form of *Tätigkeit*, one morally more desirable, is altruistic activity. Such disinterested well-doing Wilhelm performs when delivering Mignon from the custody of the rope-dancers and a brutal patron. Later, it widens into the concept of usefulness, or *Nützen*, already related to broader concepts of Palingenesia.

Bearing these different examples of *Tätigkeit* in mind, we must ask ourselves how far Carlyle was aware of them. From the general tenor of 'The Everlasting Yea,' as well as from the verbal borrowings contained in his chapter, it appears that Carlyle was conscious of the various implications. As a translator, he was intimately familiar with the text.[14] It is owing to the diversity of the creed of *Tätigkeit* that so many different aspects of activity are introduced in *Sartor*. While, in Goethe's work, these perspectives were related to different personalities, they are consolidated in Carlyle's book on the inimitable Teufelsdröckh.

Admittedly, in *Sartor* the emphasis shifts because the central issue of the spiritual struggle demands an immediate solution; the problem of personal fulfilment does not come first, as it does in Goethe's work. Carlyle was, above all, interested in the concept of *Tätigkeit* as a remedy for doubt, which Goethe had linked to the problems besetting the harper. In his essay 'Goethe' of 1828, the formula later to be applied to Teufelsdröckh is already found, affecting the life of Goethe, as well as his work. After extensive translation from *Wilhelm Meisters Wanderjahre*, Carlyle draws the following conclusion: 'By means of these quotations, we meant to make it visible that a great change had taken place in the moral disposition of the man; a change from inward imprisonment, doubt and discontent, into freedom, belief and clear activity' (*Essays I*, 242–3).

Carlyle thus finds in Goethe's life and in *Wilhelm Meister* the solution to a problem uppermost in his own mind, that of the removal of doubt. In the case of *Sartor*, this problem is depicted and solved along the same lines Carlyle believed to be applicable to Goethe. Action as a remedy for doubt, leading on to duty, is strongly brought out in the following passage: 'Most true is it, as a wise man teaches us, that "Doubt of any sort cannot be removed except by Action." On which ground, too, let him who gropes painfully in darkness ... lay this other precept well to heart, which to me was of invaluable service: *"Do the Duty which lies nearest thee,"* which thou knowest to be a Duty!' (*Sartor*, 196).

The pronouncement may be considered a step in the direction of the Gospel of Work, but not one without Goethean reservations, as the monitory 'which thou knowest to be a Duty' implies. An echo of the notion of action as a remedy can be traced even to the 'Inaugural Address': 'The most unhappy of all men is the man who cannot tell what he is going to do, who has got no work cut out for him in the world ... For work is the grand cure of all the maladies and miseries that ever beset mankind' (*Essays IV*, 455).

Well-doing, which we had met with in *Wilhelm Meisters Lehrjahre* regarding Wilhelm's actions toward Mignon, appears twice in *Sartor*: once as a 'God-given mandate' (183) and again in connection with Teufelsdröckh's personal fulfilment, ushering in his spiritual majority: 'we are henceforth to see him "work in well-doing," with the spirit and clear aims of Man' (199). This well-doing is not a personal act, as it is described by Goethe, but a vocation with altruistic tendencies. Teufelsdröckh awakens, arises, speaks forth what is in him. His writings fall into the seed-field of opinion: 'I thank the Heavens that I have now found my Calling; wherein, with or without perceptible result, I am minded diligently to persevere' (200).

A word remains to be said about the impact of the Indenture as a whole on Carlyle. He is quick to grasp the message, particularly as far as moral implications are concerned. Thus the mention made of the unconsciousness of right action remains a favourite with him: 'No one knows what he is doing, while he acts aright; but of what is wrong we are always conscious' (*Meister*, II, 76).[15] Carlyle takes this statement exclusively in the moral sense and, in 'Characteristics,' simplifies it to: 'Of the Wrong we are always conscious, of the Right never.'[16]

Even if Carlyle is inclined to misread the Indenture, he does show a full understanding for the creativity of the poet as a form of *Tätigkeit*. What he says of the Poet and the Priest, who 'in all times have spoken and suffered; bearing testimony, through life and through death, of the Godlike that is in Man' (*Sartor*, 192), comes close to what Wilhelm tells his friend Werner on the nature of the poet 'as a teacher, a prophet, a friend of gods and men' (*Meister*, I, 113),[17] although overtones of Fichte's 'perpetual priesthood' are worked into Carlyle's passage. His unqualified appreciation of creative activity is still perceived in the chapter 'Helotage,' where Carlyle differentiates between menial and spiritual labour: 'A second man I honour, and still more highly: Him who is seen toiling for the spiritually indispensable; not daily bread, but the bread of Life ... Highest of all ... when we can name him Artist; not earthly Craftsman only, but inspired Thinker, who with heaven-made Implement conquers Heaven for us' (*Sartor*, 228).

Even in the most urgent call to work, the fervent 'Produce! Produce!' (ibid., 197), some aspect of creativity are still captured, in the context, which speaks of 'the utmost thou hast in thee,' although it is not in the least Goethean in its formulation. Carlyle the preacher calls the faithful to action in the spirit of a religious duty.

On account of this great variety inherent in the meaning of activity, it might be well to keep MacCunn's admonition with regard to over-simplifications in mind: 'Work in the Carlylean vocabulary is a wide word. It includes, as a memorable passage in *Sartor* reminds us, the work for spiritual bread. The fact of the matter is not that Carlyle did not live up to his own Gospel of Work, but that the critics should learn to interpret that gospel aright' (*Six Radical Thinkers*, 161).

While MacCunn's words of caution are certainly applicable to some of the *Sartor* passages on action, they do not apply for Carlyle's further development of the initial idea of *Tätigkeit*. Action loses its connectedness with thought – so significant a relationship for Goethe – and deteriorates into work for work's sake, a cure-all for social ills. This is, however, a gradual process. In *Past and Present*, the above aspect of work for work's sake reaches its zenith.

In the following passage, the emphasis has shifted to work as fulfilment without any relation to thought or ability: 'It is, after all, the one unhappiness of a man, that he can't work, that he cannot get his destiny as a man fulfilled' (*Past and Present*, Book III, ch. 4, 156). This disassociation increases as Carlyle proceeds: 'The spoken Word, the written Poem, is said to be an epitome of the man; how much more the done work ... To work: why, it is to try himself against Nature' (ibid., ch. 5, 158). Here the written work or poem is contrasted with work, and work itself seen, in Fichte's sense, as a struggle with Nature or the 'Not-Me.'

In the chapter 'Labour,' no attempt is made to save any of the old distinctions. Instead, Carlyle serves up oversimplifications of the worst kind: 'The real desire to get work done, will itself lead one more and more to truth' (Bk. III, ch. 11, 196). This trend reaches its height in 'the latest Gospel in this World': 'The latest Gospel in this World is, Know thy work and do it. "Know thyself:" long enough has that poor "self" of thine tormented thee; thou wilt never get to "know" it, I believe! Think it not thy business, this of knowing thyself; thou art an unknowable individual: know what thou canst work at; and work at it, like a Hercules! That will be they better plan' (ibid.). As Carlyle evidently refers to the muscle-man, not 'Hercules at the cross-roads,' this looks like an intellectual sell-out. The elaborations of this theme are all taken from manual labour. Although seed-fields are among them, they no longer have much in common with Goethe's *Acker der Zeit*, into which thought is being planted. On the contrary, labour becomes a tranquillizer against the pitfalls of thought: 'Consider how, even in the meanest sorts of Labour, the whole soul of a man is composed into a kind of real harmony, the instant he sets himself to work! Doubt, Desire, Sorrow, Remorse, Indignation, Despair itself, all these like hell-dogs lie beleaguering the soul of the poor day-worker as of every man: but he bends himself with free valour against his task, and all these are stilled, all these shrink murmuring far off into their caves. The man is now a man' (ibid.).

The final outcome is the equation of work with religion: 'Truly enough a religious operation; which cannot be carried on without religion' (ibid., ch. 12, 206). In between such pronouncements as these, Carlyle not only names Goethe – quoting passages from *Wilhelm Meisters Wanderjahre* totally unrelated to the New Gospel – but decides to march out of the third Book with 'a rhythmic word of Goethe's on our lips,' which sounds like a distortion of everything Goethe's *Tätigkeit* stands for.[18]

This unfortunate development in Carlyle illustrates well the necessity of *Entsagen* as a limiting factor with regard to activity. Endless, aimless activity is, in Goethe's opinion, wasteful; activity should be determined, channelled, or curbed, for striving towards a goal is the secret of all productive work. One way of achieving this directedness is by voluntary restriction of choice, a discipline the individual imposes upon himself. In the 'Bekenntnisse,' the uncle points out the necessity for limitation: 'Whatever it may be,' said he, 'reason or feeling, that commands us to give up the one thing for the other, to choose the one before the other, decision and perseverance are, in my opinion, the noblest qualities of man. You cannot have the ware and the money both at once ... Man is intended for a limited condition' (*Meister*, I, 445).[19]

This philosophy of life lies deeply imbedded in the texture of *Wilhelm Meisters Wanderjahre*, as the subtitle, 'Die Entsagenden' indicates. Voluntarily imposed limitation for the sake of achieving a concrete goal forms part of the creed: 'Man is never happy till his vague striving has given itself a proper limitation' (*Meister*, II, 132).[20] With this comes a new conception of happiness, not as pleasure but as inner fulfilment. Those who consciously make this choice are the *Entsagenden*. Several examples are given that are supposed to illustrate *Entsagen*. These include not only actual characters in the novel but also references to the stories inserted in *Wilhelm Meisters Wanderjahre*. In the version of 1821, which Carlyle translated, these examples are only sketched but not completed, so that much remains enigmatic. It is certain, however: *Entsagen* is not restricted to 'the artist's "selecting," ordering and shaping of his materials.'[21] *Entsagen* is a frame of mind, not a method. The artist accepts it as it applies to his person, not to his work.

Entsagen is presented as a way of life in Wilhelm himself. He is a character to whom the high meaning of Renunciation, constituting his real entrance into life, becomes increasingly clear. This involves giving up things. He thus voluntarily postpones his union with Natalie by following the call to travel, as the pledged member of the Society of the Tower. This separation is a painful experience, and he naturally enough longs to be reunited with her. Wilhelm renounces personal fulfilment in order to practise 'well-doing," to which his activity within the Society is related. For he does not wander about aimlessly, but has certain tasks to fulfil that help solve other people's problems. An example is the case of Leonardo, whose mind he tries to put at ease by searching out the Nutbrown Maiden to whom the former felt an obligation. Wilhelm is aware of his commitment: 'My life is to become a restless wandering. Strange duties of the Wanderer have I to fulfil and peculiar trials to undergo' (*Meister*, II, 199).[22] The result is beneficial for his character; and the lasting gains are self-denial and altruistic acts.

It follows that Carlyle is not totally wrong when he speaks, in connection with *Entsagen*, of 'the law of self-denial, by which alone man's narrow destiny may become an infinitude within himself' (*Essays I*, 161). Nor is the moral emphasis completely inappropriate, which Carlyle stresses in his interpretation: 'for without some portion of this spirit, not of boisterous daring, but of silent fearlessness, of self-denial in all its forms, no good man, in any scene or time, had ever attained to be good' (*Essays I*, 311).

If *Entsagen* means a restriction of the total freedom of choice, it also means a gain in excellence that results from the concentration on one chosen activity. Those practising *Entsagen*, one is led to believe, must be, first and foremost, the gifted among mankind, those who have a choice to make between several latent possibilities and are able to further humanity at large. This is the final goal of the *quasi*-Masonic organization, of which the Tower Society is but a part.

Although all men make up mankind and every gift is considered valuable within a larger framework, a certain type of gift in man needs to be promoted, while other abilities look after themselves: 'The useful encourages itself; for the multitude produces it, and no one can dispense with it. The beautiful must be encouraged; for few can set it forth and many need it' (*Meister*, II, 132).[23] From this point of view it may be gathered that *Entsagen* has a special meaning for the artist within the larger pattern of life. By promoting the development of his special gifts through utmost concentration, humanity will be enriched by qualities it may not value but urgently stands in need of.

It is in these last wide-reaching effects of *Entsagen* that Goethe and Carlyle seemingly differ. In Goethe's view, a choice has to be made between a variety of talents, as Jarno informs Wilhelm: 'It is your affair to try and choose; it is ours to aid you' (*Meister*, II, 132).[24] Addressing itself foremost to the gifted, a moral decision may play a part in this choice, but does not always do so, as is clear from the case of Lothario, whose moral concepts are not of the strictest as far as his love relationships are concerned. Carlyle, in contrast, interprets choice purely in a moral sense: work for the devil or for God (*Past and Present*, Bk. II, ch. 9, 1). He also stresses the unconditional renunciation of personal happiness for the sake of well-doing, to a degree to which Goethe does not. According to Carlyle's revisionist reading, it is time to 'Close thy *Byron*; open thy *Goethe*' (*Sartor*, 192), for man should not indulge in self-pity but act for others. The poet, in particular, should not contemplate the loss of happiness, but join the preaching sages – Carlyle seeing Goethe as being one among them.

In this way, Carlyle accepted and understood Goethe's message of *Entsagen*, admittedly missing out on much of its complexity but not basically misinterpreting it. Therefore his claim to be indebted to Goethe in this regard cannot be dismissed as altogether wrong.[25] Goethe's notion remained an essential building-block for Carlyle, however much he associates other influences with what he had gained from his model's initial presentation of the concept.

Fichte: Renunciation and the 'Divine Idea'

Interpreters of Fichte's influence on Carlyle have been so absorbed with hero-worship as allegedly his main contribution to Carlyle's thought that his concept of renunciation has been left largely unconsidered.

The theme of renunciation is best expressed in Fichte's *Über das Wesen des Gelehrten,*[26] where it is related to the 'Divine Idea' and the personal morality of his leader-type, not however, to hero-worship as such. For the making of heroes and the worshipping of them are two different operations. It is one thing to set up a leader, and another to demand admiration, commitment, even submission from humanity at large as a desirable consequence. A hero does not, after all, stand in need of devout followers, as many heroic actions have been carried out single-handedly, even totally independent of any backing or approval by a loyal community. The word 'hero-worship' itself is an incorrect translation of *Heldenverehrung,* which presents admiration, not veneration. Man worships God, not man.

The heroes Fichte sets up in *Über das Wesen* are of an intellectual type, and are not once called by this name, despite what the reader gathers from some rearranged passages quoted in Harrold's *Carlyle and German Thought,* which give the impression that Carlyle not only adopted Fichte's theory of the hero but also owed his brand of hero-worship to him.[27] Fichte is, however, much more concerned with the problem of renunciation and obligation than has been recognized. The nature of these lectures already vouches for this, designed as they were, to introduce students to the ethics of scholarship. Fichte presents an ideal for the right performance of scholarly duties, which they are encouraged to follow, as well as a deficient type students are advised not to emulate. In addition, they are given intellectual and moral guidance on how to become perfect scholars and teachers.

Besides such assistance to students seeking to orient themselves in the world of learning, Fichte offers an exposition of the duties of the ruler, with a view to such among them who intend to enter active government service. A third type relevant to the aims of students is the writer, whose vocation demands additional requirements related to the unfolding of the 'Divine Idea.'

Except for the emphasis on the great responsibilities related to their calling and its connection with the Divine Will, there is nothing blatantly heroic about the personalities Fichte speaks of in a serious and sober manner. Instead, obligation to humanity is writ large in these lectures. The perfect scholar is a hero only in so far as he acts out the 'Divine Idea,' helping it to unfold before other men – in this case, before the students or 'future scholars,' as Fichte calls them, who have to be introduced to the 'Divine Idea' in order that they, in turn, may strive for truth. In this sense, and in this sense only, is the perfected scholar a member of a continuous priesthood, fulfilling a sacred duty in perpetuating this ideal. This higher type of scholar loves the 'Divine Idea,' lives for it, and is able to communicate it to others, in contrast to the *Stümper*, Carlyle's 'bungler,' who is not only deficient in knowledge but avoids independent thinking, which alone can lead to truth.

The major prerequisites for the unfolding of the 'Divine Idea' in man are free obedience to its demands and strict self-discipline. Man is its hallowed tool, its organ, a mediator between the Deity and the Idea, but not, as in Carlyle, its symbol; this notion, which Carlyle introduces, is strange to Fichte, for whom a symbol cannot take an active part in what it represents; it merely stands for a notion. Fichte's ideal scholar, in contrast, is constantly active in interpreting the 'Divine Idea' in word and deed to his students, who cannot as yet relate their studies to eternal values, not having as yet developed the inner eye. The constant progressive activity directed towards achieving something higher than self demands, according to Fichte, strict self-abnegation to the point of *Selbstvernichtung*, or destruction of self: 'His personal life has now been completely absorbed in the life of the idea, and is being destroyed in it, a self-destruction which for the student is as yet not attainable. Insofar as he is a perfected scholar there does not exist a thought with regard to his own person, but his total thought is always absorbed in the subject-matter' (*Über das Wesen*, VI, 412; Smith, 278).[28]

The person described here is really a type of saint, a martyr to his science rather than a hero in the ordinary sense. Fichte even declares him to be a sacred personality. Renunciation is the moral law under which the scholar lives. It alone induces the 'Divine Idea' to take hold of him, so that he becomes its administrator. Those chosen, therefore, must be eager and ever ready to sacrifice personal pleasure and happiness for this cause.

What is also peculiar to this interpretation is the quasi-religious nature of the doctrine of obligation of the 'sacred few.' The perfected scholar is one among the elect, but election demands merely more sacrifice and active renunciation. He explicitly states that he understands divine man to be God-inspired man. Christian humility is also the tenor of the more generally formulated concept of vocation as it pertains to all men.

Of the two variations of the scholarly hero or type of excellence – ruler and writer – who also stand under the impact of the 'Divine Idea,' a word remains to be added. Fichte states that, having so far spoken of intellectual education as an indirect furtherance of the 'Divine Idea' by way of example and teaching, he will now speak of one who acts out the precepts received. In practical life, he must therefore be considered as a direct manifestation of the 'Divine Idea' in the world because he immediately affects the affairs of men. To leave out this explanation would present a distortion of Fichte's theories. He demands that the ruler should act least himself – that is, least selfishly, always conscious that his task is to ennoble the human race as a whole. To read into this idealistic presentation unbounded veneration of the hero is far off the mark. On the contrary, the already mentioned attitude of humility is pronounced in such phrases as 'Diener der Gottheit' (*Das Wesen, Werke*, VI, 423; Smith 154) with which Fichte stresses the high calling of this type of leader. He adds a further warning that completely puts any notions of worship aside: 'this thought should in no way lead him to self-conceit puffed up by pride.'[29]

The writer's responsibilities are even greater because he writes in the light of eternity. Fichte thinks here first and foremost of the scholarly writer. In this regard, the same holds true for the written word as had been applied to the scholar's teaching and the ruler's actions, namely, that the idea itself must speak. He too must leave all selfish motives out of consideration; he too must voluntarily submit himself to the law of self-discipline, so that the idea he wishes to express may live. He stands in need of clarity and powerful language in his profession and must also, in the interest of truth, courageously correct error where he finds it, despite adverse consequences for himself as a person. Taking a long-range historical perspective, Fichte perceives that his whole age may take his approach and adopt his outlook.

It must be objectively stated that Fichte nowhere in *Über das Wesen* speaks of worship towards the 'Träger der göttlichen Idee,' as he describes them. This type of personality-cult would have been incompatible with the notion previously stated that the man disappears behind the idea he acts out. The changes Carlyle effects, with regard to the hero type and hero-worship, in particular, go far beyond this source, if indeed we can consider Fichte as a model for the latter, which is most dubious. Here Fichte and Carlyle part ways. Since hero-worship as such influences the rebirth of society, this aspect of the problem will be considered in chapter 8, on Palingenesia.

The concept of election and the emphasis on moral conduct, however, are another matter. One certainly can speak of an influence here that conforms with Carlyle's original disposition. These Fichtean notions Carlyle most effectively introduces in *Sartor*, to add to such messages as the 'Worship of Sorrow' and the idea of reverence derived from Goethe.

In his interpretation of Fichte, Carlyle leaves finer distinctions unheeded. The scholar (*Gelehrte*), of whom Fichte specifically speaks, Carlyle defines more widely as the 'literary man,' a type better suited to his purposes. When writing of the 'literal Communion of Saints' in *Sartor* (247) in connection with a thought that will never die, he follows Fichte much more closely than he does Goethe, even though the term itself occurs in *Wilhelm Meisters Wanderjahre* (II, 268). For Carlyle, the thought is part of the 'Divine Idea,' gathered from the past to be transmitted to the future. Also in the reference to 'Priest and Prophet to lead us heavenward' (*Sartor*, 222), a Fichtean interpretation seems indicated, especially as the 'Divine Idea' is elaborated in the following passages.

The contempt Carlyle shows towards personal happiness in favour of blessedness also owes something to Fichte. Renunciation is at least implied in the contention that 'there is in man a HIGHER than Love of Happiness: he can do without Happiness, and instead thereof find Blessedness' (ibid., 192). In the place where we find it 'The Everlasting Yea,' it appears to be an introduction to the following thought that 'Self ... needed to be annihilated' (ibid.), giving it a Fichtean ring. Unique to Carlyle, however, is the emphasis on the struggle that characterizes all man's efforts to live up to the demands made by the 'Divine Idea.' 'Characteristics' provides an example: 'Hard, for most part, is the fate of such men; the harder the nobler they are. In dim forecastings, wrestles within them the "Divine Idea of the World," yet will nowhere visibly reveal itself ... The Godlike has vanished from the world; and they by the strong cry of their soul's agony, like true wonderworkers, must again evoke its presence' (*Essays III*, 31).

Those who lack the capacity to bring the 'Divine Idea' to light within themselves are described in 'Voltaire,' under the image of the *philosophe*: ' "The Divine Idea, that which lies at the bottom of Appearance," was never more invisible to any man ... We find no heroism of character in him, from first to last' (*Essays I*, 414).

In light of the above, Carlyle's use of the term 'Annihilation of Self' in 'The Everlasting Yea,' called a moral act, could be aligned with Fichte's *Selbstvernichtung*, in spite of the added *Selbst-tödtung* derived from Novalis: 'The first preliminary moral Act, Annihilation of Self (*Selbsttödtung*), had been happily accomplished; and my mind's eyes were now unsealed, and its hands ungyved' (*Sartor*, 186). Related to the whole complex of the moral act is the reference made later in the same chapter linking conviction to conduct: 'But indeed Conviction, were it never so excellent, is worthless till it convert itself into Conduct. Nay properly Conviction is not possible till then' (ibid., 195). This statement reiterates Fichte's belief in man as a hallowed instrument of the 'Divine Idea', consciously directing his conduct towards achieving renunciation, to aid its unfolding.

Novalis: *Selbsttödtung*

The few studies that contain suggestions regarding *Selbsttödtung*[30] and the use Carlyle makes of this term have failed to relate its meaning to the whole concept of 'Magical Idealism' of which it forms a part. Novalis can hardly be considered as an original thinker, independent of Fichte's Idealism or Schelling's Philosophy of Nature. Aspects of both philosophers are incorporated in what one feels inclined to call Novalis's philosophical musings.[31] If he does not add new perspectives, however, he does add new dimensions to transcendental experience, in spite of his lack of methodical penetration and the unsystematic and fragmentary nature of this thoughts, as represented in *Blütenstaub* and his *Fragmente*.

Philosophy is, for Novalis, an artistic occupation he values foremost for its generally stimulating effect: 'To philosophize means to dephlegmatize, to invigorate.'[32] 'Magical Idealism' is therefore not a philosophical system but rather a poetical world-view, enriched by philosophical thought. Novalis's whole aim is to bring about a union between philosophy and art for the sake of a vicarious experience, a fuller apprehension of life. Their separation is for him a sign of sickness that must be cured by bringing about an even closer fusion with the aid of mystical vision.

In this vision, intuitive insights have a great role to play, as Novalis insists that the poet senses rather than knows the springs of life. The supernatural powers in and around him are revealed in 'aufblitzenden Enthusiasmusmomenten,'[33] that is, 'lightning flashes of inspiration.' Part of the mystery of life that must be illuminated is Nature. Only the highest form of man, the poet, can ultimately decipher her hieroglyphic writings. He alone is able to read the book of the external world, and to interpret it to others by the light from within. In this sense, Novalis, insists, 'Poetry is the absolute real. This lies at the core of my philosophy. The more poetic, the truer'.[34]

This notion of the *Ich* or Self as reflecting the world is the poetical application of Fichte's *Ich* and *Nicht-Ich* relationship, experienced on what Novalis would call a magical plain. Fichte's moral activity of the *Ich* within the realm of the *Nicht-Ich* changes into artistic activity. It employs the creative imagination, called *produktive Einbildungskraft,* to open up the secrets that lie dormant in Nature. In this profound sense, art is related to magic[35] and 'Magical Idealism' is the application of art to the idealistic philosophical system.

A prerequisite for this penetration into the sphere of the *Nicht-Ich* is an intensive development of the powers inherent in the *Ich.* As it is split into the lower Self, also called the 'empirical Me,' and the higher or 'transcendental Me,' or 'Divine Me,' the former will have to die so that the latter may unfold. This is the meaning of *Selbsttödtung,* or Annihilation of Self, an act that roots out man's selfish inclinations.

Hand in hand with this annihilation of the lower Self goes the active awakening of the 'transcendental Me,' which should be the aim of all education. This is accomplished, Novalis suggests, by exploring the innermost recesses of the 'Divine Me,' which has now been liberated. He calls it *der Weg nach Innen*: 'Inwards turns this mysterious way. Inside of us or nowhere lies eternity with her worlds, her past and her future.'[36] Only in this way is 'the transcendental Me' brought to ever-growing perfection.

Selbsttödtung, however, constitutes only the first step in a twofold process, which Novalis describes in the following manner: 'The first step is looking inward in an introspective contemplation of Self. Those who remain at this stage only go half-way. The second step must be self-active contemplation of the external world.'[37] How is this second step of Self-activity, this *Weg nach Aussen,* to be achieved? Owing to the enigmatic quality of Novalis's remarks, the answer is never fully supplied. All the reader can do is to glean explanations from other parts of the *Fragmente* by way of thought association.

An illustration of the two steps resulting in a complete metamorphosis is given in the form of poetic symbolism in the fragmentary tale *Lehrlinge zu Sais.* Here the *Weg nach Innen,* followed by the *Weg nach Aussen,* leads to a stage where *Ich* and *Nicht-Ich,* Man and Nature, are interchangeable. This state, described as the artistic process, is peculiar to Magical Idealism:

He carefully listened to his moods and his thoughts. He did not know where his longing drove him. When he grew older he strolled around, viewed other countries, other seas, new spheres, strange stars, unknown plants, animals, peoples ... Everywhere he now met with familiar things, strangely mixed and paired, and thus strange things fell into patterns for him ... He no longer observed things by themselves. – Observations by way of his senses crowded into huge colourful pictures ... sometimes the stars seemed to be men to him, sometimes the men stars, the stones beasts, the clouds plants, he played with forces and appearances, he knew where and how he could find and make apparent one or the other, and in this way he himself touched the strings for tunes and variations.[38]

In reading the hieroglyphic writing of the universe the body–soul combination in man has an important function to fulfil. From this awareness stems Novalis's worship of the body as an important part of the tool that modifies the world. 'There is but one temple in the world; that is the body of man. Nothing is holier than this high form.'[39] This pronouncement is not what it might appear to be at first sight, 'a hedonistic and sensualistic mysticism,[40] but the description of a sensitive organ the poet uses to explore the world. Man, standing as a mediator between God and Nature, acts as a Messiah: 'Man has ever expressed some symbolical Philosophy of his Being in his Works and Conduct; he announces himself and his Gospel of Nature; he is the Messiah of Nature.'[41]

Carlyle is fond of referring to both these notions. The 'Body as Temple' he quotes not only in his essay on Novalis, in *Sartor*, and in *Heroes*, but also twice in *Past and Present*.[42] From one of these hitherto unconsidered passages it can be gathered that Carlyle understood Novalis to be referring to the body as a symbol of the Divine Idea, in Fichte's sense. Prior to quoting the passage from Novalis, Carlyle states: 'It is the most reverend phenomenon under this Sun. For the Highest God dwells visibly in that mystic unfathomable Visibility, which calls itself "I" on the Earth, "Bending before men," says Novalis, "is a reverence done to this Revelation in the Flesh" ' (*Past and Present*, Bk. II, ch. 16, 124).

Carlyle's further elaboration of the 'Messiah of Nature' theme is found in 'Boswell's Life of Johnson.' Here he pictures man as a kind of Christ triumphant, who overcomes Necessity: 'Man is heaven-born; not the thrall of Circumstances, of Necessity, but the victorious subduer thereof: behold how he can become the "Announcer of himself and of his Freedom"; and is ever what the Thinker has named him, "the

Messias of Nature" ' (*Essays III*, 90). This interpretation is upheld in *Sartor*, where a connection with freedom is once more made. We hear of 'a "Gospel of Freedom," which he, the "Messias of Nature," preaches' (220). Clearly, the Messias of Nature in this instance overcomes and subdues nature, and is connected with the Gospel of Freedom, which in contrast to Novalis takes precedence over the Gospel of Nature.

From these two borrowings, it appears doubtful whether Carlyle fully comprehended the complexities of Novalis's creed, on which I have presented my own theory above. He is perplexed, but at the same time senses something new and strange worth going after: 'We find ourselves carried into more subtle regions of thought than any we are elsewhere acquainted with: here we cannot always find our own latitude and longitude, sometimes not even approximate to finding them; much less teach others such a secret' (*Essays II*, 'Novalis,' 42). Despite these misgivings, Carlyle immediately finds a niche for Novalis in his clothes philosophy: 'He loves external Nature with a singular depth; nay, we might say, he reverences her, and holds unspeakable communion with her: for Nature is no longer dead, hostile Matter, but the veil and mysterious Garment of the Unseen; as it were, the Voice with which the Deity proclaims himself to man' (ibid., 29).

Such a description of Novalis's relationship with Nature in no way takes any philosophical subtleties into account. There is also no indication that Carlyle understood *Selbsttödtung* to be a preparatory stage for the acquisition of 'Magical Idealism.' He was, of course, aware of the ability of the *Ich* to split itself up into the lower Self and the transcendental Me, but this much he would have gathered from Fichte. An eye-opener is his translation of the fragment on *Selbsttödtung*, which he quotes in full in 'Novalis': 'The true philosophical Act is annihilation of Self (*Selbsttödtung*); this is the real beginning of all Philosophy; all requisites for being a Disciple of Philosophy point hither. This Act alone corresponds to all the conditions and characteristics of transcendental conduct' (*Essays II*, 40).[43]

Novalis's text calls for the word 'action' (*Handlung*) instead of 'conduct.' The transcendental action, which Novalis deems necessary for a true communion between the *Ich* and the *Nicht-Ich*, Carlyle interprets, in Fichte's sense, as conduct. This lack of awareness of the progressive stages on the way to magical perception appears to be an indirect proof of my interpretation that Carlyle uses *Selbsttödtung* in Fichte's sense. This falls in line with his definition of Annihilation of Self' in 'Diderot,' which should settle the problem: 'Ever indeed, must Self-denial, 'Annihilation of Self' be the beginning of all moral action' (*Essays III*, 239) – that is to say, moral conduct.

Werner: Renunciation and Vision

In Zacharias Werner's dramatic works, renunciation is a key theme that appears under a variety of names, such as *Entsagen*, *Selbsttödtung*, *Selbstvergessen*, and *Selbstverneinung*. Common to all of them is their relation to vision. While renunciation strengthens man's readiness to receive the message, vision is spiritual growth brought about by mystical insights. These insights do not relate to Nature, as Novalis claimed, but exclusively to man, and usually have strong religious overtones.

Werner goes into aspects of renunciation in almost all his dramatic works. Most frequently love-renunciation is chosen as the preferred form; in it sublimated emotions turn towards spiritual goals. This is, however, not the case in his *Söhne des Thals*, which is of first importance in connection with influences on Carlyle. A lengthy play in two parts, called a dramatic poem, it deals with the decline and final destruction of the Order of the Templars. Already in the Prologue we hear of 'quiet, peaceful renunciation, the first step on the road to perfection.'[44] Within the vast framework of the story, stretching from Cyprus to Paris, and to the Hebrides, a good many opportunities present themselves to give the term a broader meaning. Renunciation is not related to Self alone; it is also considered as a prerequisite to communal living. The proud Self must be crucified for higher goals without any expectation of reward.

In the beginning of the play – substantial parts of which Carlyle translated for his essay on the 'Life and Writings of Werner' (*Essays I*, 87–145) – the spirit of renunciation is conspicuously absent in the description of the individual Templars. Self-indulgence and inactivity are the order of the day, resulting in the loss of any ability to struggle and renounce. Molay, the leader of the order, is well aware of these shortcomings in his followers, and clearly sees that there is little hope of renewal from within: 'From these sluggish masses the pure Phoenix will no longer rise.'[45] From his soliloquy, the reader gathers that renunciation must not only be practised in a passive sense as self-denial, but also must express itself actively by casting off base characteristics of the lower Self.

Werner presents both forms of renunciation in two different characters: young Adalbert dominates the action in the first part of the drama, and the Scot Robert d'Heredon in the second. Both are young knight-aspirants who have to pass through different trials prior to admission into the order. In the initiation of Adalbert, an illustration of the casting off of fear is given. The test situation consists in a confrontation with the image of the diabolic Baffometus. In a symbolical act, Adalbert is bidden to take off the figure's neckband, crown, and chains. In addition, he is required to trample on the cross he lifts from Baffometus's back. This act Carlyle does not interpret as blasphemous, but as emblematic in so far as 'the true spirit of religion is delivered from the state of thralldom and distortion under which it was held' (*Essays I*, 'Life and Writings of Werner,' 103). That fearless defiance is the actual meaning behind this action seems confirmed by a recall of the scene in Part II of the play: 'Did the monster not vanish when you gripped it with fearless hands?'[46] In view of the importance of this trial scene for Carlyle's 'Baphometic Fire-baptism' (*Sartor*, 168), it should be commented on in greater detail.

Carlyle is probably right in interpreting Adalbert's trial scene as a Protestant allegory, symbolically indicating the deterioration of the Christian Church under the papacy. Baffometus is designated as a master, a person in authority. Instead of following the Lord's command to build his temple, he completes his own dwelling on a foundation stone, suggestive of Saint Peter's rock. For 'filthy gold' he has repeatedly sold the stones set apart for this purpose, besides committing other sins to which the fiend has tempted him. He is punished by completely losing himself in worldly affairs, deteriorating into the image he serves: the Prince of This World. Faith declines; a new saviour is anxiously awaited. This saviour Werner later finds in his drama *Martin Luther*, where he picks up the idea of the deterioration of the Church and expresses the need for reform. Adalbert in a way foreshadows this act by courageously divesting the false god of his signs of power in order to redeem true faith. The guide assures Adalbert that the cross is merely a counterfeit – not Christ's true one, but that of an idol of this world. After this act of defiance Baffometus is freed from a heavy load. At this point Carlyle ends his translation while Adalbert completes his work of redemption. It is then stated that Adalbert undertook the delivery in the name of him 'who baptizes with fire' (I, V, ii). This is, without doubt, a reference to the Holy Spirit, as around 1800 the word *Feuertaufe* designated a spiritual insight, not first battle experience, a meaning it only acquired much later. Jean Paul employs it in the former sense when speaking of Holy Communion as a Fire Baptism in his *Selberlebensbeschreibung*,[47] which Carlyle knew so well.

If Carlyle built his defiance of 'the Everlasting No' to parallel Werner's trial scene, as the Baphometic reference indicates, Harrold's description of Teufelsdröckh as 'a kind of Baffometus' (*Sartor*, 168, fn. 1) does not fit the facts. As it is Adalbert who defies Baffometus, Teufelsdröckh should rather be aligned with him. Adalbert as well as

Teufelsdröckh undergo spiritual experiences of a similar kind, not Baffometus who is a symbol of deteriorated faith. Teufelsdröckh is a second Adalbert, shaking off fear of what is only seemingly divine. Fear must be overcome to destroy spiritual phantoms. This is a prerequisite for experiencing the 'Baphometic Fire-baptism' in which not only full manhood is reached, but new religious consciousness is gained: 'It is from this hour that I incline to date my spiritual Newbirth, or Baphometic Fire-baptism; perhaps I directly thereupon began to be a Man' (*Sartor*, 168).

Robert d'Heredon's spiritual insights are less spectacular. From the outset, this young Templar is baffled by the problem of renunciation and its relationship to action. Being active for action's sake, he finds it hard to understand the need to renounce as a goal for all mankind. When Molay asks the crucial question 'Strong Robert, are you prepared to practise submission, to renounce?' (I, IV, ii), d'Heredon fails to answer it in the affirmative. Although hope is held out that he will learn the secret of renunciation in the future, he leaves the order. Later, when he meets the Council of the Sons of the Valley, old Adam of Valincourt, a prototype of man, opens up broader vistas to this youthful personality in need of guidance: '... Thus you too, if you wish to rule over matter, must part with your own self by way of Self-annihilation [*Selbstertödtung*]. Only when you realize that matter and spirit are manifestations mirroring infinity, can you hope to shape creatively their fanciful interplay ... By way of Self-forgetfulness you obtain vision.'[48] Robert gets the message about the interrelatedness of the finite and the infinite, and reluctantly begins to realize that revelation can be granted only to him who can lose himself.

Renunciation also has a role to play in Werner's unfinished drama *Kreuz an der Ostsee*, which portrays the conquest of Prussia by the Teutonic Knights. The main theme consists in the clash of two cultures, and the impact of Christianity on a people living in a ruder stage of civilization. Carlyle describes the play as 'appearing to us as the best of Werner's dramas' (*Essays I*, 'Life and Writings of Werner,' 123). He was certainly familiar with the 'Historical Introduction' Werner provided for his rather unusual topic. In it, he describes the customs of the ancient Prussians and notes, among other observations: 'Their customs were as simple as was their language. For stomach and soul they used one and the same expression, as do to this day the Lithuanians and the financiers.'[49] This is the puzzling reference Carlyle repeatedly uses without giving his source. The most-often-quoted version is to be found in *Sartor* (117), where Werner's Lithuanians are matched by

Carlyle's Finns, and his financiers by Carlyle's Utilitarians, in the same kind of sentence structure, with the same kind of sardonic humour: 'If man's *Soul* is indeed, as in the Finnish language, and Utilitarian Philosophy, a kind of *Stomach*.'[50]

Renunciation in this play could not have contributed over and above what Carlyle had already learned from *Söhne des Thals*, since love-renunciation, as practised by the Prussian Prince Warmio and his lover, Malgona, would not particularly attract Carlyle. Renunciation as a standard of excellence, however, is to be found in the ranks of the Teutonic knights. Warmio, received into the order as a lay member and instructed about his duties, learns the meaning of 'erringen and entsagen' (*Kreuz an der Ostsee*, Act II, scene ii).

The drama *Söhne des Thals*, however, remains central to Carlyle's knowledge of Werner's forms of renunciation. Describing it in 'Life and Writings of Werner' as a strange phantasmagoria, Carlyle nevertheless devotes a total of fourteen pages to something he calls 'not a work of art, but little more than a rhapsodic effusion' (*Essays I*, 114). Although he strongly disapproves of its 'mass of mystical theology' (ibid., 94), he is attracted by the symbolical figures, and listens to its message.

It is obvious from his criticism that Carlyle does not deal with the initiation scenes featuring Adalbert and Robert as a functional part of the play, but considers them as significant in themselves, also with regard to renunciation. He translates Robert's final contemplation and praises Werner's 'high tenet of entire Self-forgetfulness' (ibid., 116), which Carlyle had already absorbed in a variety of forms. Werner appears to Carlyle as part of a whole school of thought, merging the Me into the idea, and aligns him also with both Stoic and Christian ethics. To his mind, Werner has expressed one particular element best: 'He will not have Happiness under any form, to be the real or chief end of man: this is but love of enjoyment, disguise it as we like ... to be admitted as an indestructible element in human nature, but nowise to be recognized as the highest; on the contrary to be resisted and incessantly warred with, till it become obedient to love of God' (ibid., 117). According to this statement it may well be that Werner had something to add to the 'Love not Pleasure; love God' (*Sartor*, 192) message of 'The Everlasting Yea' chapter, besides contributing, by way of the trial scene, to the symbolical myth of 'The Everlasting No.'

SEVEN

'Das Ewige Nein' and 'Das Ewige Ja'; Centre of Indifference

Thomas Carlyle is the only English writer on whom German literature had a direct and very significant influence. Out of mere courtesy Germans cannot leave his writings unnoticed.

(Marx/Engels, Review, 1850)

Further Contributions in Horn's Fiction

In view of Franz Horn's several apt definitions of 'das ewige Ja' and 'das ewige Nein,' contained in his literary criticism, one might presume that the application of these terms and what they stand for would also be presented in his own novels. Horn was, after all, not only a well-known literary historian of the popular kind but also a widely read mainstream writer of fiction. Goethe, who sent him the latest edition of *Werther* in 1825, in acknowledgement of his merits in the field of literature in general, names him first among other novelist (Eckermann, *Gespräche* I, 3 Dez. 1824).

This supposition is confirmed by Horn's comments in *Freundliche Schriften,* Part I (151–2), under the subheading 'Andeutungen vermischten Inhalts,' where literary topics are loosely combined, and discussed in the form of aphorisms or fragments. Here Horn defines once more his concept of the 'ewige Nein' and the 'ewige Ja.' The divine, identified with the latter, consists in calmness, clarity, determination, and affirmation of life. The *Ungöttliche* (Un-divine) is restlessness, confusion, doubt, and negation: 'The state of the perfect divine manifests itself in the "ewig-selige Ja" towards goodness; the complete demonic in the "ewig unselige Nein." '[1] Further explanations point to the destructive tendency in the 'Ewige Nein,' which Horn describes as a *Scheinleben,* a merely apparent phantom life. The only way how to overcome this 'Nein' is for man to fight it will all his might. Faith is the means to win victory in the form of the 'Ewige Ja': 'This is the point from which the devil must be judged, and this is the way poets should describe him. How many have attempted it, and how few have succeeded!'[2]

Horn leaves the question open whether he himself succeeded in doing so but insists that this goal was foremost in his mind when writing the novel *Kampf und Sieg*, and the novella 'Die diamantene Kutsche.' These two works are also mentioned by him in a footnote to the *Umrisse* (218) when discussing August Klingemann's *Faust*, where the portrayal of the devil is not to his liking. Horn insists that the negative principle is not sufficiently explored in this drama, and presumably wished to indicate that his own version of the Power of Evil was superior.

It is not to be ruled out that Carlyle picked his readings according to Horn's footnote suggestions. He was aware of the creative aspects of this author's literary activities, as he mentions 'several very deserving works of a poetic sort' in 'State of German Literature,' backing up this comment with a shrewd remark, relating Horn's character to the impression he gained: 'His character seems full of susceptibility; perhaps too much so for its natural vigour. His novels, accordingly, to judge from the few we have read of them, verge towards the sentimental' (*Essays I*, 27).

How successful was Horn in elaborating the negative principle in fiction, and do his presentations throw any light on Carlyle's way of handling it? The novel *Kampf und Sieg*, in which the title already gives away the outcome, is a conglomerate between the much favoured Gothic genre, the *Ritterroman*, and a *Bildungsroman*. However, psychologically the novel appears to be a weak imitation of Goethe's *Faust*, rather than *Wilhelm Meister*, as unlike Wilhelm the protagonist Gustav gets entangled in guilt, and is finally saved by the love of a woman, leading him to repentance. This novel presents the most ambitious undertaking of a talented epigone. Horn aims at portraying a spiritual struggle within a well-worn plot, in which the moral problem is too obviously pronounced. In the course of his travels, Gustav, a shy, withdrawn personality, enters into a league with the evil spirit, represented by Manuel. The demon helps Gustav to gain his lover Klara by giving him invisible support in a duel fought with his rival for the lady's hand. He wins and kills his opponent, remindful of the Valentin-Faust scene in Goethe's tragedy. After Gustav's marriage, Manuel reappears to claim his soul. His wife Klara, however, saves him through the power of her faithful love, here presented as an aspect of the 'ewige Ja.' The problem of guilt and how man can be redeemed through the self-sacrifice of a woman are the central themes, weakly executed. Temptation is unrelated to sensuality, but to man's willingness to employ evil means to reach a desired goal. The 'ewige Nein' and the 'ewige Ja' are not expressed in words, contrary to Horn's indications in the *Umrisse*. The solution is not one Carlyle would have chosen. Man, according to his views, must find the answers within himself, not with the aid of others.

Problems of conscience are more complicated in Horn's novella 'Die diamantene Kutsche,' subtitled 'ein deutsches Mährchen' in which the devil takes the form of a demon-lover. Judging by her godless speeches, the lady Engelberta is already committed to him before he puts in an appearance. The devil gains easy access to this soul who demands a diamond coach from any man who wishes to woo her. This the devil can supply. The trouble is that it conveys Engelberta straight to hell, on waves of fire. No hesitation, no pangs of conscience, are depicted in this female sinner, who can evoke no sympathy in the reader. The real struggle is supposed to go on in the breast of one among the throng of Engelberta's admirers, Heinrich von Auerswald, who has to choose between the girl and the peace of his own soul. His infatuation had led him to lose his belief in God: 'There is no god, there is no Christ, but a devil there is!'[3] When the devil, called 'der Fremde', appears at the inn among other guests, Heinrich alone recognizes the fiend in his cavalier costume of red and black, shot through with flames, and reads the language of his eyes: 'Look at his gaze that says *eternal No* to all that's good!' [emphasis added].[4] In vain he tries to save Engelberta by presenting the spiritual consequences of her actions to her, and dies in an abortive attempt to ward off handsome Nick. This counterpart of Evil, not unlike Gustav, is a weakling without any stamina for spiritual battle. Again the portrait of the devil within the novelistic framework is unconvincing, because he is characterized from the outside, instead of revealing the spring of inner action within his breast. Horn is clearly out of his depth in the poetic treatment of deep-seated conflicts that haunt the human soul, mainly because of his inability to characterize convincingly, aspects of the supernatural, so that they come alive. There is no sense of commitment to the values of the 'ewige Ja' that might strengthen the protagonist's resolve.

Despite his failure to come to grips with the topic of eternal negation and affirmation, it cannot be maintained that Horn merely provided the formula for Carlyle's insights into the nature of spiritual battle.[5]

Such observations as 'Yes, to me also was given, if not Victory, yet the consciousness of Battle, and the resolve to persevere therein while life or faculty is left' (*Sartor*, 184) owe something to Horn's weak attempts to reach out for the perfect phrase with which to explain supernatural connotations underlying both his own and Carlyle's works – in one case insipidly expressed, in the other forcefully rendered.

A New Source in Fouqué's 'Sängerkrieg auf der Wartburg'

Until now, Horn has been considered the only writer who used the formula of negation and affirmation of spiritual values in his works. However, according to my findings, this assumption is no longer valid: the 'Ewige Nein' and the 'Ewige Ja' were also employed by Fouqué, Horn's fellow poet and intimate friend, on whom he wrote a detailed appreciative review in his *Umrisse* (173–84). Carlyle had used this criticism for his preface to 'Aslauga's Knight' (*German Romance* I, 209). Both Horn and Carlyle mention Fouqué's *Dramatische Spiele* (1801), published under the pseudonym 'Pellegrin,' but Carlyle could not have read the *Sängerkrieg auf der Wartburg* (1828) in time for his *German Romance* preface on the poet, as it was not published until the following year. He may, however, have perused it prior to presenting spiritual problems in *Sartor*. Somewhat disapprovingly, Carlyle characterizes Fouqué's works as 'of the chivalric cast': 'The Chapel and the Tiltyard stand in the background or the foreground, in all the scenes of his universe' (*German Romance* II, 209). This caustic comment is just as inconclusive as those made in 'Sir Walter Scott,' mentioned in chapter 1, about aspects of historical fiction Carlyle disliked.

The pseudo-historical 'Contest of the Bards,' based on a medieval poem, provided a source for several German Romantics. Both E.T.A. Hoffmann[6] and Fouqué used it as a basis for their fictionalized narratives. It must also have intrigued Carlyle, who, with an air of amused sophistication, reports on it as an example of the poetry of the Swabian Era and its representatives, the *Minnesänger*:

> This War at the Wartburg took place in the year 1207, under the eye of the Landgraf and the Landgräfin of Thuringia, the sovereigns of that Castle, with their Court ... present there ... harp in hand ... the main tilters and duellists seem to have been Ofterdingen, who is forthwith opposed by a counter-puff from Eschenbach ... In this predicament the fair umpire, taking counsel with the other Harpers, sees no outlet but that Ofterdingen, the suffering party,

must travel all the way to Transylvania, and therefrom bring Klingsohr, a renowned Minstrel and even Conjuror ... as alone able for the task of passing final sentence between them. (*Unfinished History of German Literature*, 81–2)

Carlyle is evidently unaware of the meaning of the poet-magician combination in Klingsohr's personality; the latter is accompanied by his demonic servant Nasion, an uncomplimentary symbol for poetic achievements that, in the medieval version, are partly traced back to 'devilish arts'.

Fouqué's *Sängerkrieg*, loosely based on these facts, did not go unnoticed. Eckermann read the play in compliance with Goethe's request (*Gespräche* I, 3 Oct. 1828) and discussed with him the suitability of the *altdeutsche* milieu, which did not impress Goethe as well chosen. Subtitled a *Dichterspiel*, the play evolves around the problems of the poet, arising from his creative urges and the demands made on a life continuously devoted to the cause of art. The idea of making a poet the hero of a drama is related to the concept of the bard as the truest and most noble image of mankind. Having these associations for its goal, the play must be considered a counterpart to the Romantic *Künstlerroman*.

The emphasis shifts from the contest of the singers, in which Ofterdingen had a central part to play, to the personality of Klingsohr. Ofterdingen is merely his youthful, idealistic pupil, who lacks his master's wisdom and genius. This portrayal of the Poet takes on mythical dimension with the introduction of the demonic forces in Egon. This dwarf-like personality is a modernization of the medieval Nasion, servant of the devil. In a variety of ways, this spirit influences Klingsohr's poetic talent, which is based on a dualistic world-view, made up of contrary states. The true artist, Fouqué believes, must be aware of the power of evil as well as of the divine. Klingsohr is under the illusion that he can always check aspects of the demonic and make them subservient to his talent, until Egon tries to impose his demands on him. The battle of the negative begins when the artist is least prepared for the onslaught. Now Klingsohr realizes the extent to which he and Egon are *Gegenbilder*, or dual presentations of life, 'life Night and Day, like cries of wailing and rejoicing' (270).[7] Egon drops all pretences and, changing his dwarfish shape, rises in height to overtake the human form. Klingsohr is immediately aware of the designs of the 'deceiving No' in the following dialogue:

KLINGSOHR: Thunder as much as you like,
You liar, your deceitful No.
Eternal Truth rings out,
Eternal love rings out Yes! –
What are you murmuring,
Like dying thunder on
Distant mountain ranges?
Why does your eye light up
In dark defiance?
Speak up!

EGON: I will not! By the eternal No!

KLINGSOHR: You must, you must!
By the eternal Yes!
(*Sängerkrieg*, 273–4)[8]

This confrontation is reflected in Nature, where winds and thunderstorms are racing across the landscape to echo the turmoil in Klingsohr's soul. While Egon flees, he victoriously stands up against the onslaught of the 'eternal No' whose power is utterly defeated. The bard, up to now considered to be a magician by the other *Minnesänger*, is defended by the Landgräfin, who on the strength of her intuitive female sensitivity for the plight of the artist, describes his state of mind and his susceptibility to a whole range of influences good or bad, trite or meaningful, that he shapes into poetic song.

Klingsohr himself proceeds to speak about the interplay of all impressions the poet must endure to convey the duality of life. He experiences love and woe, alienates and unites all life's elements, attracts and repulses his fellow men. The danger lies in the threat that what serves him now may finally conquer him. Freed from Egon's influence and confident that the ordeal is over, he takes up his walking staff and leaves the Wartburg to return to Hungary, ready to meet new challenges, in search of 'echoes of eternity' ('Wiederklang der Ewigkeit,' 287), under divine, not demonic inspiration. Heinrich, the learner, has gained deeper insights into the complexity of poetic genius; he feels humbled, but not destroyed.

In this interesting variation of the theme, Fouqué shows the two states of being in action, but he is unable to present a believable poet on the stage. Abstract artistic theories interfere with the struggle for spiritual values. Fouqué is no Goethe, but, as Carlyle rightly stated, 'a man of genius with little more than an ordinary share of talent' (*German*

Romance I, 213). One must reach the conclusion that neither Horn nor Fouqué was able to depict the 'Ewige Nein' and the 'Ewige Ja' adequately in fiction.

Carlyle succeeds where his two predecessors failed, mainly for two reasons: his own forceful personality, which he expresses in Teufelsdröckh's brand of spiritual defiance, and his superb stylistic formulation of the struggle that leaves an echo ringing in the reader's mind, long after closing the book. With these specific faculties at his disposal, he makes full use of potent suggestions contained in his German readings.

'Centre of Indifference' and 'Gleichgewichtszentrum'

There are other possible sources to explain the original idea behind the 'Centre of Indifference' that Carlyle describes in *Sartor* to indicate Teufelsdröckh's position between two extremes than the rather far-fetched one associated with Musäus's phrase 'philosophischer Ruhepunkt,' which occurs in the fairy-tale setting of 'Dumb Love' (*German Romance* I, 80). In this story, the term is applied to Meta, an unsophisticated girl, who lacks what should have been translated as 'philosophical tranquillity,' the equivalent of *Ruhepunkt*, a term related to a sense of calm composure about life her mother has obviously reached while incessantly turning her spinning-wheel. The phrase 'philosophical centre of indifference,' which Carlyle uses to render this term in English, betrays his inadequate knowledge of shades of meaning in German. The word 'philosophical' might have misled Carlyle to use much too complex terminology for the simple situation presented in the tale.

In *Sartor*, however, taking Teufelsdröckh's intellectual background and philosophical inclinations into account, the phrase fits the German professor perfectly. His state of insight constitutes a highly complicated mental turning-point as the result of his conversion, related to the act of defiance of 'The Everlasting No.' Philosophically speaking, the *Indifferenzpunkt* – which Carlyle translates as 'centre, not point' – is a legitimate term, used in transcendental philosophy. It indicates a position in which no form of power can be transformed from one state into another. This state of things is also applicable to the 'Centre of Indifference' in *Sartor*, where one state of being has been rejected, and the new state has not yet been reached. In this philosophical sense Carlyle could not have derived the term from Musäus, for whom the 'philosophische Ruhepunkt' characterizes a Stoic outlook on life, a simple *Lebensphilosophie.*

When and where could Carlyle have come across this term, which reveals a certain familiarity with the terminology of *Transzendentalphilosophie*? It must have surfaced in his readings before or during 1827, when he translated *German Romance* and prepared himself for the writing of 'State of German Literature,' for which Schelling's *Methode des akademischen Studiums* was one of his mainstays. The same volume of *Schriften, 1801–4* that contains the *Methode* also includes his short essay on the *Über das Verhältnis der Naturphilosophie zur Philosophie überhaupt* (1802), where in a brief eighteen-page abstract, Schelling undertakes to defend his philosophical principles. Here the term 'Indifferenzpunkt' occurs twice (422, 423). It relates to the absolute unity of opposing forces on which he had already written at length in his treatise *Von der Weltseele* (1798). Carlyle mentions this work in a footnote (109, fn. 5) in his *Life of Schiller* (Chapman and Hall rev. edn., 1845), referring to it as 'Schelling's book on the "Soul of the World",' a reference that so far has not been discussed by scholars.

In this work, Schelling aligns all manifestations of Nature with a single power or force that expands in two opposite directions. According to this view on the polarity of matter, the force presents itself in specific modes that appear to the mind of man as attraction and repulsion. This is due to nature's constant renewal, which takes on two forms: forward and positive and backward and negative. The 'World-Soul,' a term borrowed from Plato, signifies this inexhaustible self-activity of Nature, which is eternally in the state of becoming.

In connection with these propelling and withdrawing forces, a state of equilibrium must be reached at some point. This Schelling calls the 'Centrum des Gleichgewichtes,' when plus and minus fall together at dead centre: 'As obviously opposed materials in our atmosphere hold their balance, somewhere the centre must lie upon which they both act.'[9]

In the same way, the 'Centre of Indifference' constitutes the moment in time when a spiritual equilibrium has been achieved. Carlyle may have considered the 'Indifferenzpunkt' (Point of Indifference) as well as the 'Centrum des Gleichgewichtes' (Centre of Equilibrium), fusing them together in order to convey a spiritual state that existed in Teufelsdröckh's mind. As in 'The Everlasting No' and 'The Everlasting Yea' formulations, a conglomerate of meanings seem to have played a part in the shaping of his concept.

EIGHT

Palingenesia or Newbirth of Society

> We are all more or less Sons of Time; from earliest infancy we have received her impressions, have learnt in her and partly through her to love, to hate and to seize upon Knowledge and Faith.
>
> (Franz Horn, *Umrisse*)

Patterns of Change

The concept of Palingenesia, which Carlyle sets forth in *Sartor,* has been examined by such scholars as Harrold, Shine, and Wellek with regard to Carlyle's view of history, but not as an extension of the Clothes Philosophy, discussing social change within this framework.[1] It is from this more specific angle of a philosophy of prophetic revelation that German sources are considered here, in so far as they contributed to the emergence of Carlyle's notions of Newbirth.

At the core of the Clothes Philosophy lies the idea of varied manifestation, or ever-present change. If the 'Divine Idea of the Universe is pleased to manifest itself' (*Sartor,* 209), it does so in recurring patterns. If Eternity looks through Time, it does so in Time-Figures (*Zeitbildern*) which evolve in order to be dissolved.

With regard to this process, it is significant that the Clothes Philosophy deals, on the one hand, with the reality of clothes in space and time, on the other, with the idea of clothes as emblems transcending it. The reality of clothes could be tentatively termed their historical manifestation, while clothes as emblems of the transcendental could be aligned with the religious spirit. The former would be under the influence of the *Zeitgeist,* the latter would follow supernatural laws. Such an alignment considerably widens the scope of the Clothes Philosophy beyond the personal sphere. It could cover whole epochs in which either clothes real or clothes ideal would be foremost cherished by humanity. In this manner, 'clothes cycles' could be established, in which one or the other predominates.

This larger vista opens up in the complex metaphysical Part III of *Sartor*, where a negative attitude becomes more and more pronounced concerning clothes in time: 'In vain, while here on Earth, shall you endeavour to strip them off; you can, at best, but rend them assunder for moments, and look through' (*Sartor*, 260). While this comment can still be applied to man on the personal level, the social context presents itself when Teufelsdröckh gives short shrift to clothes in the realm of the real. He has 'trod the old rags of Matter, with their tinsels, into the mire' (ibid., 207) and is ready – quite in keeping with the rag-fair aspect of the world – to begin the rending and burning of garments, 'through the whole compass of Civilized Life and Speculation' (ibid.). This is not a destructive process, but one that will enable mankind to look into the 'celestial Essence' of the World. It is indeed considered the first step towards Newbirth or Palingenesia.

Teufelsdröckh has devoted himself to just this kind of work. The second volume of his clothes philosophy, bearing the momentous title *Palingenesie der menschlichen Gesellschaft* – a work not yet written – will treat 'practically of the Wear, Destruction, and Retexture of Spiritual Tissues, or Garments ... the Transcendental or ultimate Portion of this my work *on Clothes*' (*Sartor*, 217). In connection with the suggested Saint-Simonian influence, we cannot but ask ourselves why Carlyle would speak of Transcendentalism, if he meant Positivism, firmly convinced, as we are, that he knew enough about both concepts so as not to confuse them. 'Palingenesie,' in Carlyle's meaning of the word, stands for social change with the aim of spiritual regeneration by way of religious faith. Therefore he connects it with the Phoenix symbol, and its Christian connotations.

Jean Paul's contribution to the emergence of Carlyle's use of both concept and symbol has not been sufficiently acknowledged.[2] Not only does Jean Paul entitle a reworked edition of his youthful writings *Palingenesien*; he also uses the term in many of his other works – *Quintus Fixlein* among them – which Carlyle translated as early as 1826, well before any Saint-Simonian contacts were established. In this instance, the term is linked to rebirth, after Fixlein has successfully overcome the crisis in what appeared to be a deadly sickness: 'Every recovery is a bringing back and palingenesia of our youth' (*German Romance* II, 256).

With regard to the Phoenix symbol, Jean Paul lets it rise no fewer than eleven times,[3] among these twice in works Carlyle translated for *German Romance* (II, 237, 136). Especially in the footnotes to *Schmelzle's Journey*, of which Carlyle made use on several occasions, the connection between Phoenix and literature is made: 'In books lie the Phoenix-ashes of a past Millenium and Paradies; but War blows and much ashes are scattered away' (*German Romance* II, 136). This same idea Carlyle expresses in a more elaborated form: 'To the perfection and purifying of Literature, of Poetry, Art, all eyes are turned; for in these times the deepest interests of man seem to be involved in it; the ashes and fact burning fragments of the whole Past lie there, from which, amid clouds and whirlwinds, the Phoenix Future is struggling to unfold itself' (*Unfinished History of German Literature*, I, 8).

Did Carlyle find other indications in Jean Paul that could have aided his Newbirth concept to emerge?

The term 'spiritual Newbirth' itself, central to the personal regeneration in 'The Everlasting No,' as well as an alternative expression for Palingenesia, is Carlyle's translation of Jean Paul's 'geistige Wiedergeburt' (Spiritual rebirth), which is used in *Schmelzle's Journey* (*German Romance* II, 147). Furthermore, it is discussed in connection with social upheaval, under the title 'Loud Clamour of the Time-Spirit': 'Reversely peoples are born and die. Their births and rebirths are heralded by a storm. War and Mars act as midwives of Time; on the other hand, close to the continuity and extinction of peoples stands old quiet Saturn and swallows them up silently' ('Vermischte Aufsätze,' 234, published together with *Wahrheit aus Jean Pauls Leben*).

This same thought is echoed in *Sartor*: 'It continues ever true ... that Saturn, or Chronos, or what we call TIME, devours all his Children: only by incessant Running, by incessant Working, may you ... escape him; and you too he devours at last' (*Sartor*, 127).

If these are possible ingredients compounding Carlyle's notions, Werner's concept of the rebirth of society and his use of the Phoenix emblem in several of his plays comes even closer to the point. Here the fusion between the two – as yet separate in Jean Paul – is accomplished. Carlyle, in the 'Life and Writings of Werner,' takes note of the dramatist's use of the Phoenix symbol in the *Mutter der Makkabäer* and observes that a new vision of salvation manifests itself with this aid (*Essays I*, 144). The self-immolation of the legendary birth takes place on the Tree of Life, causing an effusion of light, compared to which all human lightbearers are merely a feeble reflection.

In *Die Söhne des Thals*, Molay, while undergoing enormous suffering in prison, is strengthened by a vision of the Phoenix rising from the ashes, a symbolic reference to the forthcoming rebirth of the old Order in the newly formed society (*Söhne des Thals* I, V, iii). Luther, in Werner's drama, receives strength from a dream-vision, where he sees the old eagle turn into a Phoenix, as a sign of the rebirth of the old faith in a new form. (*Martin Luther,* V, ii).

If Carlyle had thus been introduced to the concept of Palingenesia and the symbol of the Phoenix, it was on his own merit that he employed both exclusively to represent the spiritual Newbirth of society at large: 'In a word, do we at length stand safe in the far region of Poetic Creation and Palingenesia, where that Phoenix Death-Birth of Human Society, and of all Human Things, appears possible, is seen to be inevitable?' (*Sartor,* 268).

This formulation contains all of Carlyle's meanings: the notion of death-birth, represented by its symbol, the Phoenix, applicable to poetic creation and human society, and the implication of a cyclic recurrence of established patterns within which Palingenesia takes place. In addition, the reader gathers from it that poetry and Palingenesia are linked to and affect each other. It foreshadows the role of the poet as prophet and seer, who will aid in the emergence of the new society.

In order to reach a higher vantage point from which to overlook the whole field of human endeavour in time, it is important for man to clear the barrier that divides the natural from the supernatural: 'Here, therefore, properly it is that the Philosophy of Clothes attains to Transcendentalism; this last leap, can we but clear it, takes us safe into the promised land, where *Palingenesia,* in all senses, may be considered as beginning' (ibid., 255).

Palingenesia being thus visualized in transcendental terms by Carlyle, it seems legitimate to turn to German Idealism in search of the philosophical pattern underlying Teufelsdröckh's concepts. Others had led the way in previous leaps. This was part of the message Carlyle retained from his study of Schelling's *Methode,* which he is known to have undertaken in 1827, in preparation for writing his essay 'State of German Literature.'

In these lectures, never formally given, Schelling suggests an overall method of study which describes all forms of knowledge as a participation in *Urwissen.* This *Urwissen* is an expression of divine power, as it emanates from a single source. All Knowledge is one, with the various sciences representing different branches of a single tree. Knowledge unrelated to *Urwissen* and directed towards immediate empirical goals Schelling rejects as unworthy, connecting such limited efforts with the notion of *Brotwissenschaft* or *Brotstudium* related to material gains. Man must not penetrate into the realm of knowledge as if on a fact-finding mission, but must strive to understand the higher unity of learning. All else Schelling considers as *Scheinwissen*.

If this is the general tenor of Schelling's theory of knowledge in relation to *Urwissen*, he is more specific, as far as cyclic patterns of change are concerned, in the chapters dealing with religion and history (*Methode*, lectures 8, 9, 10). The principle is, broadly speaking, the same: unchanging ideal values must be related to the real, and the latter interpreted in the light of the former. In the constant interplay between the real and the ideal, the esoteric, consisting of unchanging spiritual values, manifests itself to a greater or lesser degree. It is man's task to aid its unfolding, not to hinder it, in order that it may become effective and illuminate the world: 'The esoteric must be bodied forth, and freed from its hulls shine forth' (*Methode*, 305).

This principle, applied to religion, demands an unfolding of its spiritual core, to be revealed with the aid of Christian symbolism, not by an overemphasis on literal religious interpretation, which Schelling calls exoteric and limited. Only in an esoteric fashion can an effective rebirth of Christianity take place, and the annunciation of the 'absolute Evangel' be prepared.[4]

With regard to history, the principle does not vary. Man must do more than merely interpret movements and upheavals in society in a purely pragmatic fashion, for such instruction gives nothing better than a correct empirical relation, according to the laws of understanding, here used in a Kantian sense. As in the field of religion, a new vision of history in the light of the esoteric factor must ensue, which becomes 'a great mirror of the spirit of the universe, an eternal poem of divine Reason' (ibid., 309). This revelation of the divine in man's history is, in Schelling's opinion, peculiar to the Christian vision, which explains it in the light of Providence. In this view, religion and history fuse, for everything existing in time must needs be related to eternity.

Besides recognizing the esoteric to be inherent in religion as well as in history, Schelling maintains that the living spirit of creativity in man will 'body forth the infinite in ever new forms' (ibid., 305), while old forms will die once the life principle has fallen away from them. To know these laws that effect social change and are intimately connected with a revival of the religious spirit is to participate in *Urwissen* in this field. Only then is knowledge *in* time, in the sphere of the real, part of knowledge *out* of time, in the realm of the ideal.

The similarity between Carlyle's and Schelling's patterns of thought is most obvious in relation to the idea of change, coupled with the belief that the esoteric will manifest itself in perpetual rebirth, something Carlyle also terms 'evolving' in *Sartor*. The following passage is decidedly in Schelling's spirit: 'Society ... is not dead: that Carcass, which you call dead Society, is but her mortal coil which she has shuffled off, to assume a nobler; she herself, through perpetual metamorphoses, in fairer and fairer development, has to live till Time also merge in Eternity' (*Sartor*, 236).

Such beliefs are also found in much of the thought contained in Part III of *Sartor*, in the chapter 'Church-Clothes' (213), discussing the forms under which Religion is embodied. The idea that religion is produced by society and sustains it (*Methode*, lecture 8, 293) is considered by Carlyle as well, who expresses the need for symbols in clothes metaphors: 'Thus was it that I said, the Church-Clothes are first spun and woven by Society; outward Religion originates by Society, Society becomes possible by Religion. Nay, perhaps, every conceivable Society, past and present, may well be figured as properly and wholly a Church' (*Sartor*, 215).

Because of the all-inclusiveness Carlyle seeks to present, any particular identification becomes increasingly harder to find in his later works. Typically enough, he often cites Fichte and Schelling together, and as far as the application of transcendental notions to the field of social change is concerned, it is obvious that eventually Schelling's 'esoteric' fuses with Fichte's manifestation of the Divine Idea in the world. It is remarkable, however, that Carlyle does not make use of the latter's involved scheme of *Zeitalter*, as outlined in the *Grundzüge*, for which reason Fichte's historical theory is not included in this discussion of social patterns of change.

Snatches from Schelling's *Methode* appear in unlikely places; Carlyle, in his 'Inaugural Address,' delivered at Edinburgh in 1866, speaks of the higher aims of knowledge in Schelling's terms: 'In regard to all your studies here ... you are to remember that the object is not particular knowledge – not that of getting higher and higher in technical perfections ... there is a higher aim lying at the rear of all that ... you are ever to bear in mind that there lies behind that the acquisition of what may be called wisdom ... And that ... may be missed very easily; never more easily than now' (*Essays IV*, 466).

In a fumbling fashion and a somewhat mangled context, Carlyle here presents his version of wisdom as *Urwissen*. Furthermore, Teufelsdröckh's 'Science of Things in General' (*Sartor*, 18), which is considered a *Zeitbedürfnis*, might well be a version of Schelling's idea of the relatedness of all knowledge. The Weissnichtwo authorities, we are told, are well aware of this need of the age and believed to be 'in the vanguard of the world' (ibid., 19) because they suggest lectures on the subject, never actually delivered – possibly an allusion to the fate of the *Methode.*

What Schelling had expounded with regard to the esoteric – the necessity that the spiritual content in religion and the divine message in history be strengthened – fuses, for Carlyle, with Goethe's ages of Belief and Unbelief, a two-phase cycle he obviously preferred to more complicated systems:[5]

> The special, sole and deepest theme of the World's and Man's History, says the Thinker of our time, whereto all other themes are subordinated, remains the Conflict of Unbelief and Belief. All epochs wherein Belief prevails, under what form it may, are splendid, heart elevating, fruitful for contemporaries and posterity. All epochs, on the contrary, wherein Unbelief, under what form soever, maintains its sorry victory, should they even for a moment glitter with a sham splendour, vanish from the eyes of posterity; because no one chooses to burden himself with the study of the unfruitful. (*Essays III* 'Diderot,' 248: Goethe, *Werke,* II, 208)

The fact that this for Carlyle so important passage, to which he refers no less than ten times in his works,[6] is tucked away among the *Noten zum westöstlichen Divan* cannot diminish its significance. The *Westöstliche Divan* itself was an important source for Carlyle's concepts, as he also found here the 'seedfield of Time' (*Werke,* II, 'Westöstliche Divan,' 52), which supplemented his own ideas on Palingenesia. According to this formulation, man must sow seed in Time in order that it may bear fruit in dark periods of man's history in which the forces of Unbelief are all-powerful. A passage in 'Boswell's Life of Johnson' shows the connection Carlyle makes between the seedfield of Time and Palingenesia: 'All work is a seed sown; it grows and spreads, and sows itself anew, and so in endless palingenesia lives and works' (*Essays III,* 120).

It follows that whosoever is convinced of the values inherent in periods of Faith in world history would want to contribute to their manifestation in society. Carlyle aligns such utterances with others made by Goethe in *Wilhelm Meisters Wanderjahre* on the subject of reverence and religious faith. These passages left so deep an impression on Carlyle that he fills his essay 'Goethe' (*Essays I,* 198) with a seven-page translation of their essence and discusses them as guidelines through life in the 'Inaugural Address.'[7]

Wilhelm Meister, in visiting the Pedagogical Province, not only finds a sense of reverence being instilled in the pupils, but also notices that this reverence is expressed in symbolical gestures that relate it to religion and a sense of wonder. The Elders of the Province explain these relations: although man brings much into the world, reverence is not among such natural gifts that merely unfold of their own accord. 'And yet it is on this one thing that all depends for making man in every point a man ... All want it, perhaps you yourself' (*Meister* II, 265). The gestures are then explained: The first is reverence for what is above man, testimony that there is a God above, who images and reveals himself in parents, teachers, superiors. Second, reverence for what is below man; the third, reverence of self, to stand forth frank and bold, when in combination with his equals he faces the world (ibid.).[8]

The three Reverences are ultimately aligned with forms of religious worship by Goethe, and connected with the spirit of universal history in the symbolical presentation of 'sacred things' in the sanctuary of the Pedagogical Province, through which Wilhelm is led by the Elders. This is another way of showing the interrelatedness of the spheres of the natural and the supernatural, the real and the ideal, which Carlyle had already met with in Fichte and in Schelling, there expressed in philosophical, here in poetical terminology.

The Christian religion is singled out from among others as possessing values 'from which the human species cannot retrograde ... which having once appeared, cannot again vanish' (*Meister* II, 276). Its most touching expression is 'the Worship of Sorrow,' representing Christ's sufferings, over which a veil is drawn 'because we reverence them so highly' (ibid., 275). This Worship of Sorrow as the essence of Christianity grants highest spiritual insights into life. Carlyle constantly refers to these inherent values, often using the Worship of Sorrow as their ultimate symbol. He feels, in keeping with the Elders, that allusions to it in realistic terms would weaken its impact: 'Christianity, the "Worship of Sorrow" has been recognized as divine ... the Christian Religion once here, cannot again pass away; in one or another form it will endure through all time' (*Essays I*, 172). The same opinion is restated in 'Inaugural Address' (*Essays IV*, 475). In all his quotations of this Goethe text, Carlyle conveys the opinion that the Worship of Sorrow is exclusively the merit of Christianity. For this very reason Harrold's contention that Carlyle 'came to think of the whole world as such a sanctuary' (*Carlyle and German Thought*, 226) appears erroneous.

In the light of these additional passages derived from Goethe, the periods of Faith might be defined as ages in the history of the world, in which Reverence and a consequent sense of Wonder would establish a time of fruitful growth, which Goethe speaks of so hopefully as lying within the reach of mankind.

Werner is also aware of the cyclic pattern of change. Although sacred things remain forever, the garment of dust in which they are clothed must, from time to time, fall apart and make way for new garments, that is, new forms: 'If old forms are destroyed, will new ones endure any longer? ... Unfold the books of universal history. They serve as proof of constant change. Although sacred things last forever, their earthly garment of dust will be destroyed.'[9]

This formulation may have had a stimulating influence on Carlyle. Also, in *Sartor*, old spiritual clothes 'have gone sorrowfully out-at-elbows; nay, far worse, many of them have become mere hollow Shapes, or Masks, under which no living Figure of Spirit any longer dwells.' (ibid., 216). Both Werner's and Carlyle's aim is to make man aware of the nature of this process, and by way of ever renewed Faith help usher in a new dawn.

The Time-Spirit

If Schelling and Goethe provided the two most significant patterns of change Carlyle employed, he found in the notion of the *Zeitgeist* an effective means to serve his increasingly prophetic views on clothes. He would have encountered a variety of suggestions in his German readings related to the meaning of this term. While only a few of these tend to rate this force as a positive one, the majority of the other sources consider *Zeitgeist* to affect man in a negative way.

Schelling's presentation is unique, in so far as he includes both aspects. The 'Geist der neuen Zeit' is the driving force behind the 'destruction of all merely finite forms' that have outlived themselves, and thus clears the way 'for new effective forms of worship' (*Methode*, 301). This explanation of the destructive-constructive activity of the Time-spirit, which emphasizes new tasks and new solutions after a thorough spring cleaning, appealed to Carlyle. Much of what he has to say about new Church clothes relates to Schelling's interpretation of a force which, although acting ruthlessly, only destroys what has already lost its deeper meaning. The forward-looking, bold passages in *Sartor* that map out tasks for man in relation to newbirth seem to find their inspiration here: 'Nevertheless, ... who can hinder it; who is there that can clutch into the wheelspokes of Destiny, and say to the Spirit of the Time: Turn back, I command thee? – Wiser were it that we yielded to the Inevitable and Inexorable, and accounted even this the best' (*Sartor*,

235). Here, the term Carlyle uses, the 'Spirit of the Time,' is a translation of Schelling's 'Geist der Zeiten.'

On the other hand, Schelling, links the Time-spirit to the so-called Moderns, whom he connects with the Age of Enlightenment. With regard to this negative manifestation, he quotes Goethe's *Faust*: 'What they call the Time-spirit, is nothing but their own in which the times are mirrored.'[10] Accordingly, the Time-spirit, in the sphere of the ideal, consists of the judgment of one standing above the times, while, in the sphere of the real, it is the expression of short-sighted and ignorant humanity who, with limited powers of observation and penetration, apply a mediocre yardstick to measure the sublime. In this latter case, as a further quotation from *Faust* verifies, the 'Geist der Zeiten' represents the superficial notion of the march of progress, which never stops to think if its achievements are truly significant.[11]

In contrast to Schelling's twofold application of the term, Goethe, Jean Paul, and Werner emphasize its dangers rather than its constructive elements.

Goethe identifies *Zeitgeist* more often than not with the spirit of the French Revolution, in which he is inclined to see destruction and upheaval rather than significant renewal. He doubts the sincerity of motives behind the revolutionary tendencies leading to lawlessness, violence, and misrule. He even goes so far as to compare the destructive energies released with natural catastrophes such as volcanic eruptions or deluges. These, he claims, result, on the intellectual level, in the annihilation of existing cultural values. Not only does the *Zeitgeist* drown out personality in a flood of mediocrity, but it promotes unbelief and aids sham values that sell under the name of progress and result in a lack of reverence. In his *Maximen und Reflexionen*, he advises youth to use their own judgment, instead of swimming unreflectingly with the stream of time (*Werke*, XII, 388, 392). All forces must be rallied to stem this tide, which Goethe also compares to a contagious disease, the *Zeitfieber*. This alertness to dangers results in further advice to attend to immediate duties (*Meister*, I, 386), an admonition which Carlyle incorporates into his 'Everlasting Yea' chapter as 'Do the Duty which lies nearest thee' (*Sartor*, 196).

Going beyond Goethe, Carlyle strengthens the sinister aspect of the Time-spirit by associating it with the devil as its visible manifestation. In this connection he refers to life as a 'war against the *Zeitfürst*' (Prince of Time).[12] The German term strengthens the association with the name for the evil spirit.

The whole *Zeitgeist* complex includes Goethe's 'Sons of Time,'[13] who, destined to battle the Time-spirit, are nevertheless themselves subject to the law of change: 'Necessity urges him on; Time will not stop, neither can he, a Son of Time' (*Sartor*, 121). Wilhelm Meister voices this thought on his visit to the Antiquarian: 'Yet you will confess that no man withstands the change which Time produces' (*Meister* II, 256).[14] The Antiquarian reluctantly agrees with this statement, but nevertheless advises man to hold on to his own opinions.

The association of the Time-spirit with the Fiend, made by Carlyle, is quite common in the works of Zacharias Werner. *Zeitgeist* is here largely responsible for man's utter disregard of divine evidence, as well as for his inability to recognize as God-like what is clad in dust but nevertheless not of it. Man's mind being closed, his inner eye sealed, he is, because of the Time-spirit, incapable of completing the cherished dream of humanity. A blind man indeed, he cannot be awakened by the sun as long as the bandage of obliviousness hides truth. To counteract all manifestations of cold rationality, art must undertake to present the *Lichtwelt*, the World of Light, and its eternal values to man.

Most effectively the Time-spirit in Werner's works finds expression in clothes as its symbols. An instance is Robert d'Heredon's summoning before the council in *Die Söhne des Thals* where old Adam discusses clothes with him to make him aware of the difference between appearance and inner worth in a social context. Clothes become symbols of passing trends of the times, which should not affect his set of values. Adams widens the social implications of the activity of the Time-spirit to include the field of politics:

ADAM: Can you recreate me by taking away my linen coat and clothing me in a gown of velvet?

ROBERT: You confuse me.

ADAM: Are politics and other forms into which the world chooses to clothe itself like a chameleon – today in this fashion, tomorrow in another – a part of the core of our being? Or are they not merely hulls, which may they be heavier or lighter, cannot change the body itself? Can a despot deprive you of your inner worth, your true self which links you to God? Can the Republic illuminate you from above? (*Söhne des Thals*, Part II, 5, iii)[15]

In Carlyle's view, the Time-spirit embroils man more and more in activities 'in time,' from which he can hardly ever disentangle himself, until he feels completely trapped in the Time-prison: 'O Time-spirit, how hast thou environed and imprisoned us, and sunk us so deep in thy troublous dim Time-Element, that only in lucid moments can so much as glimpses of our upper Azure Home be revealed to us!' (*Sartor*, 127). Unfortunately Carlyle never takes the trouble to explain these inner connections to his readers, who would then be better able to appreciate such passages more fully.

Jean Paul deals with the Time-spirit in his visionary-dream writings as well as in his essays. More influential for Carlyle are doubtlessly the former, which he is fond of quoting in his reviews of his own age. Only Jean Paul among Carlyle's German sources speaks of his age as one of transition, a thought Carlyle shares. An immediate sense of impending danger is conveyed in the following *Hesperus* passage, which Carlyle quotes twice in 'Characteristics' (*Essays III*, 32 and 42): 'Yes, indeed, a new age will arrive when it shall grow light, when man awakens from sublime dreams and finds them [true], because he lost nothing but his sleep ... Thou Eternal Providence, wilt cause the day to dawn. As yet struggles the twelfth hour of the night: birds of darkness are on the wing, spectres uproar, the dead walk, the living dream' (Preface to *Hesperus*, I, 490).[16] In Jean Paul's opinion, the only protection against the *Zeitgeist*, and the only way to offset the confusion and chaos of conflicting times, is the maintenance of a certain aloofness from it: 'One of the aims of education which we must visualize clearly and in its magnitude, is elevation above the Time-spirit. The child must not be educated for the present Time ... but for the future; not necessarily even for the immediate future. But one must get to know the spirit which one wants to flee' (*Levana*, *Werke*, V, 567).[17]

It follows that youth must be able to recognize it. In the chapter 'On the Time-spirit,' Jean Paul elaborates this very point and comes to negative conclusions: 'What we are wont to call the Time-spirit, the ancients called the way of the world, the last times, the sign of Domesday, the empire of the Devil, of Anti-Christ. Bleak names all!' (ibid., 568).[18]

This appraisal is not far off the mark with regard to Carlyle, nor is the solution Jean Paul proposes: faith in God and a renewed acceptance of transcendental values. This suggestion is followed by a prophetic preview of the dangers inherent in an unchecked Time-spirit at work: 'Of the world will be made a world-machine, of the Aether a gas, of God a Force, and of the Second World a coffin' (ibid., 570; *Essays II*, 'Novalis,' 55).[19]

For Carlyle, the Time-spirit is connected with materialism. At least in 'Characteristics,' he uses it as a phrase that fits the materialistic philosophy as far as it is incorporated in the works of one Hope, whose life he compares with that of Friedrich Schlegel: 'If Schlegel's work is the apotheosis of Spiritualism, Hope's again is the apotheosis of Materialism: in the one all matter is evaporated into a phenomenon, and terrestial life itself ... held out as a disturbance (*Zerrüttung*) produced by the *Zeitgeist*; in the other matter is distilled and sublimated into some semblance of Divinity' (*Essays III*, 34). As Carlyle's judgment on Hope grows to be increasingly severe, while that on Schlegel waxes ever more appreciative, the connection of *Zeitgeist* with the former is hardly complimentary but condemning, particularly as reference to the 'Symptom of universal disease' is made. Such further developments of initial suggestions received from his German sources on the topic of the Time-spirit are entirely Carlyle's own.

Heroes and Their Worshippers

Heroes, whatever their qualifications, have been set up by mankind since the dawn of civilization until the advent of the anti-hero age, where the 'no-hero' is eventually being turned into a hero of no less influence than other heroes before him.[20] New visions of society have always stood in need of human models – single hero-personalities or groups of leaders – able to present these visions to mankind at large and thus to help realize them. Their followers would either devote themselves strictly to the cause or feel a personal commitment to the leaders themselves, as effective mouthpieces of the new tidings. Although in practice it would be hard, indeed, to draw a dividing line between these two attitudes, it is one thing to stress the idea or message and another to demand blind personal loyalty and devotion, on the basis of the leader's presumed superiority. Did Carlyle, in whom this latter trait of hero-worship is very much pronounced, meet with any such features in his German Romantic sources?

Generally speaking, the stress on the personality of the individual hero is far less emphasized in Carlyle's German sources than it is usually presumed. The group of outstanding persons is much more favoured by poets and thinkers alike. In this connection the modern reader should avoid associations with the term 'elitist' common in our society, usually indicating unmerited furtherance of often unworthy personalities that goes against the original meaning of the word. The élite are 'the chosen' – religiously by God, on the human level by society in need of effective leadership in times of crisis.

Schelling, for example, refrains from setting up a distinct model or hero type but speaks of appointed men, able to interpret the new values in the light of religious-historical revelation. These *höhere Naturen*, as he calls them in the *Methode* (286), constitute the elect on account of their ability to relate knowledge to meaningful action, at a time when action for its own sake dominates society: 'Action, action! this is the roll-call which resounds from many sides, most loudly from those who are lacking in knowledge.'[21] In contrast to engaging in thoughtless action that may precipitate disaster, the group is able to see beyond obvious, that is, purely pragmatic applications of knowledge. By way of this quality, they have been in the past, and shall continue to be in the future, the originators of all forms of culture and religious tradition. Artists too are among them, as devotees to art, the 'tool of the gods, the annunciator of divine secrets, the revealer of ideas' (*Methode*, 352).[22] For religion and art are one and must remain so.

Similarly, Werner stresses the leading group rather than the individual hero, who becomes effective only by forming part of and being committed to the greater whole. Robert d'Heredon, whose latent energy is channelled into the right direction by the Valley Society, is a case in point: 'The Communion of Saints does not die. From the ashes light dawns.'[23] Werner also refers to spiritual men, aware of something higher than self, as 'die Besseren.' These few guide and support mankind in search of their most needful requirement: faith in the divine power. Singly they would be destroyed by the mass of the foolish and outright malicious elements of society who deliberately set out to deface God's world. Union is therefore a prerequisite for the forces of good to be effective. To know this for a truth ennobles man and ranks him among those who attempt to overcome evil and error.

These versions of the élite group would have left their mark on Carlyle, in addition to Goethe's more elaborated thoughts on the 'Communion of Saints' in *Wilhelm Meisters Wanderjahre*. Goethe's belief in *Persönlichkeit* certainly does not rule out the heroic element, although he suggests the union between *Held and Dichter*, possibly to prevent heroism from turning into a show of strength. In his drama *Tasso*, where this problem becomes acute, Goethe claims that the same aspiration, to work for the improvement of humanity, should unite hero and poet.[24] In *Iphigenie* the idea is expressed that everybody must choose his hero in order to aspire after him towards Olympus.[25] Goethe does not specify any heroic qualities, leaving enough latitude for the individual to follow his own ideal. If we take these statements as being in keeping with the characters who express them rather than as Goethe's own views, this limitation does not apply to utterances in *Maximen and Reflexionen*, where he points out the significance of the individual in relation to the advancement of mankind. Great deeds are accordingly never accomplished by the age we live in but by outstanding personalities. Socrates and Huss stand for this type of *Geistesheld* Goethe has in mind. Carlyle expresses similar thoughts, with a tendency to generalize:

Goethe	*Carlyle*
In all ages only individuals have furthered knowledge not the age itself. The ages have executed Socrates by way of poison, the ages have burnt Huss. The ages have always remained the same. (*Maximen*)	Universal History, the history of what man has accomplished in this world, is at bottom the History of the Great Men who have worked here. They were the leaders of men, these great ones. (*Heroes*, 1)

Goethe is, however, quite aware that the faculty to identify a heroic personality, its special worth or value, is not given to all:

Goethe	*Carlyle*
It is being said that for the valet a hero is non-existent. This is due to the fact that a hero can only be known by another hero. The valet is likely able to evaluate his own kind. (*Maximen*)	The Valet does not know a Hero when he sees him! Alas, no; it requires a kind of *Hero* to do that. (*Heroes*, 184) It is written: 'if we are ourselves Valets, there shall exist no hero for us; we shall not know the hero when we see him – we shall take the quack for a hero. (*Past and Present* II, iii, 83)

The tribute Goethe pays to the poet and his role in society by way of uplifting the cultural and artistic awareness of his fellow men, was an attitude originally alien to Carlyle: 'From his heart, his native soil, springs up the lovely flower of wisdom; and if others while waking dream ... he passes the dream of life like one awake ... And thus the poet is at once a teacher, a prophet, a friend of gods and men .. Nay, if thou wilt have it, who but the poet was it that first formed gods for us; that exalted us to them, and brought them down to us?' (*Meister* I, 112–13).[26]

Admittedly, these thoughts may not be new to readers acquainted with Renaissance concepts of art and its connection with the emergence of culture or society. They would, however, strike Carlyle as such, who had been raised in a faith that put little store in poetry and aesthetic values. Furthermore, the role of the poet as mediator between God and men not only fitted in well with what Carlyle gathered from Fichte regarding the manifestation of the Divine Idea in chosen men, but also added new dimensions to the clothes philosophy, that is, the notion of the high guild of tailor-writers: 'What too are all Poets and moral Teachers, but a species of Metaphorical Tailors? Touching which high Guild the greatest living Guild-brother has triumphantly asked us: "Nay if thou wilt have it, who but the Poet first made Gods for men; brought them down to us; and raised us up to them?" ' (*Sartor*, 290). The added quote echoes the above *Meister* passage.

For Carlyle, Goethe himself acts out his role as hero-poet who plants seed in time, in an age of Disbelief, when 'whatever belonged to the finer nature of man, had withered under the Harmattan breath of Doubt' (*Essays I*, 216). In this way he had described Goethe the wise poet-herald, ushering in a new era in German letters.[27] In this sense, Goethe is introduced by name into *Sartor* in a passage in which diverse threads are skilfully intertwined: clothes philosophy as vestures of the age, Divine Idea and prophetic guidance by the announcer of new times: 'And knowest thou no Prophet, even in the vesture, environment, and dialect of this age? None to whom the God-like had revealed itself, ... even in these rag-gathering and rag-burning days, Man's Life again begins, were it but afar off, to be divine? Knowest thou none such? I know him, and name him – Goethe' (*Sartor*, 253).

Goethe the poet-prophet also figures in *The French Revolution*, as a witness of the cannonade of Valmy, where he made his famous pronouncement of the importance of this martial event for the future. For Carlyle, he is the 'World-Poet' in whose mind exists 'the spiritual counterpart of this same huge Death-Birth of the World' (III, 57).

Although Goethe stresses the mission of the poet, he nevertheless sees his place within the group as a whole, 'an inspired Communion of Saints, that is, of men in the highest degree good and wise' (*Meister* II, 268).[28] This is represented by the Society of the Wanderers, trained in renunciation, willing to give up profitable engagements, and in employing special skills, manual or intellectual, in aiding humanity at large as the most distinguished portion of active men. Only in this fashion can disinterested well-doing be planned on a large scale.

The Communion of Saints as an invisible bond linking together all those striving for faith in transcendental values is mentioned several times in *Sartor*. There, however, it appears in a heroic context, absent in Goethe. We are given to understand that the heroic heart senses the wise men to be 'a living literal *Communion of Saints*, wide as the World itself, and as the History of the World' (*Sartor*, 247).

If thus Goethe's views on the vocation of the poet – for which his own personality provided a living example – and his thoughts on the Communion of Saints served Carlyle as a foundation on which to build his heroic edifice, it is also possible that Goethe's insistence on the necessity of reverence contributed indirectly to the worshipping part of the hero-creed. In *Wilhelm Meisters Wanderjahre*, the Elders, admit that 'man does not willingly submit himself to reverence ... [however] 'in some particularly favoured individuals [it] unfolds itself spontaneously' (*Meister* II, 266).[29] Here man is designated as a divinely inspired individual because he naturally worships whereas others must be awakened to the need for reverence. Goethe does not elaborate this point any further; Carlyle stresses it. For him, reverence gradually takes on the colouring of worship for the divinely inspired personality who can neither speak nor do any wrong: 'believe not that man has lost his faculty of Reverence ... only in reverently bowing down before the Higher does he feel himself exalted' (*Sartor*, 251). Unfortunately 'the Higher' does not make any fine distinctions between man and God, distinctions Goethe is acutely aware of, while Carlyle is not: 'We all love great man; love, venerate, and bow down submissive before great men: nay can we honestly bow down to anything else? (*Heroes*, 15).

Religious adoration – and worship of this kind – is, clearly, part of Novalis's creed. The hero is, first and foremost, a saint who stands in need of a community of worshippers, eager to give themselves over to the emotions of awe and wonder. Novalis's pronouncement in the *Fragmente*, that 'Martyrs are spiritual heroes. Christ was the greatest martyr of our species,'[30] does not go unheeded by Carlyle. Not only does he translate this fragment in 'Novalis,' but he also employs the notion in *Heroes*: 'Hero-worship ... is not that the germ of Christianity itself? The greatest of all Heroes is One – whom we do not name here! Let sacred silence meditate that sacred matter' (*Heroes*, 11). He finally comes to the conclusion that 'all religion issues in due Practical Hero-worship' (*Past and Present*, Bk III, ch. 15, 227).

Besides this stress on the saintly hero and the community of worshippers, the insistence on the importance of wonder is ever present in Novalis's message: 'Magical power of Faith – all belief is wonderful and wonder-creating' (*Fragmente* II, 131). This emphasis on the miraculous is also evident in *Sartor* (67): 'the reign of wonder is perennial, indestructible in Man.' Teufelsdröckh himself is by nature a worshipper. His characteristic is, besides his 'indomitable Defiance,' 'boundless Reverence' (ibid., 205). This personal creed finds expression in the connection made between wonder and worship: 'he deals much in the feeling of Wonder; insists on the necessity and high worth of universal Wonder ... "Wonder," says he, "is the basis of Worship" ' (ibid., 67).

Where belief takes over, reason must be silenced. It follows that the hero must be believed: 'The inspiration of the Almighty giveth him understanding. We must listen before all to him' (*Heroes* II, 46). From here on Carlyle's Calvinism steps in and leaves Novalis far behind in the demands he makes on the willingness of the community to follow the God-inspired man. Ever broader generalizations are being made, such as: 'A hero is a hero at all points' (ibid., I, 28). Those reluctant to go this far are reproachfully labelled by Carlyle as part of 'sceptical Dilettantism, the curse of these ages' (ibid., III, 84). While the worshippers must accept the hero without reservation, increasing single-mindedness no longer demands any specific aptitude in the heroic personality, but only one quality, described as 'hero-stuff': 'I confess, I have no notion of a truly great man that could not be *all* sorts of men ... Burns, a gifted song-writer might have made a still better Mirabeau' (ibid., 78–9). 'Hero-stuff,' in the last instance applicable to all heroes, consists in the ability 'to read the world and its laws' (ibid., 91).

As far as Carlyle's visions of Palingenesia are concerned, the glad tidings read: 'Hero-worship is the deepest root of all, (ibid., I, 11). This message he drums out in monotonous repetitions, painful to sensitive ears. Is this indeed Fichte-inspired?

The whole concept of hero-worship is a far cry from anything Fichte suggests as regards the reaction of mankind to the divine revelation among them. Although Fichte believes in the hero's effectiveness, this cult of the great man is alien to him. If he worships anything, it is the 'Divine Idea,' not the man as Carlyle does, who, however much he builds the 'Divine Idea' into the pedigree of his heroes, is actually more interested in their reception by humanity. This basic difference cannot be ignored by those who have seriously studied Fichte's *Über das Wesen des Gelehrten*, where the word 'hero' does not appear. With almost tedious pedantry, Fichte repeats over and over again that the man disappears behind the idea he represents, a fact pointed out above, in chapter 6, in connection with the ethics of renunciation. A personality cult of the kind Carlyle propagates would be contrary to Fichte's development of the theory of the state where the idea of the institution takes priority over the individual citizen, who virtually disappears behind the abstract concept.

It should also be remembered that Fichte nowhere speaks of worship of those committed to their vocation, who are all intellectual leaders with high standards regarding obligation and sacrifice. In addition, he is acutely aware of the danger of abusing leadership qualifications by employing them in unworthy causes: 'What is nobler than the desire to be active, to inspire man and to direct his vision towards the divine? But this desire may become a temptation to present what is sacred in an unworthy manner, to desecrate it so that it would appeal to baseness' (*Über das Wesen* VI, 408; Smith, *Popular Works, I,* 272).[31]

Carlyle was possibly aware of these reservations. Partly in *Sartor,* but mainly in *Past and Present,* he repeatedly speaks of the sham hero who usurps the role he is not destined to fill and who leads mankind into error. Such references may well indicate an influence on Carlyle so far disregarded in the evaluation of the much misinterpreted Fichte. It may thus be timely to examine more specifically Carlyle's passages dealing with the false hero: 'Will not that be a thing worthy of "doing"; to deliver ourselves from quacks, sham-heroes; to deliver the whole world more and more form such. They are the one bane of the world' (*Past and Present,* I, iv).

Not only the hero-image but hero-worship is in danger of deteriorating into a worship of shams: 'Hero-worship, if you will – yes friends; but first of all, by being ourselves of heroic mind ... We for our share, will put away all Flunkyism, Baseness, Unveracity from us' (ibid., vi). This comment should be remembered before making hasty judgments. It clearly states that hero-worship does not consist in worshipping a brainless, cruel, or criminal personality with some form of real or imagined charisma. The confusion arising from hero-worship in general is tied to the unfortunate term Carlyle chose. Veneration or admiration would have been a better translation of *Heldenverehrung,* as worship indicates a form of *Anbetung.* Man worships God and venerates examples of particular excellence in men and women.

With regard to the notion of 'hero-stuff,' which Carlyle adopts in *Heroes,* Fichte cannot be considered as a model. To his way of thinking, genius always manifests itself in a specific way, never in general, as is clearly stated in *Über das Wesen*: 'Genius will always appear as a *specific* Genius, for philosophy, poetry, natural science, legislation or the like, – never clothed with an *absolute* character, as Genius in the abstract' (VI, 396; Smith II).[32]

The difference between Fichte's notion and Carlyle's oversimplified application is strikingly revealed in connection with the various forms ideas take on in different ages: 'Every idea is bodied forth in any age under a new shape and compels the surrounding world to model itself according to it' (*Über das Wesen* VI, 406; Smith, II, 271).[33] While Fichte speaks of the Divine Idea in this instance, Carlyle transfers this thought of perpetual metamorphosis to hero-worship: 'It is a thing forever changing, this of Hero-worship: different in each age, difficult to do well in any age' (*Heroes*, 49). This is a significant example of how Carlyle moulds the initial influence in progressive stages to become part of his own thoughts.

It may not be insignificant to note that, among the several hero-types presented and discussed in *Heroes*, there is a single German, who has to share the spotlight with John Knox among the 'Heroes as Priests': Martin Luther. Not even Goethe appears among the 'Heroes as Poets' beside Dante and Shakespeare. Carlyle's countryman Burns is relegated to the rank of a 'Man of Letters,' a most unsuitable place for one of the greatest lyrical talents in English literature. Odin, as heroic divinity an unknown quantity, relates to the then popular Scandinavian mythology. The Hero as Prophet deals with Mahomet in an Islamic context, where Moses should have been the obvious choice. The last presentation of the Hero-Kings – most baffling of all – names Cromwell, the executioner of kings, in one breath with Napoleon, the child of the French Revolution, placing them both under one ill-chosen and ill-fitting slouch hat.

The Promised Land

Visions of the future do not always follow in the wake of a critique of contemporary society. It is one thing to point out deficiencies and quite another to introduce an effective set of new values to replace the old ones. Often the reader must search between the lines for snatches of prophecy tucked away beneath much negative comment on the present. Not all commentators on an age wish to elaborate on an utopian structure that may easily become dated; indeed, most poets and thinkers are hardly interested in a workable plan, once the general pattern or trend of development has been established. Thus, for Goethe, there is no lasting solution within the ever-recurring cycle of change. A new birth begins in times of Belief, only to vanish in the following era of Unbelief. In this sense his remark to Eckermann must obviously be understood that retarding demons prevent the world from reaching its goals, in spite of gains in epochs of regeneration.[34] It stands to reason that even the poet cannot break through the eternal law of retardation, which the gods have seen fit to erect between mankind and themselves.

He can merely direct man's striving 'towards the noblest aim' (*Meister* II, 370). As this can be most effectively brought about in a social context, 'society remains man's highest want' (ibid., 409).

This reluctance to go beyond suggestions also applies in the case of philosophers like Schelling, who visualizes an ideal but is vague about the form it should take in the actual. In the *Methode* (261), he briefly indicates a state of existence in which mankind would not live for pleasure alone, but rather in the contemplation of esoteric values. However, here too there is no finality, but constant becoming.

Neither in Goethe nor in Schelling does the past act as an immediate source of inspiration with regard to the future. Werner, however, does look backwards for a manifestation of true spirituality and finds it in the Middle Ages: 'Therefore remain a while, musing over this lovely semblance of those pious Ages that have passed. The pleasing Paradise vanished, the child weaned from its mother's breast, covers itself with the cold shield of wisdom' (*Söhne des Thals* I, Prolog).[35] Such hints at the benefits of Primitivism are not infrequent in Werner.

More direct comments on Palingenesia are offered by Novalis, who provides elaborate suggestions regarding the rebirth of European society in his fragmentary *Die Christenheit oder Europa*. He uncovers what, in the context of the history of ideas, would be termed a Golden Age tradition, furnishing his own society with a new norm, and accordingly with a new set of values. This new ideal is, for Novalis, not a return to Nature, as it is for Rousseau, but a return to religious faith. He finds the model in the Universal Church of the Middle Ages and its spiritual leadership, which, to his way of thinking, provide all the qualities lacking in his own time. This vision, which is to serve as a guideline for the future, he presents in a new and positive light to contemporary Protestant Christians, hitherto inclined to look back at this period with an amount of distrust and prejudice against Catholicism. The glowing account Novalis gives of this rediscovered spirituality, a true *civitas dei*, is in no way a realistic description, but a nostalgic elaboration, and for this reason highly effective in bringing across to the reader the notion of true piety. The prophet turned backwards tells a tale of times of yore 'when Europe was one Christendom ... [and] one great common interest united the most distant parts of this vast spiritual empire' (*Werke*, III, 7).[36]

At the core of this spiritual unity of the Middle Ages, based on a hierarchical pattern, stands an élite group responsible for its functioning, made up of saintly heroes who administer to the people and offer help, protection, and advice: 'these [were] elect men, armed with miraculous powers as children of heaven, whose mere presence and affection dispensed manifold blessings' (ibid.).[37] Quite in keeping with Novalis's concepts in the *Fragmente*, which were discussed earlier, these saintly personalities act as mediators between God and man: 'They were experienced navigators on the vast unknown ocean under whose protection all storms could be defied as trifling, and man could reckon confidently with a safe landing on the coast of his true fatherland. The wildest and greediest inclinations had to yield to the reverence and obedience demanded by their words (*Christenheit oder Europa*, 7).[38]

This ideal type of hero-worship has for its setting a milieu that enhances the mystical element: 'With serenity men left the beautiful congregations in the mysterious churches filled with sweet fragrance, adorned with inspiring paintings, and stimulated by sacred and solemn music. There the consecrated relics of former pious men were gratefully preserved in precious shrines' (ibid., 8).[39]

Secularization destroys the web of this poetic dream of child-like faith and willing adherence of mankind to inspire leadership. Novalis goes on to trace the emergence of the Protestant spirit, not without sympathy, but with stress on the destructive elements of a new society that 'prefers limited knowledge to infinite faith and comes to despise all that is great and awe-inspiring' (ibid., 9).[40] This process is completed in the Age of Reason, when, in a barren intellectual landscape, love and faith wither and all emotional and irrational values are uprooted or ridiculed. Desire for material possession gains ground. Gone are the more splendid manifestations of the supernatural: A comparison with Carlyle's 'Mill of Death' (*Sartor*, 104) immediately comes to mind. 'The infinite creative music of the universe was changed into the monotonous clatter of a gigantic mill which turned by the stream of chance, and floating thereon, was a self-contained mill without builder and miller, properly a genuine *perpetuum mobile*, a self-grinding mill' (*Christenheit oder Europa*, 16–17).[41]

In an *Ubi sunt*? lament, all that was lost is once more recalled: 'Where is now that ancient, cherished, only redeeming faith in the government of God on earth, where is that divine trust of men in one another, that delightful devotion in the outpourings of a soul inspired by God, that all-embracing spirit of Christendom?' (ibid., 26).[42] But a firm belief in the cyclic pattern in history convinces Novalis that a renewal of faith is about to begin. This Palingenesia manifests itself in birth-throes: 'They are the first pains of labour, let everyone prepare himself for birth' (ibid., 23).[43]

This rebirth Novalis describes with a directness more radical than any of the Saint-Simonian statements on the topic: 'That the age of resurrection has arrived and that precisely those events that appeared to be directed against its vivification and seemed to complete its fall, have turned into the most favourable signs of regeneration, no historically minded person can doubt. True anarchy begets religion, and from the destruction of everything positive it raises its illustrious head as the founder of a new world' (*Christenheit oder Europa*, 18–19).[44] The practical outcome is a new history and a new mankind, able, above all else, to 'attach itself by a higher aspiration to the heights of heaven, and relate itself to the universe' (ibid., 19).[45] The way out of the imperfections and the terrifying aspects that bear witness to the decline of previous institutions is a new religiosity: 'Only religion can reawaken Europe, reconcile the people, and reinstate Christianity with new splendour visible on earth in its old office of peacemaker' (ibid., 25).[46]

The overall similarity in spirit of Novalis's essay with much of Carlyle's thought is too obvious to need further elaboration. Novalis places his saintly hero type into history, which the religiously inspired author reads like a divine revelation. Carlyle picks up this message and incorporates it into the Palingenesia chapters of *Sartor* (Book III), where he applies it to his own vision of a new society based on hero-worship. A passage from 'Characteristics' foreshadows developments in *Past and Present*: 'Polities are formed; the weak submitting to the strong; with willing loyalty giving obedience that he may receive guidance: or say rather in honour of our nature, the ignorant submitting to the wise ... Last, as the crown and all supporting keystone of the fabric, Religion arises' (*Essays III*, 11–12). Inspiration is drawn from the Middle Ages, described as a time when 'society was what we call healthy' (ibid., 15) and future progress intimately connected with the religious spirit: 'Greatly her best progress, moreover, was in the old times. In those same "dark ages," Intellect built not only churches, but a Church, *the* Church based on this firm Earth, yet reaching up, and leading up, as high as Heaven' (ibid., 18–19). This picture is contrasted with the present age of unbelief in which man's relation to the universe and to his fellow men has become doubtful. As Novalis had emphasized, society is sick to dissolution because of lack of religious faith. Carlyle's staccato outcry 'Whither has religion fled?' (ibid., 15) is no less effective in its brevity than Novalis's longer lament. The essay ends on a more optimistic note, contrary to the 'Carlyle the Pessimist' blueprint that has in the past obscured the more positive aspects of his prophecies: 'Deep and sad as is our feeling that we stand yet in the bodeful Night; equally deep, indestructible, is our assurance that the morning also will not fail. Nay already, as we look around, streaks of a dayspring are in the east; it is dawning ... The Progress of man towards higher and nobler developments of what is highest and noblest in him, lies not only prophesied to Faith' (ibid., 37).

Despite the fact that *Past and Present* deals mainly with social issues of the day, the suggestions it contains with regard to Palingenesia show similarity with Novalis's concerning general themes based on a rediscovery of the virtues of the Middle Ages. The religious spirit, fused with hero-worship focusing on Abbot Samson, who heads the saintly community, forms an indispensable part of the whole proposition of looking to the past for purposes of contrast with the present.

Already the approach to the medieval scene recalls Novalis's poetic vision of the Blessed Isles:

Novalis	*Carlyle*
The Spirit of God hovers over the waters, and a celestial island becomes visible for the first time across the receding waves as the dwelling-place of new men, as the river-basin of eternal life. (*Christenheit oder Europa,* 19)[47]	As we emerge from the trough of the sea ... there lies the Heroic Promised Land; under that Heaven's light, my brethren, bloom the Happy Isles, – there, O there! ... there dwell all Heroes and will dwell: Thither all ye heroic-minded! (*Past and Present,* Bk I, 6)

In *Past and Present* hero-worship is introduced in the same manner as in 'Christenheit oder Europa,' that is, tied to the élite group of mediators, in Carlyle's case the feudal aristocracy, not as yet identified with the 'partridge-shooters' of his own day. They represent a governing class of talent who very efficiently fulfil their task in society, as ably as Novalis's priests:

Novalis	*Carlyle*
A numerous guild [was] open to all ... Every member of that society was everywhere honoured; and if the common people sought from them comfort or help, protection or advice ... they also found support among the mighty. (*Christenheit oder Europa,* 7)[48]	A feudal aristocracy is still alive, in the prime of life; superintending the cultivation of the land, ... the adjustment of the quarrels of the land; judging, soldiering, adjusting. (*Past and Present,* Bk II, ch. 5, 65)

Carlyle's intention to illuminate the present by holding up for emulation the medieval Age of Faith becomes particularly clear in Book II, of *Past and Present,* where he leads the reader back into a somewhat remote century, where people like St Edmund 'walked humbly and valiantly with God not pridefully with Mammon' (*Past and Present,* Bk II, ch. 3, 53) and where the response of his followers is hero-worship, now qualified as true admiration: 'It is the very joy of man's heart to admire where he can; nothing lifts him from all his mean imprisonments, were it but for moments, as true admiration' (ibid., 55). Abbot Samson, although less saintly than any of Novalis's Elders, is recognized in the same manner as possessing outstanding leadership qualities. It is his authoritative rule Carlyle describes in convincing details, not the religious, contemplative side of monastic life. The Abbot's otherworldliness is largely ignored.

Here, too, there is an atmosphere of wonder that casts a spell over the whole medieval scene: 'Beautifully, in our earnest love-glances, the old centuries melt from opaque to partially translucent, transparent here and there; and the void black Night, one finds, is but the summing-up of innumerable peopled luminous *Days*' (*Past and Present,* Bk II, ch. 11, 49). This is the appropriate setting for cultural primitivism of the kind Carlyle injects into the times: 'The great antique heart: how like a child's in its simplicity, like a man's in its earnest solemnity and depth! Heaven lies over him wherever he goes or stands on the Earth; making all the Earth a mystic Temple to him, the Earth's business all a kind of worship. Glimpses of bright creatures flash in the common sunlight; angels yet hover, doing God's messages among men: that rainbow was set in the clouds by the hand of God! Wonder, miracle encompass the man; – he lives in an element of miracle' (ibid., II, ch. 15, 116).

The qualities lacking in his own time, Carlyle finds here. The contrast is made explicit: 'This is Abbot Samson's Catholicism of the Twelfth Century; – Alas, compared with any of the *Isms* current in these poor days, what a thing!' (ibid., II, ch. 15).

The part assigned by Novalis to the Age of Reason as the era of Unbelief is replaced in *Past and Present* by 'the Gospel of enlightened Selfishness,' as Carlyle defines philosophical Utilitarianism.[49] Here as there, however, God has departed from a mechanically conceived world:

Novalis	*Carlyle*
God was made an idle spectator of this great moving pageant in which	– which the Maker at most, sat looking at, in a distant singular and

the scholars performed. ('Christenheit oder Europa,' 17–18)[50]

indeed incredible manner. (*Past and Present* I, ch. 5)

Carlyle also reiterates the claim that the past had been deliberately distorted by a godless century: 'To predict the Future, to manage the Present, would not be so impossible, had not the Past been so sacrilegiously mishandled, effaced, and what is worse, defaced! ... All was inane discord in the Past; brute Force bore rule everywhere, Stupidity, savage unreason, fitter for Bedlam than for a human world! (*Past and Present,* IV, i, 239).

In this unusual spirit of reconciliation with all powers representing faith against the spectre of Unbelief, Carlyle even risks a kind word for the Jesuits, whom Novalis had also praised as the staunch supporters of the dying spirit of the hierarchy.[51]

But Carlyle does not only share with Novalis the religious interpretation of the evils of the times. He likewise heralds a return to faith as imperative for a regeneration of man's spiritual life. The inner fountains of life must again flow, 'by descending into the inner man and see if there be any traces of soul there' (*Past and Present,* I, iv).

It is also remarkable that the new vision contained in *Past and Present* applies to Europe as a whole, although the social problems dealt with previously pertained strictly to 'the matter of England': 'If the convulsive struggles of the last Half-Century have taught poor struggling convulsed Europe any truth, it may perhaps be this: That Europe requires a real Aristocracy, a real Priesthood, or it cannot continue to exist' (*Past and Present,* IV, i). Where Novalis speaks of a venerable European Council that will perform the business of religious awakening according to an all-embracing Divine plan, Carlyle demands, in like fashion, 'a spiritual guideship and practical Governorship' (ibid., IV, i) with an added emphasis on some hero-worship, in order that 'by degrees, we shall again have a Society with something of Heroism in it, something of Heaven's Blessing on it' (ibid., IV, iv).

How far Schleiermacher's *Über die Religion* may be considered as a direct source for Carlyle's theory of the hero remains to be examined in the future. The fact that he refers to Schleiermacher's views on immortality in 'Life and Writings of Werner' (*Essays I,* 117) indicates that he read the above-mentioned work, including the second speech, in which this problem is discussed. Would Carlyle, we ask ourselves, have overlooked Schleiermacher's remarks on man's role as a mediator, with the hero representing one among a variety of interpreters and reconcilers?

These various intellectual watchtower perspectives at the 'Promised Land' reveal the heavy stress laid on religion as an essential part of Palingenesia. The spirit is broadly Christian with much leeway for personal deviations. It speaks for Carlyle's powers of observation and his acute awareness of essentials that he singles out this very trait as typical for the new trend in German Romantic writings in 'State of German Literature': 'It is a common theory among the Germans, that every Creed, every form of worship is a form merely; the mortal and ever changing *body*, in which the immortal and unchanging *spirit* of Religion is expressed to the material eye, and made manifest and influential among the doings of man' (*Essays I*, 143).

Carlyle seems to have received and applied this message, which can hardly be considered a peripheral concern at the threshold of another millennium when a new European order, including ethical renewal, is about to evolve.

Part Three

STYLISTIC ASPECTS
(*Sartor Resartus*)

'Do our readers know the German Jean Paul and his style of thought?'

Carlyle, 'Mirabeau'

NINE

Jean Paul and No End

"Are you well up in your Jean Paul, Watson?"
"Fairly so, Holmes. I worked back to him through Carlyle."
"That was like following the brook to the parent lake."

(Conan Doyle, *The Sign of Four*)

Carlyle's Creative Application of Jean Paul's Style and Word Power

Carlyle's dependence on Jean Paul in matters of style can never be determined with complete certainty because we deal here with a translation into another language. The sources, in other words, have undergone a change. Is this transformation so great, we must ask ourselves, that the original is no longer recognizable? The critic who undertakes the task of examining this problem must not merely know enough German to read Jean Paul in the original, but must be an expert in both languages to detect similarities in style. Scholars on both sides of the ocean who have not been able to meet this initial requirement, have, therefore, tended to attribute Carlyle's style to influences that, according to his own utterances at a later date, he had received at his father's house. This theory has gained ground, leaving the previous school of thought claiming that Carlyle had deliberately emulated Jean Paul's style stranded on high ground, awaiting a turn of the tide.[1]

Carlyle's much-quoted statement of 1834, originally cited by Froude, declares that he was stylistically indebted to his father's speech pattern as the most important influence by far.[2] Further information on this subject is contained in *Reminiscences* (I, 8), where his father's speech is described: 'None of us will ever forget that bold glowing style of his, flowing free from his untutored soul, full of metaphors ... with all manner of potent words which he appropriated and applied with a surprising accuracy ... brief, energetic ... definite, clear, not in ambitious colours, but in full white sunlight ... The whole district knew of it and laughed joyfully over it ... The fault was that he exaggerated (which tendency I also inherit).'

From this excerpt which contains more of the passage, than is usually quoted, few readers would be able to recognize Thomas Carlyle's sartorial style, which, however, bold and glowing, is hardly known for accuracy, brevity, and clarity; for lack of ambitious colours; or for being steeped in full white sunlight. On the contrary, presented in darkling chiaroscuro, his prose employs copious variations in speech patterns, erratic sentence structure, and untamed verbosity related to the manifold intellectual and philosophical connotations that Carlyle can pull out of his 'Fortunatus hat' at will. It should also be noted that the passage describing James Carlyle's speech is brought into no relationship to his son's, except in so far as it is an example of the latter's tendency to exaggerate. James Carlyle appears in this personal eulogy 'in a certain sacred sanctified light' (ibid., 4), after his son has experienced the immediate sorrow of bereavement. What unfolds in the *Reminiscences* is a portrait of the virtues of Primitivism in 'a brave man,' with the German epithet 'ein tapferer' [*sic*] added in parentheses (14), which Jean Paul had used to characterize the poet Fouqué (*German Romance*, I, 210). Carlyle then takes a sentence part from Fichte, *das garnicht existirte* [*sic*], to explain his father's indifference to public opinion (10), and misquotes a line from Goethe, *ohne Hast aber ohne Rast*, to explain James Carlyle's 'great maxim of philosophy': 'not to speculate, or feel or dream' (10). In this fashion two German poets and one philosopher are needed to characterize this Scottish mason, where the reader would at least have expected a glowing adage of his own. Furthermore, we are told that James Carlyle's 'measured by quantity of words was a talker of full average copiousness' who could 'in a few sentences, sketch you off an entire biography' (12). That much for a style that supposedly had such a bearing on his son.

What James Carlyle gains in virtues of simple manhood he loses in intellectual and literary scope. We are told that 'my father's education was altogether of the worst and most limited. I believe he was never more than three months at any school ... Poetry, fiction in general, he had universally seen treated as not only idle, but false and criminal. This was the spiritual element he had lived in almost to old age' (19). We are furthermore disappointed to hear that even Burns's natural lyrics, loved not only by the Scottish nation as a whole, but also by its peasantry, remained a closed book to Carlyle's father, who 'never read three pages of Burns' poems' (17).

The reader begins to wonder what significant stylistic impact this honest man, rightly praised for admirable qualities related to the simple lifestyle, could have had on his famous son's literary expression in the highly sophisticated prose of *Sartor*. Old James Carlyle's imagery, besides containing biblical echoes, must have basically been of a homely kind, deft and full of Scotticisms, to keep the whole district laughing. If it was a defensive move by Carlyle to present his parent's style as the prototype of his own, it remains incomprehensible how critics could follow this lead, without considering the anomalous nature of his observations as to his stylistic roots.

The *Reminiscences* themselves are a proof that Carlyle as an experienced translator had various styles at his command. Contrary to anything presented in *Sartor*, the eulogy is written in a sober, terse, even brittle style that serves its purpose admirably. It indirectly reveals the great versatility he had achieved by the time he was about to compose and expand his own *Kunstwerk* (1832). Carlyle's comments about the origins of his style must obviously be related to the realm of personal myth, built around his venerable parent. According to the description he gives of his father's speech, they must be considered as invalid.

Another puzzling question relates to the time factor: why did he bottle up his father's style for so long, until it suddenly burst forth, uncontemplated, unintentionally, after twelve years of writing practice in which not a single trace of it could be found? The fact that we do not possess any sample of James Carlyle's style of speech or writing makes it impossible to check this alleged derivation.

After having examined the improbable foundations on which the first school of thought bases its claims, a second possibility remains, namely, that Carlyle deliberately wished to imitate Jean Paul in *Sartor* to present faithfully the style patterns of a German professor's speech, based on specimens he knew down to the minutest details. Ruling out the critical voices that merely identified the German idiom as such, the reaction to *Sartor* among his educated contemporaries immediately identified the style of the book with Jean Paul. Some of them were Englishmen with literary interests and a knowledge of German; others were Germans who recognized the style as Jean Paulian in concept and expression, and were proficient enough in the English language to identify the emulation.

A typical English representative of the first group is John Sterling who was well aware of his friend's capabilities as a translator and stylist, and never questioned his ability to employ Jean Paul's mannerism for his own literary purposes. His testimony after reading *Sartor* cannot be downplayed. Sterling appreciates the feelings and tastes of Teufelsdröckh 'or his prototype Jean Paul' (*Sartor*, 308), and immediately recognizes his 'Rhapsodico-Reflective' form of composition. Although he mentions other sources, such as Rabelais, Montaigne, Sterne, and Swift, as possible precursors, the stylistic dependence on Jean Paul is obvious to him. So was it to other less-well-known translators who had wrestled with Jean Paul's sentence structure at close quarters well enough not to mistake them in Carlyle's work. Storr dedicated his translation of 'Maria Wuz' to Carlyle 'In Memory of our English Jean Paul.'[3]

A German voice from the second group should not go unheeded either, as it emanates from two famous men – Marx and Engels – and seems to have been overlooked by Carlyle scholars: 'Outmoded and quaint turns of speech and words were brought up and newly invented, according to Jean Paul's pattern. The new style was always highflying heavenwards and tasteless, but frequently brilliant and always original. It is significant that from the whole of German literature, the mind that influenced Carlyle most was not Hegel, but the literary pharmacist Jean Paul' (Marx/Engels, *Über Kunst und Literatur*, 201–2; my translation).

This close identification with Jean Paul is not a popular theory among English critics who, as Smeed already states, show a tendency to belittle foreign influences on Carlyle's style,[4] but truth, not popularity, should be our aim. At least we do not have to take this theory on trust; the sources are at hand, for those who can read them, to reach more tangible conclusions. Carlyle himself eased the work of posterity by partly translating Jean Paul, fully conscious of his stylistic peculiarities, as he assures us in several of his Richter essays. Such specimens, from *Fixlein* and *Schmelzle* with additional translations from works Carlyle is known to have read, would lend themselves to comparison with similar passages from *Sartor*, followed by an examination of Jean Paul's and Carlyle's word power in relation to this work (see the appendix to this chapter, p. 181).

Even before his career as a translator and writer, Carlyle possessed the ability to adopt a peculiar style not his own. A letter written by his schoolfellow Thomas Murray in 1814 indicates as much by speaking of his 'Shandean turn of expression' (Froude, *First Forty Years* I, 21) in correspondence Carlyle had written at the age of nineteen. His first official publications, in the form of his contributions to *Brewster's Edinburgh Encyclopaedia*, reveal nothing of the sort. These articles are written in a formal, completely factual biographical style, employing heavily latinized vocabulary. The following relates observations on Mary Montagu's poems (1820): 'Suggested chiefly by ephemeral topics, they seem to have been written without great care. They are not polished, but across their frequent harshness and infelicity of expression, we can easily discern considerable vivacity of conception, accompanied with some acuteness in discriminating character and delineating manners. It is to be regretted that they are not always free from indelicacy' (*Essays V*, 76).

Carlyle continues in the same vein in his *Life of Friedrich Schiller*, which was serialized in *London Magazine* (1823–4) before it was published in book form (1825):

> Besides, once accustomed to attend strictly to the operations of his genius, and rigorously to try its products, such a man as Schiller could not fail in time to discover what was false in the principles by which he tried them, and consequently in the end, to retain the benefits of this procedure without its evils. There is doubtless a purism in taste, a rigid fantastical demand for perfection, a horror of approaching the limits of impropriety, which obstructs the free impulse of the faculties, and if excessive, would altogether deaden them. But the excess on the other side is much more frequent, and, for high endowments, infinitely more pernicious. (ibid., Part III, 115)

It is doubtful whether this abstract, anaemic style constitutes an advance over his first blueprint Johnsonian. Carlyle's later disparagement of the book in the 1845 reprint may have had something to do with his dissatisfaction concerning its stylistic presentation, which he may have felt did not enhance the topic as it should have done. A rewriting of the entire biography was considered as 'frightful' by him.

The next step forward in stylistic awareness is Carlyle's *Wilhelm Meister* translation (1824), which left its mark on the later novel fragment *Wotton Reinfred*; that fragment, however unevenly written, made a feeble attempt to capture Goethe's *Altersstil* in individual passages. Unfortunately, he never developed an ear for Goethe's prose, as he admitted in a letter to Sterling dated 25 November 1839: 'But the *Goethe tune*, the last perfection of translation, was not fully in it ... I translated Goethe some two years before I could discover that he had a tune ... There is nothing of it, or next to nothing, in my *Meister's Apprenticeship*; in the other *Meister* I did get hold of it' (*New Letters of Carlyle*, I, 172,

25 Nov. 1839). We might add: imperfectly so. Carlyle was uncomfortable with it, and never truly able to render its natural simplicity, which constitutes its greatest charm.

Carlyle's translation of the second volume of *German Romance*, containing Jean Paul's *Quintus Fixlein* and *Schmelzle's Journey to Flaetz*, announces a significant point of departure and a beginning in a new direction: he rids himself of his Goethe affectations, and receives the new stimulating influence of Jean Paul's style. He admits as much in a letter to Jane Welsh (19 July 1826): 'It is singular what a mock-bird I am. I am writing here unconsciously in the very note of J.P. Richter, on whose works I have been labouring for the last four weeks.'[5] As yet this realization does not substantiate itself in his preface to Richter in *German Romance* (III, 1827), but his interest is awakened and kept alive. The 'unconscious imitation' must be changed into a conscious one if it is to become a literary art form. For this reason, he has to explore it further before he experiments with it. The following period shows Carlyle at the height of stylistic greatness in the conventional English idiom in the review essays, culminating in 'State of German Literature,' but at the same time being very much aware of Jean Paul's stylistic uniqueness, of which he gives several detailed accounts.

Before examining these, it may be worthwhile to bring back to mind De Quincey's description of Jean Paul's style in his *Analects from Richter* (1821), which preceded Carlyle's translations by several years. De Quincey had been the one to introduce Jean Paul, or 'John Paul' as he calls him, to the English reading public, and had, according to Carlyle's statement, directed his attention to him as well (*Froude* I, 323–4). When speaking of Jean Paul, De Quincey shows uncommon enthusiasm, even slight levity, calling him 'the Proteus, the Ariel, the Mercury, the monster ... wild, giddy, fantastic, capricious, incalculable, springing, vaulting, tumbling' (Introduction to *Analects*, *Writings* XI, 266). In a more sober passage, he characterizes his style in detail. The following account is of great importance, as it constitutes an objective appraisal. We cannot accuse De Quincey of describing his own style when speaking of Richter, as has been said in the case of Carlyle. It follows that, if Carlyle shows a similarity of style in *Sartor* with that described by De Quincey, the former's style must be classed as obviously Jean Paulian:

> But after all, these verbal obscurities are but the necessary result and product of his style of thinking. The nimbleness of his transitions often makes him elliptical: the vast expansion and discursiveness in his range of notice and observation, carries him into every department and nook of human life, of

science, of art, and of literature; whence comes a proportionably extensive vocabulary, and a prodigious compass of idiomatic phraseology; and finally the fineness and brilliancy of his oblique glances and surface-skimmering allusions often fling but half a meaning on the mind, and one is puzzled to make out its complement ... These are causes which must affect his own countrymen no less than foreigners. (Ibid., 268)

In this analysis of Jean Paul's style by a critic who did not adopt it in any of his own works, it is not difficult to discover all the qualities *Sartor* possesses to the same degree. It is evident that Carlyle's style, for whatever reasons, has something in common with Jean Paul's or, more explicitly, that the *Sartor* style shows a similarity with Jean Paul's.

These observations bring us to Carlyle's own accounts of Jean Paul's stylistic peculiarities, which are here strictly severed from his general interest in his idol's personality, so feelingly presented by Wellek (*Confrontations*, 61-71). In his Richter Preface to *German Romance* II (1827), which presents an impressive list of Jean Paul's works, Carlyle undertakes to describe for the first time noteworthy stylistic elements merely from the point of view of an enthusiastic reader. He approves of Jean Paul's 'intellectual vigour, copious fancy, the wildest yet truest humour, the whole concocted in a style entirely his own' (ibid., 118). Speaking of his early novel, *Hesperus*, which brought him lasting recognition, Carlyle shows unreserved amazement, even bewilderment:

The style and structure of the book appear alike incomprehensible. The narrative is every now and then suspended to make way for some 'Extra-leaf', some wild digression upon any subject but the one in hand; the language groans with indescribable metaphors and allusions to all things human and divine; flowing onward, not like a river, but like an inundation; circling in complex eddies, chafing and gurgling now this way now that, till the proper current sinks out of view amid the boundless uproar. We close the work with a mingled feeling of astonishment, oppression and perplexity. (ibid., 120)

De Quincey, in his critique, had already briefly related Jean Paul's verbal expression to his 'style of thinking.' Carlyle clearly realizes that the nature of his imagination is transcendental, and the style uniquely fitted to convey these visions: 'His imagination opens for us the Land of Dreams; we sail with him through the boundless abyss, and the secrets of Space and Time and Life, and Annihilation hover round us in dim cloudy forms, and darkness and immensity and dread encompass and overshadow us ... His very language is Titanian; deep, strong, tumultuous, shining with a thousand hues, fused from a thousand elements, and winding in labyrinthic mazes' (ibid., 122).

It is hardly a coincidence that Carlyle's subsequent essays on German literature are ushered in with a Jean Paul review in connection with Heinrich Döring's *Life of Richter.* Here, his comments on style are less vague and more directly related to Jean Paul's technique:

> His language itself is a stone of stumbling to the critic; to critics of the grammarian species, an unpardonable, often an insuperable rock of offence. Not that he is ignorant of grammar ... but deals with astonishing liberality in parentheses, dashes and subsidiary clauses; invents hundreds of new words, alters old ones, or by hyphen chains and pairs and packs them together into most jarring combination; in short, produces sentences of the most heterogeneous, lumbering, interminable kind ... indeed the whole is one tissue of metaphors, and similes, and allusions to all the provinces of Earth, Sea, Air; interlaced with epigrammatic breaks, vehement bursts, or sardonic turns, interjections, quips, puns and even oaths! A perfect Indian jungle it seems; a boundless, unparalleled imbroglio ... It is in fact a chaos. (*Essays I*, 'Jean Paul I,' 12–13)

Nobody can accuse Carlyle of not having done his homework in this detailed investigation. By referring to Jean Paul's style as a 'complicated Arabesque' elsewhere (19), Carlyle reveals his knowledge of Friedrich Schlegel's characterization of Jean Paul's writings (*Athenaeum*, III, 116). With a certain audacity he describes his diversity of mood in an unacknowledged quote from *Levana*: 'Like Rubens, by a single stroke he can change a laughing face into a sad one' (*Werke*, V, 632; *Essays I*, 'Jean Paul I,' 15).[6]

This detailed analysis of Jean Paul's manner is followed by its partial application in the 'Burns' essay (1828), which gave cause for Jeffrey's censorial remarks.[7] The following passage exemplifies the inroad Carlyle had made into Jean Paul's stylistic expression: 'Alas, his Sun shone as through a tropical tornado; and the pale Shadow of Death eclipsed it at noon! Shrouded in such baleful vapours, the genius of Burns was never seen in clear azure splendour, enlightening the world: but some beams from it did, by fits, pierce through; and it tinted those clouds with rainbow and orient colours, into a glory and stern grandeur, which men silently gazed on with wonder and tears!' (*Essays I*, 263).

This breakthrough is followed by 'Jean Paul Friedrich Richter Again' (1830), which brings a full appreciation of this writer's genius. In reviewing *Wahrheit aus Jean Pauls Leben*, the unfinished autobiography of the author, edited by his friend Joh. Chr. Otto, Carlyle's concern with Jean Paul's style is immediately brought to our attention:

Far from appreciating and appropriating the spirit of his writings, foreigners find it in the highest degree difficult to seize their grammatical meaning. Probably there is not in any modern language so intricate a writer; abounding without measure, in obscure allusions, in the most twisted phraseology; perplexed into endless entanglements and dislocations, parenthesis within parenthesis; not forgetting elisions, sudden whirls, quips, conceits and all manner of inexplicable crotchets: the whole moving on ... in huge parti-coloured mob-masses. (*Essays II*, 98)

Carlyle particularly relishes Jean Paul's invention of promoting himself to the rank of Professor in his own history, presented in several lectures; Professor Teufelsdröckh will do the same, if not in the form of lectures in the form of scraps extracted from Jean Paulian paper bags. In fits and starts, Jean Paul's style elements cross Carlyle's pages, as in the following passage on Professor Richter's poverty: 'Of all literary phenomena, that of a literary man daring to believe that he is *poor*, may be regarded as the rarest. Can a man without capital open his lips and speak to mankind? Had he no landed property, then; no connection with the higher classes; did he not even keep a gig? By these documents it would appear so. This was not a nobleman, nor gentleman, nor gigman; but simply a man!' (*Essays II*, 130). Extensive translations from Jean Paul are wrought into the fabric of this essay, the important passage 'I am a ME' (111) that lies at the spiritual core of *Sartor* (53) among them.

The last description of Richter's style as such is contained in *Lectures on the History of Literature* (1838) the published version of lectures given in the year *Sartor* had finally appeared in book form. In nostalgic retrospect Carlyle falls into metaphorical language to characterize it, with Richter's 'Indian jungle' changed into an 'American forest':

He cannot get half the things said that he has to say – a confused, strange, tumultuous style! It is like some tangled American forest, where the axe has never been, and no path lies through it. For my part I tried to understand him over and over gain before I succeeded; but I got finally to perceive his way of thinking, and I found a strange kind of order in him at last, and it was quite easy after that to make him out. His is a most gorgeous style; not like an articulate voice, but like the sound of cataracts falling among the wild pine-forests! It goes deep in the human heart. (*Lectures on the History of Literature*, 222)

After these various descriptions of Jean Paul's style, by De Quincey, and in profusion by Carlyle himself, the last link in the chain of evidence must be added: the English editor's illustration of Teufelsdröckh's characteristic manner of writing:

In respect of style our Author manifests ... a rich idiomatic diction, picturesque allusions, fiery poetic emphasis, or quaint tricksy turns; all the graces and terrors of a wild Imagination, wedded to the clearest Intellect, alternate in beautiful vicissitude. Were it not that sheer sleeping and soporific passages; circumlocutions, repetitions, touches even of pure doting jargon, so often intervene! On the whole, Professor Teufelsdröckh is not a cultivated writer. Of his sentences perhaps not more than nine-tenths stand straight on their legs; the remainder are in quite angular attitudes, buttressed-up by props (of parentheses and dashes) ... a few even sprawl-out helplessly on all sides, quite broken-backed and dismembered ... A wild tone pervades the whole utterance of the man, like its keynote and regulator; now screwing itself aloft as into the Song of Spirits, or else the shrill mockery of Fiends. (*Sartor*, 31)

We are most fortunate that Carlyle was a critic before he became a creative writer; that he set down his critical observations on Jean Paul's style in a detached way before he attempted to emulate him in the same vein. At that stage, someone as yet unaware of his own future development unwittingly let the cat out of the bag, committing himself in a way no author would have done. In the description of Teufelsdröckh's style cited above, Jean Paul's manner of writing is once more recaptured. The reader merely has to compare the features to realize the undeniable similarity.

It cannot go unnoticed that *Sartor* is the only work in which Carlyle employs two distinct styles, that of the English editor and that of Teufelsdröckh. The German professor's utterances are modelled on Jean Paul in keeping with the German milieu and the all-important aspects of transcendental thought for which it is the obvious vehicle. Carlyle did not have to adapt the style to suit the subject-matter; Jean Paul had already done this in his presentation of the new *Weltbild* that went with it and could not be separated from it. This *Weltbild* presented as its subject-matter the picture of the universe related to transcendental thought. It too is a vesture or garment that changes everything it touches. Carlyle is, by now, not only able to grasp it, but to handle it in a superb fashion in his native language. It runs parallel with that of the Editor, which is overshadowed by the former's uniqueness and very pronounced coinage. The following is an example of the Editor's normal style of reporting: 'Directly on the first perusal, almost on the first deliberate inspection, it became apparent that here a quite new Branch of Philosophy, leading to as yet undescried ulterior results, was disclosed; farther, what seemed scarcely less interesting, a quite new human Individuality, an almost unexampled personal character, that, namely of Professor Teufelsdröckh the Discloser' (*Sartor*, 10). This passage should be contrasted with Teufelsdröckh's style in another in which he describes his ideas himself: 'Of this thing, however, be certain: wouldst thou plant for Eternity, then plant into the deep infinite faculties of man, his Fantasy and Heart; wouldst thou plant for Year and Day, then plant into his shallow superficial faculties, his Self-love and Arithmetical Understanding, what will grow there' (ibid., 225). His comments are usually Romantic, heightened by transcendental associations and artistic vision of the Jean Paulian kind:

Jean Paul	*Carlyle*
this immeasurable nearly helpless feeling with which the silent spirit appears to stand in the wild giant-mill of the Universe, stunned and alone. He sees innumerable unsurmountable world-wheels circling in succession – and he hears the roaring of an eternally driving stream – ... and thus he stand forlorn in the all-powerful, blind, lone machine. (*Ästhetik*, *Werke*, V, 96)[8]	To me the Universe was all void of Life, of Purpose, of Volition, even of Hostility: it was one huge, dead, immeasurable Steam-engine, rolling on, in its dead indifference, to grind me limb from limb. O, the vast, gloomy, solitary Golgotha, and Mill of Death! Why was the Living banished thither, companionless, conscious? (*Sartor*, 164)

Although Jean Paul's style is at its most restrained in this quotation, the resemblance between the two passages is obvious. The mood is one of perplexed despair, presented in a transcendental context. Carlyle heightens the effect by the added Christian note of lament.

Even vaster vistas open up in the following starscapes, both conveying the same sense of wonder for the cosmic order:

Jean Paul	*Carlyle*
Then my heart comprehended that immortality dwelled in the spaces between the worlds, and death only among the worlds ... In the Zaarahs of Creation I saw, I heard, I felt, the glittering, the echoing, the breath-	*Ach Gott*, when I gazed into these Stars, have they not looked down on me as if with pity, from their serene spaces; like Eyes glistening with heavenly tears over the little lot of man! Thousands of human

ing, of life and creative power; the suns were but as spinning-wheels, the planets no more than weaver's shuttles, in relation to the infinite web which composes the veil of Isis, – which veil is hung over the whole creation, and lengthens as any finite being attempts to raise it. (*Komet*, *Werke*, VI, 685–6)[9]

generations, all as noisy as our own, have been swallowed-up of Time, and there remains no wreck of them any more; and Arcturus and Orion and Sirius and the Pleiades are still shining in their courses, clear and young ... Pshaw! what is this paltry little Dog-cage of an Earth. (*Sartor*, 182)

There are undeniable points of resemblance underlying these reflections on childhood in both authors.

Jean Paul

Childhood, and rather its terrors than its raptures, take wings and radiance again in dreams, and sport like fire-flies in the little night of the soul. Crush not these flickering sparks! – Leave us even our dark painful dreams as higher half-shadows of reality! – And wherewith will you replace to us *those* dreams that bear us away from under the tumult of the waterfall into the still heights of childhood, where the stream of life yet ran silent in its little plain, and flowed towards its abysses, a mirror of the Heaven? (*Siebenkäs*, *Werke*, II, 267)[10]

Carlyle

The young spirit has awakened out of Eternity, and knows not what we mean by Time ... ah! the secret of Vicissitude, of that slower or quicker decay and ceaseless down-rushing of the universal World-fabric, from the granite mountain to the man or day-moth, is yet unknown; and in a motionless Universe, we taste, what afterwards ... is forever denied us, the balm of Rest. Sleep on, thou fair Child, for thy long rough journey is at hand! (*Sartor*, 90)

The subsequent sublime landscapes end this comparative selection of a few representative samples chosen to show not direct but general similarities in mood and stylistic presentation:

Jean Paul

I stepped gloomily and wild out on the Brocken. The stars burnt down

Carlyle

Silence as of death ... for Midnight, even in the Arctic latitudes, has its the heavens and glowed around the sombre mountain-side. The mists of ancient days opened up, and I saw therein below on the wide plain innumerable stakes burning, chewing up innocent men. Around me lay piled up blocks of stone, like masonry of dismantled giant castles; and the Islandic moss of the cold zones covered the old naked mountainhead like mould of the earth. The storm snorted around me and my fluttering airship and blew wildly among the stars ... inside of me, I felt sublime and darkling, and I wished the devil would appear – .... I felt suddenly as if all the world and my life had dripped away in a few dreams, and my Me said to itself: I surely *am* the devil. (*Titan, Werke*, III, 965)[11]

character: nothing but the granite cliffs ruddy-tinged, the peaceable gurgle of that slow-heaving Polar Ocean, over which in the utmost North the great Sun hangs low and lazy ... yet does his light stream over the mirror of waters, like a tremulous fire-pillar, shooting downwards to the abyss ... In such moments, Solitude also is invaluable; for who would speak or be looked on, when behind him lies all Europe and Africa, fast asleep, except the watchmen; and before him the silent Immensity, and Palace of the Eternal, whereof our Sun is but a porch-lamp? (*Sartor*, 179)

There are other passages by Jean Paul that could easily be interwoven into the *Sartor* fabric without being detected as substitutes, not to mention the many acknowledged and unacknowledged quotes from Jean Paul C.F. Harrold partly annotated in his *Sartor* edition. Carlyle also takes an extensive loan of Jean Paul's vocabulary, a strange conglomeration of gifts, dropping out of a Horn of Plenty: Naphtafire, boluses, Gygersrings, a pair of *Gallia Braccata*, Dr Graham's Celestial-Bed, Rhizophagen, pagodas, *vomissement de la reine, Putz, an Entenpfuhl*, a reverberating furnace, Jacob's-ladder, Adamites, an *orbis pictus*, the Serpent of Eterity, Otaheitan, Memnon Statues, a Schreckhorn, Blumine, Staubbach Falls, Tartarean black, a Flowerclock, Fermenting vats, *a lit de justice, Handthierendes Thier* [*sic*], Crestomathie, a Loretto-shrine, a charnel house, Papin's Digester, *Gottesacker*, Dog-grottoes, a *Hiobspost*, Montgolfieren, Ugolino's Hungertower, *Kraftmänner*, Harmattan-winds, Basilisk-glances, *Wiener Schub, Springwurzeln*, Rikoschet-shots, Dionysius Ears, *Gukguk*, an iron ring of Necessity, Fetish-worship, *Kuhreigen*, a Phoenix, Dr Faust's mantle, four Russian sailors of Nova Zembla, and many others that occur and reoccur in Jean Paul's works as part of 'a style which, whether understood or not, could not even by the blindest be overlooked' (*Sartor* 8).

Unfortunately, after the serialization of *Sartor* in *Fraser's Magazine* (1833–4), the expected success of this innovative style turned out to be a barrier rather than an enticement for English readers. De Quincey's observation that Richter's style-was quite unfitted for general popularity proved to be right. Carlyle therefore decided to abandon the Jean Paulian model and headed for Carlylese. He announced this fact curtly to his brother John – 'I am altering my style' – on 21 September 1834.[12]

In *The French Revolution* the first modification is noticeable, but it lingers on, especially in the first volume: 'Yes, poor Louis, Death has found thee ... He is here, here at thy very life-breath, and will extinguish it. Thou, whose whole existence hitherto was a chimera and scenic show, at length becomes a reality: sumptuous Versailles bursts asunder, like a dream into void immensity' (I, 3). Jean Paul's *Weltbild* had made his style effective; now it waned, and for good reason. Carlyle was no longer concerned to the degree he had been previously with primarily transcendental and poetico-philosophical ideas. He had 'done with the Germans' and turned to less ethereal and more tangible topics for new inspiration, such as the matter of France and the matter of England. Never again did he employ two different styles in his works, except for brief and ineffective interludes by Sauerteig and his kin. Only then does his prophetic style, based on the preaching pattern of Elizabethan and Puritan divines, take over, characterized by strong polemics, which as an afterthought, he identified with James Carlyle's speech.

Carlyle had never slavishly followed Jean Paul. Several aspects of Richter's style remained unexplored by him. He never adopted it in its entirety, but Jean Paul provided the Jacob's-ladder on which Carlyle ascended to reach his own height.

APPENDIX

Table of Carlyle's Favourite Passages from Jean Paul's Works

These are by no means all of Jean Paul's passages that occur in Carlyle's writings, but they appear to be favourites. They have been chosen partly because of the frequency with which they occur and partly for their significance in the general context of Carlyle's works. Quotations appear in chronological order of publication in Jean Paul, *Werke*, vols. I–VI, edited by Norbert Miller (München: Carl Hanser 1959–63). *Wahrheit aus Jean Paul's Leben* (Breslau: Max 1825–8) and Jean Paul's 'Review of Mme de Stael's *De l'Allemagne*,' are quoted from the Berend Edition, Jean Paul, *Sämtliche Werke*, vol. 1/16 (Weimar: Böhlau 1927). Single matching Carlyle passages appear opposite the Jean Paul citation. In the case of several examples, a blank space is left beneath the initial source for easier identification. New passages found by the author are marked by an asterisk. Carlyle's two Richter essays are referred to as: '1st Richter' ('Jean Paul Friedrich Richter') and '2nd Richter' ('Jean Paul Friedrich Richter Again').

Jean Paul, *Hesperus*, vol. I, 490: Unendliche Vorsicht, du wirst Tag werden lassen. – Aber noch streitet die zwölfte Stunde der Nacht: die Nachtraubvögel ziehen; die Gespenster poltern; die Toten gaukeln; die Lebenden träumen.	Carlyle, *Essays II*, '2nd Richter,' 154: Infinite Providence, Thou wilt cause the day to dawn. But as yet struggles the twelfth-hour of the Night; nocturnal birds of prey are on the wing, spectres uproar, the dead walk, the living dream.
	Carlyle, *Essays III*, 'Characteristics,' 32: As yet struggles the twelfth hour of the Night: birds of darkness are on

	the wing, spectres uproar, the dead walk, the living dream. – Thou Eternal Providence, wilt cause the day to dawn!* Ibid., 42: Well might Jean Paul say in this his twelfth hour of the Night 'the living dream'; well might he say, 'the dead walk!'* Carlyle, *Hist. of Literature*, 225: But as yet are struggles.It is now the twelfth hour of the night; birds of darkness are on the wing, spectres uproar, the dead walk; the living dream. Thou, Eternal Providence wilt cause the day to dawn.* Carlyle, *Latter-Day Pamphlets*, Motto, 1850: But as yet struggles the twelfth hour of the night. Birds of darkness are on the wing; spectres uproar; the dead walk; the living dream. Thou, Eternal Providence, wilt make the day dawn!* Ibid., 231: (Variation on Jean Paul) Twelfth hour of the Night; ancient Graves yawning; pale clammy Puseyisms screeching in their winding sheets; owls busy in the City regions; many goblins abroad! Awake ye living; dream no more.*
Jean Paul, *Hesperus*, vol. I, 490: Ja, es wird ein anderes Zeitalter kommen, wo es licht wird und wo der Mensch aus erhabenen Träumen erwacht und die Träume – wiederfindet, weil er nichts verlor als den Schlaf.	Carlyle, *Essays II*, '2nd Richter,' 154: 'But there will come another era', says Paul, 'when it shall be light, and man will awaken from his lofty dreams, and find – his dreams still there, and nothing is gone save his sleep.'

Jean Paul, *Hesperus*, vol. I, 1132: Darum wird ja diese Erde alle Tage verfinstert, wie Käfige der Vögel, damit wir im Dunkeln leichter die höheren Melodien fassen.	Carlyle, *Essays II*, '2nd Richter,' 122: Fate manages Poets, as men do singing birds; you overhang the cage of the singer and make it dark, till at length he has caught the tunes you play to him, and can sing them rightly. Carlyle, *Essays I*, 'Burns,' 314: The canary bird sings sweeter the longer it has been trained in a darkened cage.*
Jean Paul, *Siebenkäs*, vol. II, 269: ('Rede des toten Christus') ... aber ich hörte nur den ewigen Sturm, den niemand regiert, und der schimmernde Regenbogen aus Wesen stand ohne eine Sonne, die ihn schuf, über dem Abgrunde und tropfte hinunter.	Carlyle, *Essays II*, '2nd Richter,' 157: But I heard only the everlasting storm which noone guides, and the gleaming Rainbow of Creation hung without a Sun that made it, over the Abyss, and trickled down. Carlyle, *Sartor*, 54: Creation, says one, lies before us, like a glorious Rainbow; but the Sun that made it lies behind us, hidden from us.

This passage dwells on the terrifying aspect of the cosmic scene:

Jean Paul, *Siebenkäs*, vol. II, ibid.: ('Rede des toten Christus') Und als ich aufblickte zur unermesslichen Welt nach dem göttlichen *Auge*, starrte sie mich mit einer leeren bodenlosen *Augenhöhle* an ...	Carlyle, *Essays II*, '2nd Richter,' 157: And when I looked up to the immeasurable world for the Divine *Eye*, it glared on me with an empty, black, bottomless *Eyesocket* ... Carlyle, *Essays III*, 'Diderot,' 230: (Combines this passage with the previous one) The unhappy man had ... felt only the rain-drops trickle down; and seen only the gleaming rainbow of Creation, which originated from the Sun; and heard only the everlasting

storm which no one governs; and looked upwards for the DIVINE EYE, and beheld only the black, bottomless, glaring EYE-SOCKET.*

Carlyle, *Sartor*, 216 (unidentified as J.P.'s):
'... hollow Shapes, or Masks, under which no living Figure or Spirit any longer dwells; but only spiders and unclean beetles, in horrid accumulation, drive their trade; and the mask still glares on you with its glass-eyes, in ghastly affectation of Life, –'*

Carlyle, *Sartor*, 235 (parts in quotes but unidentified as J.P.'s):
'... what with the so hateful "empty Masks," full of beetles and spiders, yet glaring out on him, from their glass eyes, "with a ghastly affectation of life" – '*

Carlyle, *French Rev*. I, 37 (as above re J.P.):
Meanwhile it is singular how long the rotten will hold together, provided you do not handle it roughly. For whole generations it continues standing, 'with a ghastly affectation of life', after all life and truth has fled out of it.*

Carlyle, *French Rev*. III, 223 (as above re J.P.):
... *shapes* some of which have bodies and life still in them; most of which, according to a German Writer, have only emptiness, 'glass-eyes glaring on you with a ghastly affectation of life, and in their interior unclean accumulation of beetles and spiders!'*

	Carlyle, *Essays IV*, 'Opera,' 402: Behind its glitter stalks the shadow of Eternal Death; through it too, I look not 'up into the divine eye', as Richter has it, but down into the bottomless eye-socket.'
Jean Paul, *Siebenkäs*, vol. II, 431: Die unendlichen Kräfte ziehen wie Ströme gegeneinander und begegnen sich wirbelnd und brausend, und auf den ewigen Wirbeln laufen die kleinen Erden um den Sonnenstrudel.	Carlyle, *Essays II*, 'Signs of the Times,' 59 (unidentified as J.P.'s): The poorest Day that passes over us is the conflux of two Eternities; it is made up of currents that issue from the remotest Past and flow onwards into the remotest Future. Carlyle, *Sartor*, 65–6 (unidentified): Stands he not thereby in the centre of Immensities, in the conflux of Eternities? Carlyle, *French Rev.* I, 9: ... he stood thereby, though 'in the centre of Immensities, in the conflux of Eternities', yet manlike towards God and man.* Ibid., I, 134 (not identified): As indeed what wonders lie in every Day, – had we the sight ... to decipher it: for is not every meanest Day 'the conflux of two eternities!*
Jean Paul, *Siebenkäs*, II, 271: ... sah ich die emporgehobenen Ringe der Riesenschlange der Ewigkeit, die sich um das Welten-All gelagert hatte – und die Ringe fielen nieder, und sie umfasste das All doppelt –	Carlyle, *Essays II*, '2nd Richter,' 158: I saw the upborne Rings of the Giant-Serpent, the Serpent of Eternity, which had coiled itself round the All of Worlds, – and the rings sank down, and encircled the All doubly. Carlyle, *Sartor*, 203: '... mistaking the ill-cut Serpent-of-Eternity for a common poisonous reptile.'

Jean Paul, *Siebenkäs*, II, 299: Ein Mann kann ein Weltbürger sein und ... seine Brust an den ganzen Erdball drücken.	Carlyle, *Sartor*, 32: ... he could clasp the whole Universe into his bosom, and keep it warm.
Jean Paul, *Siebenkäs*, vol. II, 270: Wie ist jeder so allein in der weiten Leichengruft des Alles! Ich bin nur neben mir – O Vater!	Carlyle, *Essays II*, '2nd Richter,' 157: How is each so solitary in this wide grave of the All! I am alone with myself! O Father! Carlyle, *Past and Present*, Bk IV, ch. 4, 275: 'How is each of us', exclaims Jean Paul, 'so lonely in the wide bosom of the All! Encased each as in his transparent "ice-palace!" '*
Jean Paul, *Siebenkäs*, vol. II, 271: ('Rede des toten Christus') Und als ich niederfiel und ins leuchtende Weltgebäude blickte ... und alles wurde eng, düster, bang – und ein unermesslich ausgedehnter Glockenhammer sollte die letzte Stunde der Zeit schlagen und das Weltgebäude zersplittern ... als ich erwachte.	Carlyle, *Essays II*, '2nd Richter,' 158: And as I fell down and looked into the sparkling Universe – and all grew straight, dark, fearful – and an immeasurably extended Hammer was to strike the last hour of Time, and shiver the Universe asunder, ... WHEN I AWOKE.
Jean Paul, *Titan* (*Anhang*), vol. III, 956: Die deutsche Geschichte sagt uns, dass der Adel sonst vom 'Sattel oder Stehgreif' lebte, nämlich vom Rauben unter freiem Himmel.	Carlyle, *Essays II*, 'Early Germ. Lit.,' 311 Herein dwelt a race of persons ... who boasting of an endless pedigree, talked familiarly of living on the produce of their 'Saddles' (*vom Sattel zu leben*), that is to say, by the profession of highwayman.*
Jean Paul, *Fixlein*, vol. IV, 18: Überhaupt denkt der Mensch hundertmal, er habe den alten Adam ausgezogen, indes er ihn nur zurückgeschlagen.	Carlyle, *Sartor*, 183: Not so easily can the old Adam, lodged in us by birth, be dispossessed.*

Jean Paul, *Fixlein*, vol. IV, 161: ... den Übergang vom Nichts zum Sein, von der Ewigkeit in die Zeit ...	Carlyle, *Germ. Romance*, II, 299–300: ... the transition from nothingness to Existence, from Eternity to Time. Carlyle, *Sartor*, 21: *Aus der Ewigkeit, zu der Ewigkeit hin*: From Eternity, onwards to Eternity!
Jean Paul, *Fixlein*, vol. IV, 81: Am Morgen hatt' er perennierende, feuerbeständige Freuden, das heisst, Geschäfte.	Carlyle, *Essays IV*, 'Dr. Francia,' 290: Francia, like Quintus Fixlein, had 'perennial fire-proof joys,' namely employments.*
Jean Paul, *Fixlein*, vol. IV, 190: Mein Freund entwich mit der Seele die er liebt – ich blieb allein zurück bei der Nacht.	Carlyle, *Essays I*, '1st Richter,' 23–4: My friend retired with the soul whom he loves. I remained alone behind with the night. Carlyle, *Sartor*, 151: '... in my friend Richter's words, *I remained alone, behind them, with the Night.*'
Jean Paul, *Fixlein*, vol. IV, 116: ... bis die zwei Seelen, in vier Arme verstrickt, wie Tränen ineinanderrannen.	Carlyle, *Germ. Romance*, II, 253: ... and their two souls, like two tears, melted into one. Carlyle, *Sartor*, 145: ... their two souls, like two dewdrops, rushed into one, –
Jean Paul, *Fixlein*, vol. IV, 151: O du, der du noch einen Vater oder eine Mutter hast, danke Gott an dem Tage dafür, wo deine Seele voll Freudentränen ist, und eine Brust bedarf, an der sie sie vergiessen kann ...	Carlyle, *Essays I*, '1st Richter,' 8: O thou who has still a father or a mother, thank God for it on the day when thy soul is full of joyful tears, and needs a bosom wherein to shed them.
Jean Paul, *Fixlein*, vol. IV, 91: ... sind der furchtsam-andächtigen Phantasie Klänge aus dem Himmel, Singstimmen der Engel in den Lüften, Kirchenmusik des morgentlichen Gottesdienstes.	Carlyle, *Germ. Romance*, II, 226–7: ... for the timidly devout Fancy, sounds out of Heaven; singing voices of the Angels in the air, church music of the morning worship.

	Carlyle, *Sartor*, 254: Listen, and for organ-music thou wilt ever, as of old, hear the Morning Stars sing together.
Jean Paul, *Fixlein*, vol. IV, 74: Wie in Indien die Pagode zugleich den Tempel und den Gott bedeutet.	Carlyle, *Germ. Romance*, II, 207: ... as in India the Pagoda at once represents the temple and the God. Carlyle, *Sartor*, 240: Even as, for Hindoo Worshippers, the Pagoda is not less sacred than the God.
Jean Paul, *Fixlein*, vol. IV, 73: Nirgends sammelt man die Not- und Belagerungsmünzen der Armut lustiger and philosophischer als auf der Universität: der akademische Bürger tut dar, wie viel Humoristen und Diogenesse Deutschland habe.	Carlyle, *Essays II*, '2nd Richter,' 120: Nowhere can you collect the stress-memorials and siege-medals of Poverty more pleasantly than at College: the Academic Bursche exhibit to us how many Humorists and Diogeneses Germany has in it. (Includes a long footnote on the topic)
Jean Paul, *Fixlein*, vol. IV, 157: Damals wars die Wintergeschichte der vier russischen Matrosen auf Nova Zembla.	Carlyle, *Germ. Romance* II, 295: On the present occasion it was the winter history of the four Russian sailors on Nova Zembla. Carlyle, *Essays III*, 'On History Again,' 168: From Cape Horn to Nova Zembla.' Carlyle, *Sartor*, 188: Sweeter than Dayspring to the Shipwrecked in Nova Zembla.
Jean Paul, *Fixlein*, vol. IV, 76: Mädchen ohne grosse Welt ... verehren uns unendlich ...	Carlyle, *Germ. Romance* II, 209: Young women without the polish of high life ... reverence us unfinitely. Carlyle, *Past and Present*, 55: Thus it has been said, 'all men, especially all women, are born worshippers.'*

Jean Paul, *Fixlein*, vol. IV, 72: Der Senior kam dann ... auf die Aktenstücke seines akademischen Lebens, dessen sich solche Leute so gern wie Dichter der Kindheit erinnern.	Carlyle, *Germ. Romance*, II, 204: The Senior made a soft transition ... to the golden age of his Academic life, of which such people like as much to think, as poets do of their childhood. Carlyle, *Essays II*, '2nd Richter,' 107 (not marked as J.P. quote): To our professor, as to poets in general, the recollections of childhood had always something of an ideal, almost celestial character. Carlyle, *Sartor*, 91: In such rose-coloured light does our Professor, as Poets are wont, look back on his childhood.*
Jean Paul, *Fixlein*, vol. IV, 191: ... und alles ist göttlich oder Gott.	Carlyle, *Sartor*, 188: ... but godlike, and my Father's! Carlyle, *Heroes*, 9: 'All was Godlike or God:' – Jean Paul still finds it so.*
Jean Paul, *Vorschule d. Ästhetik*, vol. V, 277: Luthers Prose ist eine halbe Schlacht; wenige Taten gleichen seinen Worten.	Carlyle, *Essays II*, 'Luther's Psalm,' 161 (unacknowledged): Whose words, it has been said, were half battles. Carlyle, *Essays II*, 'Goethe's Works,' 425: The Luther, 'whose words were half battles,' and such half battles as could shake and overset half Europe.* Carlyle, *Hist. of Lit.*, 138: ... and though his words were half battles, as Jean Paul says, stronger than artillery.*

	Carlyle, *Heroes*, 139: Richter says of Luther's words, 'his words are half-battles.' They may be called so.*
Jean Paul, *Levana*, vol. V, 632: Wenn Rubens durch einen Strich ein lachendes Kind in ein weinendes verkehrte.	Carlyle, *Essays I*, '1st Richter,' 15 (unacknowledged): Like Rubens, by a single stroke he can change a laughing face into a sad one.*
Jean Paul, *Levana*, vol. V, 639: Wenn in euerer letzten Stunde, bedenkt es, alles im abgebrochenen Geiste abblüht und herabstirbt, Dichten, Denken, Streben, Freuen: so grünt endlich nur noch die Nachtblume des Glaubens fort und stärkt mit Duft im letzten Dunkel.	Carlyle, *Notebooks*, 114–15: When in your last hour (think of this) all within the broken spirit shall fade away, and die into inanity, Imagining, Thinking, Endeavouring, Enjoying – then at last blooms on the night-flower of Belief alone, and refreshes with its perfume in the last darkness.* Carlyle, *Essays I*, '1st Richter,' 22–3: 'When in your last hour' says he, (think of this), all faculty in the broken spirit shall fade away and die into inanity, – imagination, thought, effort, enjoyment, – then at last will the night-flower of Belief alone continue blooming, and refresh with its perfumes in the last darkness.'
Jean Paul, *Levana*, vol. V, 570: ... aus der Welt wurde uns ein Weltgebäude, aus dem Äther ein Gas, aus Gott eine Kraft, aus der zweiten Welt ein Sarg.	Carlyle, *Notebooks*, 114 (marked 'Jean Paul, *Levana*'): Of the world for us, is made a world-edifice; of the Aether a Gas; of God a Power; and of the second world a Coffin. – Carlyle, *Essays II*, 'Novalis,' 54: As Jean Paul has it, 'of the World will be made a world-machine, of the Aether a gas, of God a Force, and of the Second-World – a Coffin.'

	Carlyle, *Essays III*, 'Characteristics,' 34 (unacknowledged): But whether is Virtue a fluid, then, or a Gas?* Carlyle, *Essays III*, 'Diderot,' 234 'of the aether make a gas, of God a Force, of the second world a coffin'; of man an aimless nondescript.* Carlyle, *Essays IV*, 'Chartism,' 196: Is God, as Jean Paul predicted it would be, become verily a Force; the Aether too a Gas!* Carlyle, *Hist. of Lit.*, 191: As Jean Paul says, 'Heaven became a gas, God a force, the second world a grave.'*
Jean Paul, *Levana*, vol. V, 566: Friedrich der Einzige soll die Flöte nehmen, und Napoleon den Ossian.	Carlyle, *Notebooks*, 114 (not identified): Thus let Frederick the Only (der Einzige) take his flute, and Napoleon his Ossian.*
Jean Paul, *Schmelzle*, vol. VI, 65: 'O, du Löwin', sagt' ich im Liebesrausch, 'warum bist du in keiner Todesgefahr, damit ich dir nun den Löwen zeigte als Gemahl.'	Carlyle, *Germ. Romance*, II, 189: 'O thou Lioness!' said I, in the transport of love, 'why hast thou never been in any deadly peril, that I might show thee the Lion in thy husband?' Carlyle, *Essays I*, 'Life of Heyne,' 341: 'O thou lioness!' said Attila Schmelzle ... 'why hast thou never been in any deadly peril, that I might show thee the lion in the husband?'*
Jean Paul, *Schmelzle*, vol. VI, 20: Ich geriet ... nach Matzleinsdorf (einer Wiener Vorstadt).	Carlyle, translates, in *Germ. Romance*, II, 142, 'I arrived in Malzleins,' instead of 'Matzleinsdorf,' as in the original, and repeats this mistake in *Sartor*.

	Carlyle, *Sartor*, 155): I have awakened in Paris *Estrapades* and Vienna *Malzleins* ...
Jean Paul, *Schmelzle*, vol. VI, 30, fn. 103: Oder sind alle Moscheen, Episkopalkirchen, Pagoden, Filialkirchen, Stiftshütten und Panthea etwas anderes als der Heidenvorhof zum unsichtbaren Tempel und zu dessen Allerheiligsten?	Carlyle, *Essays I*, '1st Jean Paul,' 22: Or are all your Mosques, Episcipal Churches, Pagodas, Chapels of Ease [!] Tabernacles, and Pantheons, anything else but the Ethnic Forecourt of the Invisible Temple and its Holy of Holies?
Jean Paul, *Schmelzle*, vol. VI, 44, fn. 11: Das goldne Kalb der Selbstsucht wächst bald zum glühenden Phalaris-Ochsen, der seinen Vater und Anbeter einäschert.	Carlyle, *Germ. Romance*, II, 166, fn. 11: The Golden Calf of Self-love soon waxes to be a burning Phalaris' Bull, which reduces his father and adorer to ashes. Carlyle, *Essays IV*, 'Scott,' 53: The Golden Calf of Self-love has grown into a burning Phalaris' Bull, to consume its owner and worshipper.* Carlyle, *Heroes*, 173: ... 'wherein, as in the detestable belly of some Phalaris'-Bull of his own contriving, he the poor Phalaris sits miserably dying!'* Carlyle, *Past and Present*, Bk. III, ch. 13, 210–11 (unidentified): Laissez-faire: it is to die slowly all our life long, imprisoned in a deaf, dead, Infinite Injustice, as in the accursed iron belly of a Phalaris' Bull!*
Jean Paul, *Selberlebensbeschr.*, vol. VI, 1061: An einem Vormittag stand ich als ein sehr junges Kind unter der Haustüre und sah links nach der Holzlege, als auf einmal das innere	Carlyle, *Essays II*, '2nd Richter,' 111: One forenoon, I was standing, a very young child, in the outer door, and looking leftward at the stack of the fuel-wood, – when all at once the internal vision, 'I am a ME (*Ich*

Gesicht 'ich bin ein Ich' wie ein Blitzstrahl vom Himmel vor mich fuhr und seitdem leuchtend stehen blieb.	*bin ein Ich*), 'came like a flash from heaven before me, and in gleaming light ever afterwards continued.
Jean Paul, *Siebenkäs*, vol. II, 430: Was bist du jetzo, Ich?	Carlyle, *Sartor*, 53: 'Who am I; what is this ME?' A loose rendering of both passages is presented by Carlyle in *Sartor* (ibid.): 'With men of a speculative turn,' writes Teufelsdröckh, 'there come seasons, meditative, sweet, yet awful hours, when in wonder and fear you ask yourself that unanswerable question: Who am *I*; the thing that can say "I" (*das Wesen das sich* ICH *nennt*)? ...' Much of Jean Paul's context is worked into this passage. Carlyle, *Heroes*, 54: – no hearsays could hide that unspeakable fact 'Here am I! '... What am I? What is this unfathomable thing I live in, which men name Universe?'
Jean Paul, *Selberlebensbeschr.*, vol. VI, 1044: Reichtum lastet mehr das Talent als Armut und unter Goldbergen und Thronen liegt vielleicht manch geistiger Riese erdrückt begraben ... so wird wenig mehr als Asche vom Phönix übrig bleiben.	Carlyle, *Essays II*, '2nd Richter,' 122: 'Wealth bears heavier on talent than Poverty; under gold-mountains and thrones, who knows how many a spiritual giant may lie crushed down and buried!' – little will remain of the Phoenix but his ashes.*
Jean Paul, *Selberlebensbeschr.*, vol. VI, 1046: ... dieselben Sonnenstrahlen des Genius, die am Morgen seines Lebens in ihm wie in einem Memnons-Bild Wohllaute weckten.	Carlyle, *Sartor*, 143: As from Aeolian Harps in the breath of dawn, as from the Memnon's Statue struck by the rosy finger of Aurora, unearthly music was around him ...

Jean Paul, *Selberlebensbeschr.*, vol. VI, 1044: In meinen historischen Vorlesungen wird zwar das Hungern immer stärker vorkommen.	Carlyle, *Essays II*, '2nd Richter,' 122: 'In my Historical Lectures,' says Jean Paul, 'the business of Hungering will in truth more and more make its appearance.' Carlyle, *French Rev.*, I, 232: As Jean Paul says of his own life 'to a great height shall this business of Hungering go.'*
Jean Paul, *Selberlebensbeschr.*, vol. VI 1048: Leider weiss ich seinen Namen längst nicht mehr; aber da es doch möglich wäre, dass er noch lebte und als Gelehrter diese Vorlesungen im Druck vorbekäme ...	Carlyle, *Sartor*, 89: since books ... permeate the whole habitable globe ... may not some Copy find out the ... Stranger, who in a state of extreme senility perhaps still exists ...
Jean Paul, *Wahrheit*, Bd. I, Heft 2, fn. 15 Ich war in der Jugend schlimmer daran als ein Gefangener, der Wasser und Brot hat; denn nur erstes hatt' ich.	Carlyle, *Essays II*, '2nd Richter,' 120: 'The prisoner's allowance,' says he, 'is bread and water; but I had only the latter. Carlyle, *Essays III*, 'Heyne,' 202: The Heynes dining on boiled peascods, the Jean Pauls on water.* Carlyle, *Past and Present*, 263: ... as I have known brave Jean-Pauls, learning their exercise, to live on 'water *without* the bread.'* Carlyle, *Hist. of Lit.*, 223: He says: 'In gaols the prisoner's allowance is bread and water. I had the latter but not the former.'* Carlyle, *Essays I*, 'Burns,' 314: 'I would not for much,' says Jean Paul, 'that I had been born richer' ... he adds 'The prisoner's allowance is bread and water, and I had often only the latter.'*

Jean Paul	Carlyle
Jean Paul, *Wahrheit*, Bd. I, Heft 2, 33: Ich habe vieles geschildert, aber ich sterbe ohne die Schweiz gesehen zu haben und das Meer und, etc. Doch das Meer der Ewigkeit werd' ich in jedem Fall zu sehen bekommen.	Carlyle, *Essays II*, '2nd Richter,' 141: 'I have described so much,' he says elsewhere, 'and I die without ever having seen Switzerland and the Ocean, and so many other sights. But the Ocean of Eternity I shall not fail to see.'
Jean Paul, *Wahrheit*, Bd. I, Heft 2, 37: Die Stelle im Shakespear: 'Mit Schlaf umgeben', von Plattner aus-gesprochen, erschuf ganze Bücher von mir.	Ibid., 154: 'The passage of Shakspeare,' says he, '*rounded with a sleep*' (*mit Schlaf umgeben*), in Plattner's mouth, cre-ated whole books in me.'
Jean Paul, *Wahrheit*, Bd. III, Heft 3, 46: Wer einen Gott in der physischen Welt findet, findet auch einen in der moralischen, welches die Geschichte ist: die Natur dringt unserm Herzen einen Schöpfer, die Geschichte eine Vorsehung auf.	Carlyle, *Essays II*, '2nd Richter,' 113 fn.: He who finds a God in the physical world will also find one in the moral, which is History. Nature forces on our heart a Creator; His-tory a Providence.
Jean Paul, (Behrend edn.) Bd., I/16, 302 (*Rezensionen*: 'Mme de Staël, De l'Allemagne'): da unsere gelehrten Lichter von den Franzosen nicht als Leuchtsterne an-gebetet wurden, sondern als Leucht-käfer angesteckt, so wie man die surinamischen zum Wegbeleuchten aufgespiesst trägt.	Carlyle, *Essays I*, 'Mme de Stael,' 481: Our learned lights have been by the French not adored like light-stars, but stuck into like light-chafers, as people carry those of Surinam, spit-ted through, for lighting of roads.* Carlyle, *Heroes*, 195: Richter says, in the Island of Suma-tra there is a kind of 'Light-chafers', large Fireflies, which people stick upon spits, and illuminate the ways with at night. Great honour to the Fire-flies! But –!*

The following entries give two examples of rather unique combination passages, employing a phrase from Goethe and three from Jean Paul, resulting in very effective adaptations by Carlyle.

Goethe, *WM Lehrjahre*, vol. VII, *Werke*, 495:
Der Vorhang riss sich schneller auf ...

Carlyle, *Meister*, II, 74:
The curtain dashed asunder ...

Jean Paul, *Siebenkäs*, vol. II, 266:
Das ganze geistige Universum ... zersprengt und zerschlagen.

Carlyle, *Essays II*, '2nd Richter,' 155:
The whole spiritual universe is dashed asunder ...

Jean Paul, *Siebenkäs*, vol. II, 268:
Am Himmel hing in grossen Falten bloss ein grauer schwüler Nebel.

Carlyle, *Essays II*, '2nd Richter,' 156:
Over the whole heaven hung, in large folds, a grey sultry mist.

Jean Paul, *Siebenkäs*, vol. II, 269:
– die zitternden Tempelmauern rückten auseinander.

Carlyle, *Essays II*, '2nd Richter,' 157:
– the quivering walls of the Temple parted asunder.

Adaptation I

Carlyle, *Sartor*, 145–6:
– 'thick curtains of Night rushed over his soul, as rose the immeasurable Crash of Doom; and through the ruins as of a shivered Universe was he falling, falling, towards the Abyss.'

Adaptation II

Carlyle, *Past and Present*, 125:
impenetrable Time-Curtains rush down; in the mind's eye all is again dark, void; with loud dinning in the mind's ear, our real-phantasmagory of St Edmundsbury plunges into the bosom of the Twelfth Century again, and all is over.

TEN

Concluding Remarks

> And how he studied us Germans! He is almost more at home in our literature than we ourselves.
>
> (Eckermann, *Gespräche*)

It appears from this reinterpretation of Carlyle's affinities with German Romantic writers that he is not only indebted to them for transcendental ideas and poetic-emblematic vision, but also for their critical approaches and fictional techniques in a manner that cannot be written off as negligible. By grouping these influences according to themes, their breadth as well as the intensity of their impact becomes increasingly clear. In some instances, it appears that Carlyle gleaned similar impressions from several writers, so that one might speak of a collective or cumulative effect; in other cases, a novel idea attracts Carlyle in a single author. Regardless, these writers have all contributed to his unified view of German Romantic literature.

Novelty in concept and form in his German sources attracted Carlyle. Here he found new ideas and new means to express them. From his immediate response at the time of the first impact, it seems unlikely that he approached German literature in order to seek confirmation of his beliefs. More or less stumbling into it in an effort to acquaint himself with German scientific writings, he unexpectedly met with spiritual illumination. Nobody who had merely run into old familiar truths would speak of a 'New Evangel.' If Carlyle was a born Calvinist, he was far from being a practising one when he was introduced to these sources. Indeed, it was precisely his dissatisfaction with orthodox religion that led him to appreciate these broader vistas of spirituality that had suddenly opened up to him.

The stimulating influence of this new literature was, however, not restricted to transcendental verities applicable to his own personal struggles, but resulted in general intellectual growth. It is time to discard the notion of Carlyle the ignoramus blindly perusing works that would yield their deeper meaning only to those capable of intense and searching study. Instead of belittling his mental faculties, one is inclined to agree with Goethe's judgment: besides recognizing Carlyle as a great moral force, long before this tendency had clearly manifested itself, he spoke to Eckermann of Carlyle's penetrative literary interpretations.[1]

This brings us to the share individual German Romantic writers had in influencing Carlyle's literary and moral vision. Within the field of criticism, Friedrich Schlegel is a contributor by way of the critical standards and techniques he adds to Carlyle's native biographical notions. Franz Horn, no longer to be classed as 'an exceedingly unimportant critic,'[2] foreshadows several of Carlyle's critical judgments and provides more than mere tags for 'the Everlasting No' and 'the Everlasting Yes' by presenting insights into the whole process of the dynamic struggle Carlyle had left unexplained. The same holds good for Fouqué, in the sense of a feasible hypothesis.

From the evidence presented, Goethe's seminal influence emerges as second to none, so that Carlyle's outbursts of gratitude, his 'endless indebtedness' appear to be more than just an empty phrase. Besides acting as a *Lebensführer* in *Wilhelm Meister*, with broader vistas of spirituality in the 'Schöne Seele' chapters, he contributes most fruitfully to Carlyle's 'Seedfield of Time,' especially through the 'Garment of God' symbolism in *Faust*, and the Doubt-Faith pattern, as it reveals itself in personal spiritual struggle, and evolves in different periods of history.

Jean Paul's importance is restricted to *Sartor Resartus* where he makes a considerable contribution by way of his theory of humour, evident in the eccentric personality of Teufelsdröckh, besides adding to the idyllic setting of his youth, and to the love concept that unfolds in the Blumine chapters. Above all, he leaves his mark on Carlyle's style by supplying extravaganzas of technique that suited the latter's temperament and humorous disposition.

Moving away from the purely theoretical *Wissenschaftslehre*, Fichte reveals himself most effectively in his popular works, such as *Die Bestimmung des Menschen*, which is shown to have provided much of the philosophical backbone of the autobiographical *Sartor* chapters, lending strength and conviction to the process of spiritual despair and rebirth. His influence on the notion of hero-worship appears to be slight. The 'Divine Idea,' applied as an overall concept, is more important for the clothes philosophy than for *On Heroes*, where the personalities chosen by Carlyle have little in common with Fichte's Stoic scholars described in *Über das Wesen des Gelehrten*.

Schelling's notions on the cyclic pattern of Palingenesia, or rebirth of Society, as discussed in *Über die Methode*, must be considered as a more likely source for Carlyle than Fichte's *Grundzüge des gegenwärtigen Zeitalters*. Additional light has been shed on Carlyle's 'Centre of Indifference' by arguments related to the use of the term 'Centrum des Gleichgewichts' that appear in Schelling's book *Von der Weltseele*, which Carlyle had read.

Novalis's influence goes beyond the few striking *Fragmente* he is usually given credit for. While his magical idealism in its initial form is practically lost on Carlyle, he leaves a visible mark on Carlylean notions of Palingenesia, and the religiously conceived hero-worship underlying *Past and Present* through his contribution in *Die Christenheit oder Europa*.

Tieck, Hoffmann, and Hauff must be considered as secondary influences, less spectacular but no less effective, as evinced in numerous noteworthy details. A presentation of the neglected Werner yielded a more satisfactory explanation of the test situation behind the 'Baphometic Fire-baptism,' besides solving the 'stomach-soul' riddle that has long perplexed scholars as to its origins.

It goes without saying that Carlyle does not use these various influences in a mechanical fashion. His method may tentatively be called one of selective application. In other words, there is growth beyond the initial stimulus received. The creative act, in the Coleridgean sense, begins where Carlyle absorbs and reshapes the newly discovered materials to suit his own vision. In the course of this transformation, significant changes occur, but not always. It therefore must be considered as a generalization when Harrold insists that Carlyle 'touched nothing that de did not alter.'[3] Goethe's concept of reverence remains basically unchanged, as do Fichte's 'Divine Idea' and Jean Paul's notions on the idyllic. The above statement therefore needs to be qualified to the effect that the novel context in which Carlyle employs ideas as well as techniques makes all the difference. In addition, the undefinable, ever-active quality of genius prevents him from deteriorating into an imitator of Goethe, Jean Paul, or Fichte.

A word from the poet whom Carlyle considered to be his spiritual guide may be fitting here, to set the nature of any influences into proper perspective: 'We bring certain abilities with us, but our development we owe to a hundred impressions of a great world from which we gather what we can and what is in conformity with our own nature.'[4] Interpreted in this light, Carlyle's peculiar talent was enhanced, not impaired, by the 'spiritual commerce' that took place between himself and his German sources. For this reason they will always remain of value to scholars and general readers interested in the genesis of Thomas Carlyle's early works.

Notes

Preface

1 As late as 1989, I read in the Introduction to the Oxford University Press paperback edition of *The French Revolution*, edited by Fielding and Sorensen, that Goebbels tried to console Hitler in the Berlin bunker by reading *Frederick the Great* to him. Such comments do not serve any literary purpose. Hundreds of unworthy characters have read Carlyle, and as many worthy ones, each according to his or her own wit, without affecting his standing as a writer. Who would fairly evaluate Seneca's *Epistolae morales* in the light of his having had Nero as a pupil?

2 Wellek, *Confrontations*, 36

3 Storrs, *Relation of Carlyle to Kant and Fichte*, 61, 100

4 Carlyle, *Essays I*, 'State of German Literature,' 83

5 Within my framework it is impossible to deal with them, especially when they lack legitimate foundations. The so-called correspondences between Carlyle's utterances and those of the French Romantics appear far-fetched, as such claims completely disregard the time factor. Romantic theories originate in England and Germany first and are adopted much later in France and Italy, because of the strong neoclassical roots in these countries. For this reason, any similarities appear *after*, not *before* the time span in question, and could not have served as a model for Carlyle, who unequivocally proclaimed his indebtedness to his German authors.

6 Harrold, *Carlyle and German Thought*, Preface, v

7 Espinasse, *Literary Recollections*, 220

8 Carlyle, *Essays I*, 'State of German Literature,' 77

9 Espinasse, *Literary Recollections*, 220

10 MacCunn, *Six Radical Thinkers*, 141

Introduction

1 Although R. Wellek has, in passing, drawn attention to Carlyle's unified view of German literature, he does not probe into the reasons for his taking this approach; nor does he investigate how it relates to other contemporary opinion (Wellek, *Confrontations*, 50). R. Ashton, in *The German Idea*, where only thirty-two pages are given to a discussion of Carlyle's contribution, avoids the issue. Restricting her comments to Goethe and German philosophy, as far as German influences are concerned, she offers no more than a few generalizations, in a study best classified as being of the historical-survey type. In her brief section on *Sartor Resartus* she concedes that Carlyle, in later years, 'still followed the custom of heading his works and rounding off articles with German phrases,' (p. 99), but offers no evidence.

2 *Correspondence between Goethe and Carlyle*, 190–1

3 Joachimi, *Weltanschauung*, 3: 'Die Romantik und der Klassizismus eines Goethe und Schiller sind deshalb nicht als Gegenteile, sondern als zwei sich ergänzende Seiten zu verstehen.'

4 Carlyle, *Essays I*, 'State of German Literature,' 65

5 Ibid., 'Goethe,' 212

6 Ibid., 'Goethe,' 208

7 F. Schlegel, *Kritische Ausgabe II*, 'Über Goethes *Meister*,' 133

8 Ibid., 'Gespräch über die Poesie,' 346

9 Carlyle, *Essays I*, 'Goethe,' 230

10 Goethe, *Maximen und Reflexionen*, no. 863 *Werke*, XII, 487

11 Eckermann, *Gespräche*, 21 March 1830, vol. 2, 31–2: 'Der Begriff von klassischer und romantischer Poesie, der jetzt über die ganze Welt geht und so viel Streit und Spaltungen verursacht ... ist ursprünglich von mir und Schiller ausgegangen ... [Schiller] bewies mir, dass ich selber wider Willen romantisch sei ... Die Schlegel ergriffen die Idee und trieben sie weiter, so dass sie sich denn jetzt über die ganze Welt ausgedehnt hat und nun jedermann von Klassizimus und Romantizismus redet, woran vor fünfzig Jahren niemand dachte.' The English translation is mine, as is the case hereafter unless stated otherwise.

12 Carlyle, *Essays I*, 'Helena,' 146. Written for the *Foreign Review*, 1828. Carlyle points out the significance of Goethe's subtitle and translates it as 'a classico-romantic Phantasmagoria.'

13 F. Schlegel, *Kritische Ausgabe* II, 333: '... was uns einen sentimentalen Stoff in einer fantastischen Form darstellt.'

14 Horn, *Umrisse*, 66: '... die Vernichtung alles irreligiösen, antiphilosophischen und antipoetischen 'Philisterthums' ... das nicht errötet selbst dem höchsten Wesen mittelmässige Zwecke zu leihen.'

15 Carlyle, *German Romance I*, 261
16 Carlyle, *Essay III*, 'Characteristics,' 41
17 Carlyle, *Unfinished History of German Literature*, 11
18 De Staël, *Germany*, II, 370
19 Carlyle, *Essays I*, 'State of German Literature,' 33
20 Ibid., 'Goethe,' 246
21 Carlyle, *German Romance II*, 118
22 Carlyle, *Essays II*, 'Novalis,' 28–9
23 Carlyle, *Essays I*, 'Life and Writings of Werner,' 115

Chapter One

1 Kellner, *Die englische Literatur*, 'Carlyle,' ch. 5, 133
2 Roe, *Carlyle as a Critic*, 59
3 Friedrich Schlegel, *Prosaische Jugendschriften*, Introduction, v
4 Mme de Staël, *Germany*, vol. 2, ch. xxxi
5 See Carlyle, *Notebooks*: on F. Schlegel, 37, 42, 83, 104, 129, 135; on A.W. Schlegel, 258.
6 *Athenaeum* I, 106
7 F. Schlegel, *Kritische Ausgabe II*, 257, no. 8: 'Ganz recht, die Fantasie ist das Organ des Menschen für die Gottheit.'
8 All quotes taken from F. Schlegel, *Kritische Ausgabe II*, 256–72:

Nur durch Beziehung aufs Unendliche entsteht Gehalt und Nutzen; was sich nicht darauf bezieht, ist schlechthin leer und unnütz. (no. 3)

Also heiligen Samen streuet in den Boden des Geistes, ohne Künstelei und müssige Ausfüllungen. (no. 5)

Wie die Kaufleute im Mittelalter so sollten die Künstler jetzt zusammentreten zu einer Hanse, um sich einigermassen gegenseitig zu schützen. (no. 142)

Das Universum kann man weder erklären noch begreifen, nur anschauen und offenbaren. Höret nur auf das System der Empirie Universum zu nennen, und lernt die wahre religiöse Idee desselben. (no. 150)

O wie armselig sind eure – ich meine die Besten unter euch – eure Begriffe vom Genie. Wo ihr Genie findet, finde ich nicht selten die Fülle der falschen Tendenzen, das Zentrum der Stümperei. (no. 141)

Nur diejenige Verworrenheit ist ein Chaos, aus der eine Welt entspringen kann. (no. 71)

Als Bibel wird das neue Evangelium erscheinen, von dem Lessing geweissagt hat ... Das kann es nicht ohne Göttliches, und darin stimmt der esoterische Begriff selbst mit dem exoterischen überein. (no. 95)

Ihr staunt über das Zeitalter, über die gährende Riesenkraft, über die Erschütterungen, und wisst nicht welche neue Geburten ihr erwarten sollt. (no. 50)

Ein Geistlicher ist, wer nur im Unsichtbaren lebt, für wen alles Sichtbare nur die Wahrheit einer Allegorie hat. (no. 2)

Poesie und Philosophie sind ... verschiedne Sphären, verschiedne Formen, oder auch die Faktoren der Religion. Denn versucht es nur beide wirklich zu verbinden, und ihr werdet nichts anders erhalten als Religion. (no. 46)

Wer Religion hat wird Poesie reden. Aber um sie zu suchen und zu entdecken, ist Philosophie das Werkzeug. (no. 34)

Nicht auf der Grenze schwebst du, sondern in deinem Geiste haben sich Poesie und Philosophie innig durchdrungen. (no. 156)

9 Carlyle, *Essays I*, 'Goethe,' 230" 'Some day we may translate Friedrich Schlegel's essay on *Meister* by way of contrast to our English animadversions on that subject.'

10 F. Schlegel, 'Nachrichten von den poetischen Werken des J. Boccaccio,': *Charakteristiken, Kritische Ausgabe* II, 373–4: Wir wissen, dass wir etwas tun, was zu tun nicht unbedeutend und nicht unwürdig ist, wenn wir das Eigentümliche eines originellen Geistes mit aller Sorgfalt charakterisieren, sein Leben gleichsam in der Fantasie wiederholen, und an allen Erweiterungen und Beschränkungen seines Wesens Anteil nehmen. Wir werden uns auch seine fehlgeschlagenen Versuche nicht verbergen wollen ... Das Genie eines Dichters kann oft durch seine falschen Tendenzen ebensosehr und mehr noch beglaubigt und dargestellt werden, als durch seine gelungensten Werke.'

11 See also Eichner, *Friedrich Schlegel*, 32, who, independent of any connection with Carlyle, acknowledges Schlegel's originality in this critical approach.

12 F. Schlegel, *Kritische Ausgabe II*, 69: 'Wer also den Geist des *Woldemar* verstehen will ... muss Jacobis sämmtliche Schriften, und in ihnen den individuellen Charakter, und die individuelle Geschichte seines Geistes studieren.'

13 Ibid., 57: 'der kein Philosoph von Profession sondern von *Charakter* ist.'

14 Ibid., 58: 'Unfug kalter Vernünftler ohne Sinn, Herz und Urteil.'

15 Georg Forster (1754–94) accompanied his father on his travels around the world with Captain James Cook. Later he participated in the French Revolution and died in Paris in poverty, possibly under the guillotine. His main literary works are *Reise um die Welt* and *Ansichten vom Niederrhein*.

16 F. Schlegel, *Kritische Ausgabe II*, 85: 'nicht bloss diese oder jene Ansicht, aber die herrschende Stimmung aller seiner Werke, ist echt sittlich.'

17 Ibid., 83: 'jenes lügenhafte Bild des Glücks.' Ibid., 81: 'Jeder Pulsschlag seines immer tätigen Wesens strebt *vorwärts*. Unter allen noch so verschiednen Ansichten seines reichen und vielseitigen Verstandes, bleibt *Vervollkommnung* der feste Grundgedanke, durch seine ganze schriftstellerische Laufbahn.'

18 See Carlyle on: Jean Paul, Fichte, Lessing, *Essays I*, 15f., 77f., 47f.

19 F. Schlegel, *Kritische Ausgabe II*, 112: 'Er selbst war mehr wert als alle seine Talente.'

20 For unacknowledged passages from Tieck's 'Vorrede zur ersten Auflage von Novalis' Schriften' compare Carlyle, 'Novalis,' *Essays II*, 11:11.10–13 with Tieck, *Werke* I (Suhrkamp edn.), 86; Carlyle, 'Novalis,' 12:11.16–24 with Tieck, ibid., 88-9; Carlyle, 'Novalis,' 19:11.22–36 with Tieck, ibid., 93–6.

21 This quote on Hume, wrongly attributed to A.W. Schlegel by Carlyle, was originally detected by Leopold ('Die religiöse Wurzel,' 59) and also discussed by Wellek (*Confrontations*, 93–4). F. Schlegel, *Kritische Ausgabe VI*, 342: 'Denn seit Hume ist nichts weiter geschehen, als dass man durch allerlei Bollwerke den schädlichen praktischen Einfluss jener skeptischen Denkart abzuwehren und durch verschiedene Stützwerke, und Nothülfen das Gebäude aller sittlich notwendigen Überzeugungen aufrecht zu erhalten suchte.'

22 See Leopold, 'Die religiöse Wurzel,' 55–6, and 'Thomas Carlyle and Franz Horn,' 215.

23 'I have merely been reading Horn, somewhat of Fichte, Schelling etc.,' (*Letters of Thomas Carlyle*, 1826–1836, 53). Carlyle's comment refers to his preparatory reading for 'State of German Literature, (*Essays I*, 26–86).

24 See Carlyle's footnote to 'Early German Literature' (*Essays II*, 292) where he mentions Horn's *Geschichte und Kritik der deutschen Poesie und Beredsamkeit* (44) as source for his quote from Hugo von Trimberg, whom he also refers to in *Sartor* (181). Hill Shine wrongly takes this work to be *Die Poesie und Beredsamkeit der Deutschen* (*Carlyle's Early Reading*, entry no. 2440), overlooking the fact that Carlyle had also used Horn's previous book on German Literature before Luther with a similar title.

25 With regard to Carlyle's editorial methods, it must be stated that he allowed himself great latitude with the texts he quoted. Frequently, without acknowledging the author, he simply presents lines contained by single quotation marks that issue forth out of nowhere. Sometimes such phrases as 'we are informed' (*Essays II*, 'Schiller,' 206) or 'as a wise critic [poet] remarks' (*Essays II*, 'Early German Literature,' 305) leave the reader in the dark as to the source. From time to time, he quotes lines from his own previous reviews, introducing them as the opinion of a critic. In the worst case there is no acknowledgement at all. A translated

stanza from Goethe's 'Künstlerlied' ('Song of the Artist'), contained in *Wilhelm Meister* (*Werke*, VIII, 255), is presented without the slightest hint as to who the author might be (*Essays I*, 'State of German Literature,' 67). Credit goes to Leopold to have recognized it ('Die religiöse Wurzel,' 93). Carlyle also translates an acknowledged passage from Tieck in his 'Novalis' essays, for example, with unacknowledged ones sandwiched in between (see note 20 above).

26 See Harrold, *Carlyle and German Thought*, appendix: 'Carlyle's Handbooks on the "History of German Literature," ' 238–47.

27 Horn, *Umrisse*, 98: 'Umherschauen nach allen Seiten. – Aesthetischer Kosmopolitismus. – Pause. – Wurzelung in sich selbst. – Wiedergeburt. – Ernster tiefer Katholicismus ... Reine Erfassung Gottes und Christi.'

28 *Poesie*, II, 105: 'Ein gewisser Pater Bouhours ... liess ein Gespräch in Druck ausgehen, in welchem die Frage "ob ein Deutscher ein *bel esprit* sein könne," aufgeworfen und ... verneint wurde.'

29 Carlyle, *German Romance I*, 6; *Unfinished History of German Literature*, 15

30 See fn. on German Hymns (*Essays I*, 32): 'Two facts on this head may deserve mention: In the year 1749 there were found in the library of one virtuoso no fewer than 300 volumes of devotional poetry, containing, says Horn, "a treasure of 33,712 German hymns." ' Carlyle neglects to say that the beginning of the sentence is already a paraphrase of Horn (*Die Poesie* II, 214), as is the continuation, where he speaks of Hans Sachs (*Die Poesie* I, 92–4).

31 Horn, *Umrisse*, 175: 'Mit Recht nannte deshalb Friedrich Richter in der berühmten Recension jenes Werkes (in den Heidelberger Jahrbüchern) diesen Dichter den Tapfern, und es hat sich späterhin immer bestätigt, dass diese Tugend den Mittelpunkt seiner Dichtungen bilde.'

32 Ibid., 54: 'Mögen wir ... den Principien der Wissenschaftslehre und ihrem eigentlichen Inhalte beistimmen oder nicht, so wird doch jeder Literaturhistoriker nicht bloss Fichtes grosses Verdienst ... anerkennen, sondern ihn auch als einen der ersten Heroen der neueren Zeit ... zu betrachten haben.'

33 Ibid., 278: 'Ein solches Wesen, welches so ganz aus dem Geisterkostüm geht, dass es den armen alten Grafen Borotin, da er sich eben ein wenig zum Schlummer hingelegt ... grausam aufweckt,'

34 Ibid., 105: 'Unreif in den meisten Partien zeigt [er] im Grossen und Ganzen eine tragische Stimmung ... mit dem hier so manche trübe "Fragen an das Schicksal", aufgeworfen werden.'

35 Ibid., 110: 'Tieck giebt hier auf einem durchaus heiteren Grunde höchst tragische Charaktere.'

36 Ibid., 115–16: 'Es ist wohl gar hier und da eine Stimme vernommen worden, man dürfe diesen Roman dem *Wilhelm Meister* gleichsetzen ...

Dennoch ist die ruhige Klarheit des Styls in Goethe keineswegs erreicht, sondern nur mit sichtbarem Fleisse nachgeahmt worden.'

37 Why does Carlyle choose the form 'Everlasting No'? He evidently has in mind the German word *immerwährend*, which he prefers as a new coinage in English to the less conspicuous 'eternal,' the equivalent to *ewig*.

38 Horn, *Umrisse*, 198: 'Der Vater der Lüge ist ganz besonders schwer zu zeichnen, und wer kein ewiges Ja in der Brust hat, der vermeide sorgsam die Darstellung des ewigen Nein.'

39 Horn, *Die Poesie* II, 333: 'Nur wer das ewige Ja in der Brust hat, begreift und übersieht den verneinenden Geist (vergl. Goethes Faust) und nur wer des tiefsten philosophischen so wie des rein religiösen Ernstes fähig ist, kann wahrhaften Humor und heiteren Witz haben.'

40 Ibid., III, 45: 'Aber er findet nicht immer jene vollendete Befriedigung, jenes ewig selige Ja.'

41 Ibid., IV, 162: 'Dumm im tiefern Sinne des Worts hat er notwendig werden müssen, weil das ewige Nein, in welchem er waltet, der entschiedenste Gegensatz aller Weisheit ist. Ich gebrauche mit Fleiss den allgemeinen, unbestimmten Ausdruck "waltet", denn die präcisen Worte "ist", "lebt" sind für ihn ganz unpassend ... dazu bedürfte es eines schöpferischen Ja, in dessen Bekämpfung er doch allein walten kann. Da er aber immer kämpft, so zeigt sich dadurch ein Scheinleben, welches für jeden, der jenes ewige selige Ja in der eigenen Brust nicht mitbringt, von weitem aussehen kann wie wirkliches Leben. Der Teufel bekämpft aber nicht bloss jenes Ja in Gott und den Menschen, sondern er kämpft auch für sein Nein, als sei es die einzige Weisheit.'

In spite of the fact that Carlyle only lists three volumes of Horn's *Die Poesie und Beredsamkeit* which had appeared up to 1827 (1822, 1823, 1824), in fn. 1 of 'State of German Literature' (*Essays I*, 26), professing to review them, it is unlikely that he did not read vol. IV, which was published 1829, that is, prior to the serial publication of *Sartor* in 1833/4.

Chapter Two

1 Carlyle did read Nicolai's *Reise durch Deutschland und die Schweiz* (1781), as he quotes from it in his *Unfinished History of German Literature* (38, fn.). and received data on both Nicolai and Hippel from Horn's *Poesie und Beredsamkeit*, III.

2 Carlyle, *Essays I*, 'Jean Paul Friedrich Richter,' 10: 'Of this work we could speak long.' See also *German Romance II*, 121: 'His *Vorschule der Ästhetik* abounds with deep and sound maxims of criticism.'

3 Jean Paul, *Werke*, IV, 10: 'Der erste, der in die Höhe geht, ist: so weit

über das Gewölke des Lebens hinauszudringen, dass man die ganze äussere Welt mit ihren Wolfsgruben, Beinhäusern und Gewitterableitern von weitem unter seinen Füssen nur wie ein eingeschrumpftes Kindergärtchen liegen sieht. – Der zweite ist: – gerade herabzufallen ins Gärtchen und da sich so einheimisch in eine Furche einzunisten, dass, wenn man aus seinem warmen Lerchennest heraussieht, man ebenfalls keine Wolfsgruben, Beinhäuser und Stangen, sondern nur Ähren erblickt, deren jede für den Nestvogel ein Baum oder ein Sonnen- und Regenschirm ist. – Der dritted endlich – den ich für den schwersten und klügsten halte – ist der, mit den beiden andern zu wechseln.'

4 Ibid., , 21: 'Scherz ist der Ring von Gold, den man an den Finger ansteckt, damit der Ring von Diamanten nicht abgleite.'

5 Ibid., 474: 'Die gedruckten Namen sind ... ein Charakter indelebilis jeder Person.'

6 Ibid., 475: 'den teuflischen oder den englischen Charakter zu bestimmen ... als nur immer die Sternbilder der Jungfrau, des Löwen, des Skorpions und Wassermanns.'

7 Goethe, *Werke*, VIII, 33: 'Wandre nur hin, du zweiter Diogenes! Lass dein Lämpchen am hellen Tage nicht verlöschen!'

8 *Luthers Werke in Auswahl*, IV, edited by O. Clemen, Berlin: Gruyter, 1959 (329, 367).

9 Goethe, *Sämmtliche Werke*, VII, Stuttgart: Cotta, 1840. 'Ein Fastnachtsspiel von Pater Brey' (202).

10 G.B. Tennyson, in *Sartor Called Resartus* (221), obviously went to Grimm's *Wörterbuch* for his reference, where this one usage is listed, but did not comb through Jeal Paul's works, where he would have found all others: *Grönländische Prozesse* (52), with reference to publishers; *Auswahl aus des Teufels Papieren* (527), where Virtue discovers Teufelsdreck in man's heart as one of its components; *Hesperus Vorrede* (482), a lemon sauce added to sweet praise; *Palingenesien* (826), refers to the Jewish custom of adding a few pinches of it to the sacrifice; *Ästhetik* (467), a medicinal purgative causing vomiting; *Titan* (63) is the one case cited by Tennyson.

11 Jean Paul's references to J.M. Schröckh (1733–1808), who was a church historian, occur in *Die Unsichtbare Loge*, I, 125, 396; *Des Leben Fibels*, VI, 430; and *Siebenkäs*, II, 341.

12 Jean Paul, *Werke*, I, 424–5: 'aus dem unabsehlichen Gewölbe des Universums herausgeschnitten oder hineingebaut ... so warm, so satt, so wohl.'

13 Ibid., VI, 546: 'Und Morgen und Abend, Anfang und Ende, standen die Farbentore der Zeit und der Ewigkeit gegeneinander aufgetan.'

14 Ibid., II, 216–17: 'Nichts macht humoristischer ... als wenn man sein Inneres mit Philosophie gleichsam wie ein Diogenesfass gegen äussere Verletzungen überzieht.'

15 Ibid., III, 905: 'Der ungestüme, durchreissende Giannozzo ... so recht erbittert von der allgemeinen freundlichen Auswechslung gegenseitiger Lüge und Tücke ... hat die Sättigung der tiefen Kerker- und Gassenluft aufgejagt in die Bergluft.'

16 Hoffmann, *Werke*, IX, 38: ' "Das ist arg – das ist zu arg", rief Kreisler, indem er eine rasende Lache aufschlug, dass die Wände dröhnten.'

17 Ibid., V, 77: 'lebte er anachoretisch mit einer alten Haushälterin in einem finstern Hause.'

18 Ibid., VI, 91: 'einen altfränkisch gekleideten Mann muntern Ansehens, dessen kleine graue Augen unangenehm stechend blickten, und um dessen Mund ein sarkastisches Lächeln schwebte, das eben nicht anzog.'

19 See also Goethe's use of the tower image in *Wilhelm Meisters Lehrjahre*: 'Ich war froh von meiner Warte dem Getümmel von weiten zuzusehen' (*Werke*, VII, 391). Carlyle translates: 'It was pleasant for me to behold the tumult off my watch-tower, from afar' (*Wilhelm Meister* I, 431). Carlyle also refers in *Essays I*, 'Goethe's *Helena*,' 186, to the tower as 'an emblem of the Product of the Teutonic Mind.'

20 Hoffmann, *Werke*, XII, 164: 'Dieser Markt ist auch jetzt ein treues Abbild des ewig wechselnden Lebens. Rege Tätigkeit, das Bedürfnis des Augenblicks trieb die Menschenmasse zusammen; in wenigen Augenblicken ist alles verödet, die Stimmen, welche im wirren Getöse durcheinanderströmten, sind verklungen, und jede verlassene Stelle spricht das schauerliche: "Es war!" nur zu lebhaft aus.'

21 Ibid., XV, 87: 'Aus ihrem tiefen Grunde stieg allerlei hässlicher, schmutzig grauer Dampf zu mir herauf. Als der zusammengeballt sich nun über meinen Turmknopf hinweg zu dem leichten golden Morgengewölk gesellte ... da konnte ich sehen wie das Volk unter mir in den Strassen sich schwirrend drängte und trieb.'

22 Ibid., 89: 'Mein Turm warf einen langen schwarzen Riesenschatten über den Markt und über die Häuser, indem heller die Lichter aus den Fenstern hervorleuchteten. Unerachtet Mitternacht schon längst vorüber, ging es doch überall lustig her, ich hörte deutlich Gläser erklingen und das verworrence Getöse des lauten Gesprächs.'

23 Tieck, *Schriften*, XXII, 12: 'Wer weiss was er sich aus all dem heidnischen Zeuge noch in den Kopf setzt, denn so ein Klassiker, mein liebes Kind, ist eben nichts anderes, als ein Heide. In die Kirche geht er auch gar nicht, er sagt er könne die Orgel nicht vertragen ... Ja,

Lenchen, ich bin manchmal schon nachdenklich und traurig, denn ich bin dem lieben Herrn doch gar zu gut.'

24 Jean Paul, *Werke*, IV, 472: 'so wie man mehr *Hefen* und *Sauerteig* bedarf, wenn ein feiner Teig zu heben ist.'

25 It is to be noted that Carlyle translated the first version of Goethe's novel *Wilhelm Meisters Wanderjahre oder die Entsagenden*, a continuation of *Wilhelm Meisters Lehrjahre*. It was published in 1821 in eighteen chapters, without division into books. The second version appeared in 1829. It no longer containted the 'Words from the Editor' Carlyle had translated from the early version. As I was unable to obtain it, a German translation cannot be provided; we have to rely on Carlyle's rendering for the two examples quoted here.

26 Carlyle leaves out twelve of these footnotes in his translation. One might guess that they were too difficult to translate.

27 Jean Paul, *Werke*, IV, 81: 'Ich will blindlings in seine Tage greifen und einen herausfangen: einer lächelt und duftet wie der andere.'

28 Ibid., III, 61: 'den mir das Gesandten-Corpo posttäglich in festen Düten schickt.' The zodiac signs are introduced in the Preface to the first edition of the *Ästhetik*, v, 28, and p. 475 of the text.

29 Hoffmann, *Werke*, II, 22: 'Nachdem ich die Papiere des Kapuziners Medardus recht emsig durchgelesen, welches mir schwer genug wurde, da der Selige eine sehr kleine unleserliche mönchische Handschrift geschrieben, war es mir auch, als könne das, was wir insgemein Traum und Einbildung nennen, wohl die symbolische Erkenntnis des geheimen Fadens sein, der sich durch unser Leben zieht.'

30 Ibid., IX, 108: '– für den Herausgeber dieser Blätter [war es] das angenehmste Ereignis dieser Welt, dass er das ganze merkwürdige Gespräch Kreislers mit dem kleinen Geheimen Rat brühwarm wieder erfuhr. Dadurch wurde er in den Stand gesetzt, dir, geliebter Leser, wenigstens ein paar Bilder aus der frühern Jugendzeit des seltnen Mannes, dessen Biographie aufzuschreiben er gewissermassen genötigt, vor die Augen zu bringen.'

31 Ibid., 185: 'Der Biograph erschrickt abermals über das total Abrupte der Nachrichten, aus denen er gegenwärtige Geschichte zusammenstoppeln muss.'

32 This work has never been examined as a source study for *Sartor*. Herr von Natas (Satan) studies theology because he wants to find out why and when he was given a bad name. He visits the home of his professor, an elderly man in a flowered dressing gown, smoking a meerschaum pipe. His room contains a selection of old pieces of furniture, with clothes and linen lying around on chairs in picturesque array.

There is a chaotic order on the desk. The professor relates the devil to *Dreck* in his lecture, calling him 'der Herr im Dreck,' 'der Unreinliche,' 'der Stinker.' In utter disgust, Natas changes his curriculum, as he does not have to study for a *Brotstudium*. Here he meets Dr Schnatterer (Dr Gabber) who is in the habit of visiting a pub on the outskirts of town, where he passes the time in much the same way as Teufelsdröckh in the 'Grüne Gans.' Later Satan turns into a demagogue and gets arrested for Sansculottism. In the second part of the book, he meets Baron Grünacker, who is the son of a tailor turned critic – more precisely, reviewer.

33 Hauff, *Werke*, IV, 23: 'übersetzte unsterbliche Werke fremder Nationen fürs liebe deutsche Publikum.'

34 Ibid., 28: 'Sodann die Unordnung, in welcher er alles vorbringt! Ein anderer, wie z.B. der Herausgeber, hätte doch, wenn auch nicht mit dem Taufschein, was nun freilich beim Teufel nicht gut möglich ist, doch wenigstens mit der Begebenheit angefangen, die der Chronologie nach die erste ist. Ich habe das Manuskript flüchtig durchblättert (zu lesen ehe jeder Bogen hinlänglich geweiht, nehme ich mich wohl in acht.)'

Chapter Three

1 Jean Paul, *Werke*, V, 258: 'eine lange harte Dornenleiter führt am Rosenstocke endlich über weichere Stacheln zu einigen Rosen hinauf.'

2 Carlyle, *Sartor*, 146: 'Thick curtains of night rushed over his soul, as arose the immeasurable Crash of Doom.' This is in essence a passage from Jean Paul, 'Rede des toten Christus' (*Werke*, II, 'Siebenkäs,' 269). Carlyle had translated the piece in his second Jean Paul essay, 'Jean Paul Friedrich Richter Again,' (*Essays II*, 156–8). Harrold identified it in his edition of *Sartor* (146, fn. 1).

3 *Wahrheit aus Jean Paul's Leben*, the first published account of the poet's autobiography (presented in three small volumes), remained incomplete. It was only partly incorporated in Jean Paul's works under the title 'Selberlebensbeschreibung' and consists of three chapters, called 'Lectures.' Other parts of the *Wahrheit* were not included; among others, the author's jottings in his *Vita-Buch* from which Carlyle quotes frequently. This is a collection of fragmentary utterances never elaborated. It also contains excerpts from Jean Paul's *Andachtsbüchlein* of 1784, which Hill Shine could not identify (*Carlyle's Early Reading*, item no. 2073). Carlyle quotes extensively from both sources in his second Jean Paul essay, 'Jean Paul Friedrich Richter Again' (*Essays II*, 118).

4 Jean Paul, *Werke*, VI, 1061: 'Nie vergess' ich die noch keinem Menschen erzählte Erscheinung in mir, wo ich bei der Geburt meines Selbstbewusst-

seins stand, von der ich Ort und Zeit anzugeben weiss. An einem Vormittag stand ich als ein sehr junges Kind unter der Haustüre und sah links nach der Holzlege, als auf einmal das innere Gesicht "ich bin ein Ich" wie ein Blitzstrahl vom Himmel vor mich fuhr und seitdem leuchtend stehen blieb: da hatte mein Ich zum ersten Male sich selber gesehen und auf ewig.'

5 Ibid., 1040: 'Aber jetzo mag der Held und Gegenstand dieser historischen Vorlesungen unbesehen in der Wiege und an der Mutterbrust so lange liegen und schlafen – da doch dem langen Morgenschlaf des Lebens nichts für allgemein-welthistorisches Interesse abzuhören ist.'

6 Ibid., 1044: 'In meinen historischen Vorlesungen wird zwar das Hungern immer stärker vorkommen ... aber ich kann doch nicht umhin, zur Armut zu sagen: sei willkommen, sobald du nur nicht in zu späten Jahren kommst. Reichtum lastet mehr das Talent als Armut ... Wenn in die Flammen der Jugend ... zugleich noch das Öl des Reichtums gegossen wird: so wird wenig mehr als Asche vom Phönix übrig bleiben ... Der arme historische Professor hier möchte um vieles Geld nicht in der Jugend viel Geld gehabt haben.'

7 Ibid., 1048: 'Aber da es doch möglich wäre, dass er noch lebte hoch in den sechzigern und als vielseitiger Gelehrter diese Vorlesungen in Druck vorbekäme und sich dann eines kleinen Professors erinnerte ... ach Gott, wenn dies wäre und er schriebe oder der ältere Mann zum alten käme! –'

8 Carlyle, *Sartor*, 91. The word 'Entenpfuhl' appears twice in Jean Paul: 1. *Quintus Fixlein* (*Werke*, IV, 159) which Carlyle had translated. 2. *Kampanertal* (*Werke*, IV, 586). Carlyle's spelling 'Entepfuhl' is incorrect, as he uses the singular, not the required plural. His own translation (German Romance II, 298) is 'Duck-pool.'

9 Jean Paul, Selberlebensbeschreibung, Werke, VI, 1052" 'Auf dessen Deckel schon mit wahren goldnen Buchstaben (und nicht ohne Recht) der Inhalt der ersten Seite geschrieben war.'

10 Ibid., 1061: 'In der künftigen Kulturgeschichte unsers Helden wird es zweifelhaft werden, ob er nicht vielleicht mehr der Philosophie als der Dichtkunst zugeboren war.'

11 Ibid., 1077: 'Noch erinnert er sich eines Sommertages, wo ihn, da er auf der Rückkehr gegen zwei Uhr die sonnigen beglänzten Anhöhen, und die ziehenden Wogen auf den Ährenfeldern und die Laufschatten der Wolken überblickte, ein noch unerlebtes gegenstandloses Sehnen überfiel ... Ach er war der ganze Mensch, der sich nach den himmlischen Gütern des Lebens sehnte, die noch unbezeichnet und farbelos im tiefen weiten Dunkel des Herzens lagen.'

12 Ibid., 1081: 'Die jungen Schwalben priess er glücklich, weil sie in ihrem ummauerten Neste innen so heimlich sitzen konnten in der Nacht.'

13 Ibid., 1094: 'Aber so sind die Menschen durch alle Ämter hinauf; sie haben keine Lust, knechtische Maschinen zu freien Geistern zu machen und dadurch ihre Schöpf-, Herrsch- und Schaffkraft zu zeigen, sondern sie glauben diese umgekehrt zu erweisen, wenn sie an ihre nächste Obermaschine aus Geist wieder eine Zwischenmaschine ... anzuschliessen vermögen ... Alles nur *eine* Zusammenhäkelung desselben Maschinenmeisters. Gott, der Reinfreie, will nur Freie erziehen; der Teufel, der Reinunfreie, will nur seinesgleichen.'

14 Harrold (*Sartor*, 137, fn. 3) points to *Quintus Fixlein* where the schoolmaster refers to his bride in Carlyle's translation as a 'Lily of Heaven' (Lilie des Himmels). See *German Romance II*, 287, and Jean Paul, *Werke*, IV, 149, evidently unaware of the fact that Carlyle derived the name Blumine from Jean Paul's essay collection, entitled *Herbst-Blumine* which he had read as early as 1825. Incorporating the German word *Blume* it indicates 'autumnal flowers'.

15 Jean Paul, *Werke*, I, 297: 'Ein Regenbogen von Sonnen, die wie zu einer Perlenschnur aneinander gereihet waren, fasste die Erden ein und drehte sich um sie ... Haine und Alleen von Riesen-Blumen, die so hoch wie Bäume waren, durchzogen im durchsichtigen Zickzack die Aue ... Ein magischer Abendschimmer wallete wie ein freudiges Erröten zwischen den Schattenufern ... Gustav fühlte, das sei der Abend der Ewigkeit und die Wonne der Ewigkeit.'

16 Ibid., 299: 'Da kam der überirdische durch tausend Himmel auf die Erde fallende Augenblick hier unten an, der Augenblick, wo das menschliche Herz sich zur höchsten Liebe erhebt und für zwei Seelen und zwei Welten schlägt ... die verwandten Seelen, die wie zwei hohe Flammen ineinanderschlugen.'

17 Ibid., IV, 116'' 'das gute blasse himmlische Angesicht, dessen Lippen er blöde drückte, ohne sie zu küssen, bis die allmächtige Liebe ... beide enger und enger zusammenzog, und bis die zwei Seelen ... wie Tränen ineinanderrannen.'

18 Carlyle, *Sartor*, 145; see also Teufelsdröckh's 'Proem' to Carlyle's translation of Goethe's *Märchen*, elaborated with comments, signed D.T., so far not referred to by scholars. In one of these Carlylean interpretations in disguise, Jean Paul's phrase is echoed once more; in this case applied to the bridge formed by the snake: 'The divided Two shall clasp each other as flames do, rushing into one' (*Essays II*, 'The Tale by Goethe,' 453).

19 Jean Paul, *Werke*, V, 427: 'Der stärkste Einwand *gegen* die Ausmalerei der sinnlichen Liebe ist kein sittlicher, sondern ein poetischer.'

20 Ibid., III, 123: 'endlich sprang er von der obersten Sprosse seiner Jakobsleiter mit allen Sinnen in einen unbedeckten lebendigen Himmel hinaus; ein lichter Berggipfel, nur von Blumenkelchen bunt gesäumt, empfing ihn und wiegte ihn unter den Sternen.'

21 Ibid., II, 823 and 887: 'Eine Menschen-Blume seh' ich, die ohne Bewusstsein prangt ... weil sie die Liebe selber ist und wieder die Liebe selber sucht; sie zieht alles Leben an sich heran ... Blühend von Träumen trat er ins helle Zimmer; halb geblendet sah er die weisse schlanke Wina mit dem leichten weissen Hute wie eine Blumengöttin.'

22 Ibid., I, 535: 'einer Freundschaft welche um zwei Seelen nicht erdige, metallene und schmutzige Bande legt, sondern geistige, die selber diese Welt mit einer andern und den Menschen mit Gott verweben.'

23 Hoffmann, *Werke*, IX, 35: 'Wann wird endlich der verwüstende Brand in deiner Brust zur reinen Naphtaflamme werden, genährt von dem tiefsten Sinn für die Kunst?'

24 Ibid., 246: 'Wenn du entsagst, so rettest du dich vom Verderben; niemals kannst du, wirst du des eingebildeten Glücks der irdischen Liebe teilhaftig werden.'

25 Tieck, *Werke*, I, 78 (Thalmann edn.): 'Als zuerst meine Gedanken erwachten, traf ich mich in einem kleinen Hause eines Dorfes. Ich erinnere mich noch deutlich einer Weide, die vor unsrer Tür stand, und in deren Zweigen der Schein der Sonne flimmerte. Ein bräunlicher Mann, den ich Vater, und eine sehr freundliche Frau, die ich Mutter nannte, waren meine täglichen Gesellschafter.'

26 Ibid., 80: 'Meine Mutter sagte mir nämlich, dass sie und mein Vater nicht meine *wahren*, sondern meine *Pflegeeltern* wären, dass sie mir aber den Namen meines wirklichen Vaters, verschiedener Ursachen wegen, nicht nennen könne.'

27 Ibid., 91: 'In ihrem Wesen heschte eine unbeschreibliche Sanftheit, die fast ans Melancholische grenzte. Ein Wort, das sie sagte, klang wie Musik in meinen Ohren.'

28 Ibid., 95: 'Wer sind Sie? Was für ein Glück besitzen Sie, dass Sie ihr anbieten könnten – Sie sind Herr Lebrecht, und weiter nichts, und von Ihrer Liebe möchten Sie gar armselige Zinsen ziehn.'

29 Ibid., 98: 'Manche Sachen, die sich von selbst verstanden, sagten wir uns tausendmal und wiederholten sie immer von neuem, ohne nach einer Erklärung einiger poetischer Phrasen zu fragen, die der offenbarste Unsinn waren. Das Gespräch zweier Liebenden ist wie die Melodie der Äolusharfe, stets dieselben Töne ohne Rhythmus und Anordnung, die

aber trotz ihrer Einförmigkeit dem Ohre in einer schönen Gegend wohltun.'

30 Ibid., 98–9: 'Wenn der Verliebte einmal in das Gebiet der Poesie hineingeraten ist, so ist es unmöglich, ihn in die Prosa des gewöhnlichen Lebens herunterzuziehn. Er ist wie ein Luftball, der sich den festhaltenden Stricken entrissen hat; geduldig müssen die Zuschauer unten warten, bis die leichte Luft nach und nach aus ihm verflogen ist und er von selbst auf die Erde zurückfällt.'

Chapter Four

1 Judging by Harrold's Introduction to his *Sartor* edition, one would not know that such a tradition existed. R. Pascal, in *Die Autobiographie*, also neglects to look into these sources, owing to his preoccupation with precedents along the lines of Rousseau's *Confessions*, which lack the religious inspiration prominent in the German genre.

2 Goethe's novel *Wilhelm Meisters Lehrjahre* and its sequel, *Wilhelm Meisters Wanderjahre*, were translated by Carlyle under the titles *Wilhelm Meister's Apprenticeship* and *Wilhelm Meister's Travels*, usually referred to as *Wilhelm Meister I* and *II*. 'Die Bekenntnisse einer schönen Seele,' which forms a part of the *Lehrjahre*, was rather awkwardly rendered by Carlyle as 'Confessions of a Fair Saint' (*Wilhelm Meister I*, 397).

3 Goethe, *Werke*, VII, 364: 'Die Empfindungen für den Unsichtbaren waren bei mir fast ganz verloschen.'

4 Ibid., 364: 'Ich lebte in sinnlicher Munterkeit nur so hin, ich sammelte mich nicht, ich betete nicht, ich dachte nicht an mich noch an Gott.'

5 Ibid., 371: 'Ich hatte diesen Gott während vier wilder Jahre ganz vergessen; nun dachte ich dann and wann wieder an ihn, aber die Bekanntschaft war erkaltet; es waren nur Zeremonienvisiten, die ich ihm machte, und da ich überdies wenn ich vor ihm erschien, immer schöne Kleider anlegte, meine Tugend, Ehrbarkeit und Vorzüge, die ich vor andern zu haben glaubte, ihm mit Zufriedenheit vorwies, so schien er mich in dem Schmucke garnicht zu bemerken.'

6 Ibid., 374: 'Er gab mir öfters Schriften, die alles, was man Zusammenhang mit dem Unsichtbaren heissen kann, mit leichten und schweren Waffen bestritten.'

7 Goethe, ibid., 376: '... war auch unser Frühling dahin. Der Sommer kam, und alles wurde ernsthafter und heisser.'

8 Ibid., 377: 'Nun aber wie herauskommen in einer Welt, wo alles gleichgültig oder toll ist?'

9 Ibid., 378: 'dass es höhere Empfindungen gebe, die uns ein Vergnügen

wahrhaftig gewährten, das man vergebens bei Lustbarkeiten sucht, und dass in diesen höhern Freuden zugleich ein geheimer Schatz zur Stärkung im Unglück aufbewahrt sei.'

10 Ibid., 377: 'Ich war nun einmal in einen Kreis hineingesperrt.'

11 Ibid., 379: 'Aber da ich endlich nach tausendfältigem Streit, nach immer wiederholter Betrachtung auch scharfe Blicke auf das Band warf ... erkannte ich auf einmal, dass es nur eine Glassglocke sei, die mich in den luftleeren Raum sperrte; nur noch soviel Kraft, sie entzwei zu schlagen, und du bist gerettet!'

12 Ibid., 387–8: '... dass ich nicht ohne Gott auf der Welt sei! Er war mir nahe, ich war vor ihm. Das ist's, was ich mit geflissentlicher Vermeidung aller theologischen Systemsprache mit grösster Wahrheit sagen kann.'

13 Ibid., 394–5: 'Im kurzen war ich überzeught, dass mein Geist eine Fähigkeit sich aufzuschwingen erhalten habe, die ihm ganz neu war.'

14 Ibid., 416: 'Wie gerne sah ich nunmehr Gott in der Natur, da ich ihn mit solcher Gewissheit im Herzen trug, wie interessant war mir das Werk seiner Hände.'

15 Ibid., 414: 'sah ich dass das unschätzbare Glück der Freiheit nicht darin besteht, dass man alles tun kann was man tun mag ... sondern was man für recht und schicklich hält.'

16 Goethe, ibid., 404: 'und trachtete nur das eine, was not ist, erst recht ins reine zu bringen.'

17 Ibid., 404: 'Wenn wir uns', sagte er einmal, 'als möglich denken können, dass der Schöpfer der Welt selbst die Gestalt seiner Kreatur angenommen und auf ihre Art und Weise sich eine Zeitlang auf der Welt befunden habe, so muss uns dieses Geschöpf schon unendlich vollkommen erscheinen, weil sich der Schöpfer so innig damit vereinigen konnte. Es muss also in dem Begriff des Menschen kein Widerspruch mit dem Begriff des Gottes liegen.'

18 Ibid., 405: 'ein in seinem Geist entsprungenes Urbild ... zusammenstellt.'

19 Ibid., 415: 'Als ein ihr fremdes Wesen an, wie man etwa ein Kleid ansieht ... der Körper wird wie ein Kleid zerreissen.'

20 Ibid.: 'Tätig zu sein, ist des Menschen erste Bestimmung.'

21 Harrold (*Sartor edition*, 166, fn. 3) points out that neither Carlyle nor Teufelsdröckh experiences a conversion to any particular religious belief. The 'Schöne Seele' also steers clear of any theological definitions at the time of the initial impact of the new spiritual convictions.

22 Carlyle, 'Faustus,' *New Edinburgh Review*, 1822; reprinted in *Archiv* 96 (1896), 241–68

23 Norton, *Correspondence between Goethe and Carlyle*, letter 20 August 1827

24 See L. Metzger, 'Sartor Resartus: A Victorian *Faust*,' *Comp. Lit.* 13 (1961), 316–31

25 Harrold, in his Preface to *Carlyle and German Thought* (p. viii), speaks of striking parallels that point to Carlyle's familiarity with Fichtes *Bestimmung* but does not follow up on the comparison. The same is true of J.W. Beach, who in *Concept of Nature* (p. 361) asserts that Fichte's solution is the same as Carlyle's. As Carlyle intended to write an essay on Fichte, he had acquired *J.G. Fichte's Leben und literarischer Briefwechsel*, edited by the philosopher's son, I.H. Fichte. In this work, *Die Bestimmung* is recommended for containing Fichte's doctrine of the *Ich* in its most comprehensive form (p. 172). In 'Novalis,' Carlyle defines the *Nicht-Ich* as 'a manifestation of power from something which is not *I*' (*Essays II*, 25). This is a translation of Fichte's 'eine Kraft ausser mir' (*Werke*, II, 222), which occurs in *Die Bestimmung*. The same holds good for the tree-passage of the 'Novalis' essay (p. 25) which Carlyle uses to explain the nature of reality: 'There is, in fact, says Fichte, no Tree there.' Harrold breaks off the quotation (96), which he wishes to derive from Berkeley's *Principles of Human Knowledge*, one sentence prior to Carlyle's reference to Fichte as the source.

26 As a student, Fichte had been totally dejected by the impact Determinism had made on him. A period of spiritual anguish followed, but was overcome by his reading of Kant's *Kritik der reinen Vernunft*. The following excerpt from a letter may profitably be compared with Carlyle's spiritual state after 'the new Evangel': 'The last four or five months ... have been the happiest in my life. Since I could not alter my outward circumstances, I resolved upon internal change. I threw myself into philosophy, and as you know into the Kantian. Here I found the remedy of all my evils ... The influence of this philosophy, and particularly the moral part of it upon the whole spiritual life, cannot be described ... I am also firmly convinced that there is no land of enjoyment here below, but a land of labour and toil, and that every joy of life should be only a refreshment and an incentive to greater exertion' (*Fichtes Leben and Briefwechsel*, 248).

27 Fichte, *Werke*, I, 434: 'Was für eine Philosophie man wähle, hängt davon ab, was man für ein Mensch ist: denn ein philosophisches System ist nicht ein toter Hausrat, den man ablegen oder annehmen könnte, wie es uns beliebte, sondern es ist beseelt durch die Seele des Menschen der es hat.' (As Smith translated only Fichte's *Popular Works*, the English translation is supplied by the author.)

28 Fichte, Werke, II, 169: 'Nur der übereinstimmenden Aussage meiner Sinne, nur der beständigen Erfahrung, habe ich Glauben zugestellt; ich habe betastet was ich erblickt, ich habe zerlegt was ich betastet hatte.'

29 Ibid., 179: 'Ich selbst mit allem was ich mein nenne, bin ein Glied in dieser Kette der strengen Naturnotwendigkeit.'

30 Ibid., 195: 'Bin ich frei und selbständig, oder bin ich nichts an mir selbst, und lediglich Erscheinung einer fremden Kraft?'

31 Ibid., 196: 'Das System der Freiheit befriedigt, das entgegengesetzte tötet und vernichtet mein Herz. Kalt und tot dastehen, und dem Wechsel der Begebenheiten nur zusehen, ein träger Spiegel der vorüberfliegenden Gestalten – dies Dasein ist mir unerträglich, ich verschmähe und verwünsche es. Ich will lieben, ich will mich in Teilnahme verlieren, mich freuen und mich betrüben.'

32 Ibid., 198: 'Welche Macht kann mich von dir, welche Macht kann mich von mir selbst retten?'

33 Ibid., 199: 'Ich suchte, und fiel stets tiefer in das Labyrinth.'

34 Ibid.: 'Unmut und Angst nagte an meinem Innern.'

35 Ibid., 196: 'Ich erröte vor dem was ich für das Beste an mir erkenne, und um wessen Willen ich allein sein mag, als vor einer lächerlichen Torheit. Mein Heiligstes ist dem Spotte preisgegeben.'

36 Ibid., 201: 'In aller Wahrnehmung nimmst du zunächst nur dich selbst, und deinen eigenen Zustand wahr.'

37 Ibid., 222: 'Du siehst sonach ein, dass alles Wissen lediglich ein Wissen von dir selbst ist, dass dein Bewusstsein nie über dich selbst hinausgeht, und das dasjenige, was du für ein Bewusstsein des Gegenstandes hältst, nichts ist als ein Bewusstsein deines Setzens eines Gegenstandes, welches du nach einem inneren Gesetze deines Denkens mit der Empfindung zugleich notwending vollziehst.'

38 Ibid., 225: 'Wie kann, da das Ding nicht von sich weiss, ein Wissen vom Ding entstehen; wie kann ... ein Bewusstsein des Dinges in mir entstehen?'

39 Ibid., 240: 'Und mit dieser Einsicht, Sterblicher, sein frei und auf ewig erlöset von der Furcht, die dich erniedrigte und quälte. Du wirst nun nicht länger vor einer Notwendigkeit zittern, die nur in deinem Denken ist, nicht länger fürchten von Dingen underdrückt zu werden, die deine eignen Produkte sind ... So lange du glauben konntest, dass ein solches System der Dinge wie du es dir beschrieben, unabhängig von dir ausser dir wirklich existiere, und dass du selbst ein Glied in der Kette dieses Systems sein möchtest, war diese Furcht gegründet ... Von dieser Furcht nur wollte ich dich befreien.'

40 Ibid., 241: 'Ich könnte mir gefallen lassen, dass diese Körperwelt ausser mir in eine blosse Vorstellung verschwände, und in Schatten sich auflösete ... aber nach allem bisherigen verschwinde ich selbst nicht minder denn sie.'

41 Ibid., 245: 'Es gibt überall kein Dauerndes, weder ausser mir, noch in mir, sondern nur einen unaufhörlichen Wechsel ... Bilder, die vorüberschweben ... Ich selbst bin eins dieser Bilder ... Alle Realität verwandelt sich in einen wunderbaren Traum.'

42 Ibid., 246–7: 'Die Realität, die du schon erblickt zu haben glaubtest, eine unabhängig von dir vorhandene Sinnenwelt, deren Sklav du zu werden fürchtetest, ist dir verschwunden ... Nun suchst du denn doch etwas, ausser dem blossen Bilde liegendes Reelles ... Aber du würdest dich vergebens bemühen, sie durch dein Wissen zu erschaffen, und mit deiner Erkenntnis zu umfassen. Hast du kein anderes Organ, sie zu ergreifen, so wirst du sie nimmer finden.'

43 Ibid., 310: 'Aber in dem einigen Vorsatze, um dadurch der Pflicht in mir einen grössern Umfang, und eine weitere Wirkungssphäre zu bereiten ... Ich soll meine Kraft und Geschicklichkeit in jeder Rücksicht üben, aber lediglich um an mir der Pflicht ein tauglicheres und geschickteres Werkzeug zu verschaffen.'

44 Ibid., 253: 'Ich habe das Organ gefunden, mit welchem ich diese Realität ... ergreife. Nicht das Wissen ist dieses Organ ... jedes Wissen setzt ein noch Höheres voraus ... Der Glaube ist es.'

45 Ibid., 249: 'Nicht bloss Wissen, sondern nach deinem Wissen *Tun* ist deine Bestimmung: so ertönt es laut im innersten meiner Seele ... Nicht zum müssigen Beschauen und Betrachten deiner selbst, – nein, zum Handeln bist du da; dein Handeln und allein dein Handeln bestimmt deinen Wert.'

46 Ibid.: 'auf etwas, das da mehr und höher ist, denn alles Wissen, und den Endzweck des Wissens selbst in sich enthält.'

47 Ibid., 299: 'Die Stimme des Gewissens, die jedem seine besondere Pflicht auflegt, ist der Strahl, an welchem wir aus dem Unendlichen ausgehen.'

48 Ibid., 288–9: 'Dies sonach ist meine ganze erhabene Bestimmung, mein wahres Wesen. Ich bin Glied zweier Ordnungen; einer rein geistigen, in der ich durch den blossen reinen Willen herrsche, und einer sinnlichen, in der ich durch meine Tat wirke ... die erstere allein gibt dem letztern Bedeutung, Zweckmässigkeit, und Wert'.

49 Ibid., 261: 'Meine Welt ist Objekt und Sphäre meiner Pflichten, und absolut nichts anderes.'

50 Ibid., 315: 'Das Universum erscheint meinem Auge in einer verklärten Gestalt. Die tote lastende Masse ... ist verschwunden, und an ihrer Stelle fliesst, und woget und rauscht der ewige Strom von Leben, und Kraft und Tat.'

51 Ibid., 318: 'Stürbe kein vernünftiges Wesen auf der Erde, das da nun

einmal ihr Licht erblickt hätte, so wäre kein Grund da, eines neuen Himmels und einer neuen Erde zu harren.'

52 The healing sleep into which Teufelsdröckh falls, 'doubtless by benignant upper Influence' (*Sartor*, 186), is reminiscent of Faust's reviving slumber at the beginning of *Faust II* (11. 4630–3), known to Carlyle from Goethe, *Werke*, Ausgabe letzter Hand, 1827, which he owned.

53 Harrold, *Carlyle and German Thought*, 14

Chapter Five

1 Jonathan Swift, *A Tale of a Tub*, section II

2 Carlyle, *German Romance* I, 17; *Essays I*, 'Jean Paul,' 17

3 Carlyle, *Essays III*, 'The Diamond Necklace,' (328, 330, 344), where he repeatedly employs the loom symbol.

4 Goethe, *Faust* II, ll. 12104–5: 'Alles Vergängliche ist nur ein Gleichnis.' Carlyle was not acquainted with this phrasing at the time of writing *Sartor*, as *Faust* II was not published until after Goethe's death in 1832.

5 Metzger, 'Sartor Resartus: A Victorian *Faust*'

6 Compare Goethe, *Werther*, 18, 8 where the same cosmic mood prevails: 'Ha! nicht die grosse seltene Not der Welt, diese Fluten die eure Dörfer wegspülen, rühren mich ... Himmel und Erde und ihre webenden Kräfte um mich her!'

7 Harrold, *Carlyle and German Thought*, 79

8 Goethe, *Faust* I, 672–5: 'Geheimnisvoll am lichten Tag / Lässt sich Natur des Schleiers nicht berauben, / Und was sie deinem Geist nicht offenbaren mag, / Das zwingst du ihr nicht ab mit Hebeln und mit Schrauben.'

9 Goethe, *Faust* I, 3456–7: 'Gefühl ist alles; / Name ist Schall und Rauch, / Umnebelnd Himmelsglut.'

10 Froude, *Carlyle*, vol. II, 284. Harrold does not seem to have recognized this emendation, as he does not refer to it in *Carlyle and German Thought* (112), where he presents Carlyle's wrong version, evidently unaware that it constitutes a complete misrepresentation of the Goethe passage which deals with man's notion of God, not of nature.

11 Carlyle takes Fichte's phrasing literally. It is therefore possible that he senses a clothes symbol in Fichte's use of the verb *kleiden*, while in context it means 'to shape' or 'to give verbal expression.' The only passage Carlyle could have had in mind is the following: 'Der akademische Lehrer hat den Beruf die Idee nicht nur in dem einen Begriff, wie der Schriftsteller mitzuteilen; sondern er muss sie auf das mannigfaltigste

gestalten und kleiden, um sie in irgendeiner dieser zufälligen Hüllen anzubringen' (Fichte VI, 435). The reference is to varied expression in language in the lecture.

12 Harrold, *Carlyle and German Thought*, 221

13 Goethe, *Werke*, VIII, 151: 'Die grosse Mannigfaltigkeit in Schnitt und Farbe der Kleider fällt mir auf, und doch seh' ich nicht alle Farben, aber einige in allen ihren Abstufungen, vom Hellsten bis zun Dunkelsten. Doch bemerke ich, dass hier keine Bezeichnung der Stufen irgendeines Alters oder Verdienstes gemeint sein kann, indem die kleinsten und grössten Knaben untermischt so an Schnitt als Farbe gleich sein können.'

14 Ibid., 165–6: 'Er löst sich darin auf, dass es ein Mittel ist, die Gemüter der Knaben eigens zu erforschen ... die Zöglinge dürfen nach beliebiger Farbe greifen, so auch innerhalb einer mässigen Beschränkung Form und Schnitt wählen; dies beobachten wir genau, denn an der Farbe lässt sich die Sinnesweise, an dem Schnitt die Lebensweise des Menschen erkennen.'

15 Ibid., 166: 'Nun hat man Fälle gesehen, wo die Gemüter sich ins Allgemeine neigten, wo eine Mode sich über alle verbreitet ... wir lassen die Vorräte ausgehen ... wir schieben etwas Neues, etwas Reizendes herein, durch helle Farben und kurzen, knappen Schnitt locken wir die Muntern, durch ernste Schattierungen, bequeme, faltenreiche Tracht die Besonnenen und stellen so nach und nach ein Gleichgewicht her.'

16 This *Sartor* passage comes closer than *Wilhelm Meister* II, 276–7, to Goethe's original, quoted in note 14 above.

17 Jean Paul, *Werke*, IV 70: 'ihm war ein Kleid ein halber ausgebälgter Mensch, dem bloss die edlern Teile und die ersten Wege fehlten; er verehrte diese Düten und Hülsen um unsern Kern.'

18 Jean Paul, *Werke*, I, 1 (Berend), 186–7: 'Boileaus Bisse rechne dem Schnabel eines indianischen Hahnes an.' Fussnote von Jean Paul: 'Nach dem *l'année litteraire* wurde Boileau in seiner Kindheit von diesem Thiere an einem empfindlichen Orte verwundet; nach Helvetius lässt sich aus dieser Verwundung seine Bitterkeit gegen Weiber u.s.w. erklären.'

19 Ibid., 448: 'die Welt erwartet [von den Grossen] vielmehr, dass sie unter allen ihren Ohren, die sie dem tausendzüngigen Elende verschliessen müssen, doch das Ohr des Dionysius offen erhalten und eine Selbstanklage ... lieber hören als eine Selbstvertheidigung.'

20 Ibid., 99–100: 'Ich weiss, dass der Rock der Ehre bloss gemacht ist, um die Blösse des Unverdienstes zu bedecken ... Man nehme ernstlich nur die Mode. Denn die Narrheit ist der Schneider Europens ... Selber die stolze Philosophie im zynischen Mantel muss dem seidnen Mäntelchen

weichen ... Der Gehalt der meisten Idolen guter Gesellschaften wohnet auf ihrer Oberfläche, und ihre äussere Seite ist die beste.'

21 Jean Paul, *Werke*, IV, 780–1: 'Und überhaupt schenk' ich dem Elegant mein ganzes Mitleiden und kann ihm doch nicht helfen. Was hat ein solcher Mensch getan, dass ihm jeden Morgen – in Gerichtsstuben die gewöhnliche Zeit der Folter – der Haarkräusler mit glühenden Zangen die tadellosen Haare zwickt ... dass ihm der Schuster an die kranken Füsse, da der Kriminalist sonst nur gesunde foltert, kürzere spanische Stiefel anlegt ... er bekommt die Dornenkrone aus Haarnadeln und ein Sanskulotten-Zepter zur Schmach, dass er Essig an seinem Kreuze fodert (um seine Taille mager zu machen) ... er ist ein schuldloser Blutzeuge des Putzes.'

22 Ibid., 651: 'der menschlichen Oberwelt voll oberer Seelenkräfte, die er lutherisch bekleidet ... schafft er sich Platz, der Culotte und Unterwelt des Bischofs das Pallium umzuhängen.'

23 Ibid., 653; Carlyle, *Sartor*, 44.

24 As so much is made of the fatal *Futteral* of the guitar, Carlyle may have used it as surname for old Sergeant Futteral, a name otherwise non-existent as a family name in German. As Teufelsdröckh's stepfather, he is in reality no more than a case or casing.

25 Jean Paul, *Werke*, IV, 660–1: 'Das Langkinn liegt auf dem Feldbette der Erde als Sanskulott oder *gallus togatus* indes der Holzschneider und Streithahn, angekleidet als *gallus braccatus*, den Sturmbalken schwingt.'

26 Tieck, *Werke* (Thalman edition), I, 775: 'Ausserdem scheint es mir gut, wie ich auch immer gesucht habe, die Tracht der Menschen physiognomisch zu brauchen ... Ich muss gestehen, ich setze gern einem wilden bösen Kerl eine Mütze von seltsamer Figur aufs Haupt, und gebe ihm sonst im Äussern noch ein Abzeichen.'

27 Hoffmann, *Werke*, II, 56–7: 'Glauben Sie mir, es liegt eine geheimnisvolle Kraft in diesen äusserlichen Dingen; es kann Ihnen nicht missfallen ... wenn ich der Schauspieler gedenke, die oft, wenn sie sich in das Kostüm geworfen, wie von einem fremden Geist angeregt fühlen und leichter in den darzustellenden Charakter eingehen ... Meinen Sie denn nicht, dass, wenn dieses lange Kleid nicht mehr Ihren Gang zur düstern Gravität einhemmen würde, Sie wieder rasch und froh dahinschreiten, ja laufen, springen würden wie sonst? ... Herunter mit dem schwarzen Gewande, dass Ihnen nicht ansteht!'

28 Ibid., 92: 'Sie erblicken den modernen Elegant in allen möglichen Nuancen, wie er, bald keck und kühn alles überleuchtend, bald, in sich versunken, nichts beachtend, bald naiv tändelnd, bald ironisch, witzig,

übellaunigt, schwermütig, bizarr, ausgelassen, zierlich, burschikos erscheinen will. Der Jüngling der sich zum erstenmal einen Rock machen lassen ohne einengenden Rat der Mama oder des Hofmeisters; der Vierziger, der sich pudern muss des weissen Haares wegen; der lebenslustige Alte, der Gelehrte, wie er sich in der Welt bewegt, der reiche Kaufmann, der wohlhabended Bürger: alles hängt in meines Damons Laden.'

29 Ibid., X, 126: 'Ein Schneider, der sich in die phantastischen Habite, die er zu verfertigen wusste, auch phantastische Menschen hineinwünschte.'

30 Werner, *Söhne des Thals*, II, act 5, i, p. 284 (The reference is to man): 'Schneidern, was er erschaffen kann? – Zerfetzte Lumpen in das zerriss'ne Kleid der Menschheit flicken, wenn er für sich Beruf und Kräfte fühlt, sie zu vergöttlichen? – Sag' soll er das?'

31 See also *Sartor* 44, fn. 3, where Harrold mentions the similarity of the passages.

32 Jean Paul, *Werke*, IV, 88–9: 'Eben diese Achtung für alle Makulatur nahm ihn für die Vorschürzen gallischer Köche ein, welche bekanntlich aus vollgedrucktem Papier bestehen; und er wünschte oft, ein Deutscher übersetzte die Schürzen: ich berede mich gern, dass eine gute Version von mehr als einem solchen papiernen Bürzel und Schurz unsere Literatur emporbringen und ihr stattt eines Geifertuches dienen könnte.'

33 Ibid., III, 989: 'Allein bei den Büchern ist der Kleiderluxus ebenso klar als enorm. Geistliche, andächtige Werke, die sonst im bescheidnen Priester-Ornat und Trauermantel einherwandelten, kleiden sich wie Gecken nach englischem Schnitt und tragen Tressen und reden doch von Gott.'

34 Jean Paul, *Werke* (Berend edn.), I, 1, 202: 'Völlig unnötig wär' es, aus Papier mit der Schere scheinbare Helden zuzuschneiden, solange man noch Schneider hätte, die aus Tuch mit der Schere wirkliche Helden zuzuschneiden im Stande sind.'

35 Ibid., 113: 'Die Philosophie erfindet, die Poesie verschönert die Erfindung; die eine ist Kolumb, der Amerika endeckt, die andere Vespuzius Amerikus, der es benennt; die eine Tuchmacher, die andre Schneider.'

36 Horn, *Poesie und Beredsamkeit*, II, 196: 'Die äussere Tracht, in der wir uns und andere täglich sehen, ist für die Fantasie, ja selbst für Geist und Herz von grösserer Wichtigkeit, als man meistens zu glauben pflegt, indem die gewöhnlichen Geschichten der deutschen Bildung gänzlich davon schweigen.'

37 Fichte, *Werke*, VI, 440: 'Dieser neue Luxus fordert von Zeit zu Zeit neue Modewaaren; denn es ist ja unmöglich, dass einer widerum lese, was er schon einmal gelesen hat, oder auch dasjenige, was unsere Vorgänger vor uns gelesen haben; – so wie es unanständig ist, in demselben Kleide

zu wiederholten Malen in grosse Gesellschaft zu kommen, oder sich nach der Sitte der Grossältern zu kleiden.'

Chapter Six

1 Goethe, *Werke*, VII, 495: 'dass ich da Bildung suchte, wo keine zu finden war, dass ich mir einbildete ein Talent erwerben zu können, zu dem ich nicht die geringste Anlage hatte.'

2 Ibid., 494: 'Nicht vor Irrtum zu bewahren ist die Pflicht des Menschenerziehers.'

3 Ibid., 495: 'Wer seinen Irrtum nur kostet, hält lange damit haus ... er freuet sich dessen als eines seltenen Glücks, aber wer ihn ganz erschöpft, der muss ihn kennenlernen.'

4 Ibid., 495: 'Du wirst keine deiner Torheiten bereuen und keine zurückwünschen, kein glücklicheres Schicksal kann einem Menschen werden.'

5 Ibid., 520: 'Er behauptete: das Erste und Letzte am Menschen sei Tätigkeit, und man könne nichts tun, ohne die Anlage dazu zu haben, ohne den Instinkt der uns dazu treibe.'

6 Ibid., 496: 'Handeln ist leicht, Denken ist schwer; nach dem Gedanken handeln unbequem.'

7 Ibid., 497: 'deine Lehrjahre sind vorüber; die Natur hat dich losgesprochen.'

8 Ibid., 550: 'Es sind nur wenige, die den Sinn haben und zugleich zur Tat fähig sind. Der Sinn erweitert, aber lähmt; die Tat belebt, aber beschränkt.'

9 Ibid., 431: 'In Amerika glaubte ich zu wirken, über dem Meere glaubte ich nützlich und notwendig zu sein ... Wie anders seh' ich jetzt die Dinge, und wie ist mir das nächste so wert, so teuer geworden.'

10 Ibid., 431; *Wilhelm Meister*, II, 11: 'Ich werde zurückkehren und in meinem Hause, in meinem Baumgarten, mitten unter den Meinigen sagen: "Hier oder nirgend ist Amerika".' Besides the application of the above in *Sartor* (196) – 'America is here or nowhere' – a less-well-known one occurs in *Past and Present* (Book III, 14) where this Goethean remnant is found in connection with Cromwell: 'Oliver knew that his America lay THERE, Westward Ho.'

11 G. Lukács (*Goethe und seine Zeit*, 38) misses the inner connection between contemplation and action, in keeping with Pietistical concepts of active love. He interprets the call to action at the end of the *Bekenntnisse* as a rejection of spirituality by Goethe ('Abkehr von reiner Innerlichkeit').

12 Goethe, *Werke*, VII, 436: 'bloss in sich gekehrt, betrachtete er sein hohles, leeres Ich, dass ihm als ein unermesslicher Abgrund erschien. Wie rührend war es, wenn er von diesem traurigen Zustand sprach! "Ich sehe nichts vor mir, nichts hinter mir," rief er aus, "als eine unendliche Nacht, in der ich mich in der schrecklichsten Einsamkeit befinde ... Doch da ist keine Höhe, keine Tiefe, kein Vor und Zurück, kein Wort drückt diesen immer gleichen Zustand aus ... Kein Strahl einer Gottheit erscheint mir in dieser Nacht.'

13 Ibid., 405: 'Tief in uns liegt diese schöpferische Kraft, die das zu erschaffen vermag, was sein soll, und uns nicht ruhen und rasten lässt, bis wir es ... auf eine oder die andere Weise dargestellt haben.'

14 C.F. Harrold (*Carlyle and German Thought*, 203) seems to suggest that Carlyle had been merely 'browsing around in *Wilhelm Meister*, studying isolated passages, here a sentence, there a chapter.' This seems a rather naïve judgment on the labours of translation, for which an intensive study of the text is a necessary prerequisite.

15 Goethe, *Werke*, VII, 496: 'Niemand weiss, was er tut, wenn er recht handelt; aber des Unrechten sind wir uns immer bewusst.'

16 Carlyle, *Essays III*, 7; see also *Wotton Reinfred*, 73: 'One of the wisest men now living has told us, "Of what is wrong we are always conscious, of what is right, never" ' (*Last Words of Thomas Carlyle*).

17 Goethe, *Werke*, VII, 83: 'Lehrer, Wahrsager, Freund der Götter und des Menschen.'

18 Carlyle refers here to Goethe's poem 'Symbolum,' which he also quotes in the 'Inaugural Address.' The last line of the last stanza Carlyle translates as 'Work and despair not,' instead of Goethe's 'Wir heissen Euch hoffen' (We bid you hope). This distorted translation does not come close to Goethe's meaning. Goethe's disapproval of such work ethics is expressed in *Maximen und Reflexionen*, Werke XII, numbers 249 and 250: 'Es ist nichts furchtbarer anzuschauen als grenzenlose Tätigkeit ohne Fundament' and 'Es ist nichts schrecklicher als eine tätige Unwissenheit' (There is nothing worse than to observe limitless activity without foundation. There is nothing worse than active ignorance.)

19 Goethe, *Werke*, VII, 406: ' "Was es auch sei", versetzte er, "der Verstand oder die Empfindung, das uns eins für das andere hingeben, eins vor dem andern wählen heisst, so ist Entschiedenheit und Folge nach meiner Meinung das Verehrungswürdigste am Menschen. Man kann die Ware und das Geld nicht zugleich haben ... Der Mensch ist zu einer beschränkten Lage geboren." '

20 Ibid., 553: 'Der Mensch ist nicht eher glücklich, als bis sein unbedingtes Streben sich selbst seine Begrenzung bestimmt.'

21 This view, which C.F. Harrold expresses (*Carlyle and German Thought*, 216), is based on Bielschowsky (*Goethe*), who reaches this judgment by evaluating *Entsagen* with a view to the totality of Goethe's *own* work, and from this perspective is justified in making such a statement.

22 Goethe, *Werke*, VIII, 11–12: 'Mein Leben soll eine Wanderschaft werden. Sonderbare Pflichten des Wanderers habe ich auszuüben und ganz eigene Prüfungen zu bestehen.'

23 Ibid., VII, 552: 'Das Nützliche befördert sich selbst, denn die Menge bringt es hervor, und alle können's nicht entbehren; das Schöne muss befördert werden, denn wenige stellen's dar und viele bedürfen's.'

24 Ibid., 553: 'Es ist Ihre Sache, zu prüfen und zu wählen, und die unsere, Ihnen beizustehen.'

25 Norton, *Correspondence between Goethe and Carlyle*, 228, letter of 23 October 1830.

26 This lecture series of 1806 is not to be confused with an earlier one (1974) *Über die Bestimmung des Gelehrten.*

27 Harrold (*Carlyle and German Thought*, 182–3) introduces *Grundzüge des gegenwärtigen Zeitalters* into the discussion, but does not give his reasons for doing so. It is true that Fichte uses the term *Heroen* in this work, partly designating warriors of the Heroic Age with it, but not in *Über das Wesen* where Hero-worship is not discussed at all; neither is the word 'hero' used.

28 Fichte, *Werke*, VI, 412: 'Sein persönliches Leben ist nun wirklich in dem Leben der Idee aufgegangen, und in demselben vernichtet, welche Selbstvernichtung in der Idee von dem Studierenden nur angestrebt wurde. So gewiss er ein vollendeter Gelehrter ist, giebt es für ihn gar keinen Gedanken mehr an seine Person, sondern sein sämmtliches Denken geht immerfort auf im Denken der Sache.'

29 Ibid., 423: 'Nicht etwa dass dieser Gedanke ihn zu hochmütiger Selbstüberhebung aufblähe.'

30 Harrold (*Carlyle*, 220) speaks of *Selbsttödtung* as a rational act 'ridding oneself of a purely personal point of view.' In his article 'Carlyle and Novalis,' Harrold states that, for Novalis, Nature is 'symbolical of spirit' (49), but not how it got there or how it relates to the 'Me,' if at all. The transcendental Self is mentioned in a sentence. Wellek (*Confrontations*, 58) is vague on the subject, offering a half-sentence, 'the submergence of the individuality in the ecstasy of mysticims' as an explanation. Korff (*Geist der Goethezeit*, III, 255) overlooks the fact that Novalis speaks of *Selbsttödtung* as a philosophical act, interpreting it as a death wish. He even goes so far as to speak of doing away with the natural world.

31 Fichte was Novalis's main source of inspiration, as he states in his diary

(Reich, *Novalis,* 21). He called him a Newton, a lawgiver of the inner universe: 'Fichte bin ich Aufmunterung schuldig. Er ist's der mich weckte.'

32 Novalis, *Schriften,* II, 113 (Schlegel-Tieck edition): 'Philosophiren ist dephlegmatisiren, vivificiren.'

33 Novalis, *Tagebuch, Deutsche Literatur in Entwicklungsreihen,* Romantik, IV, 275

34 Novalis, *Schriften,* II, Fragmente, 158: 'Die Poesie ist das echt absolut reele. Dies ist der Kern meiner Philosophie. Je poetischer, je wahrer.'

35 Ibid., III, 246: 'Der Zauberer ist Poet' (The Magician is a Poet).

36 Ibid., II 'Blütenstaub,' 255: 'Nach Innen geht der geheimnisvolle Weg. In uns oder nirgends ist die Ewigkeit mit ihren Welten, die Vergangenheit und Zukunft.'

37 Ibid., III, 'Blütenstaub,' 304: 'Der erste Schritt wird Blick nach Innen, absondernde Beschauung unsers Selbst. Wer hier stehn bleibt, gerät nur halb. Der zweite Schritt muss ... selbsttätige, gehaltne Beobachtung der Aussenwelt sein.'

38 Ibid., II, *Die Lehrlinge zu Sais,* 56: 'Auf sein Gemüt und seine Gedanken lauschte er sorgsam. Er wusste nicht wohin ihn seine Sehnsucht trieb. Wie er grösser ward, strich er umher, besah sich andre Länder, andre Meere, neue Lüfte, fremde Sterne, unbekannte Pflanzen, Tiere, Menschen ... Nun fand er überall Bekanntes wieder, nur wunderlich gemischt, gepaart, und also ordneten sich selbst in ihm oft seltsame Dinge ... Nun sah er bald nichts mehr allein. – In grosse bunte Bilder drängten sich die Wahrnehmungen seiner Sinne ... Bald waren ihm die Sterne Menschen, bald die Menschen Sterne, die Steine Tiere, die Wolken Pflanzen, er spielte mit den Kräften und Erscheinungen, er wusste, wo und wie er dies und jenes finden und erscheinen lassen konnte, und griff so selbst in den Saiten nach Tönen und Gängen umher. (English transl. by author); see Carlyle, *Essays II,* 31.

39 Ibid., 'Fragmente,' 169: 'Es gibt nur einen Tempel auf der Welt und das ist der menschliche Körper. Nichts ist heiliger als diese hohe Form.'

40 Wellek, *Confrontations,* 59

41 Novalis, *Schriften,* II, 'Fragmente,' 169: 'Der Mensch hat immer eine symbolische Philosophie des Daseins in seinen Werken und seinen Handlungen ausgedrückt. Er kündigt sich selbst und sein Evangelium der Natur an. Er ist der Messias der Natur.'

42 Wellek (*Confrontations,* 59), refers only to *Essays II,* 'Novalis,' 39; *Sartor,* 190; *Heroes,* 10. The additional references occur in *Past and Present,* Bk II, ch. 16, 124, and Bk. IV, ch. 6, 286.

43 Novalis, *Schriften* II, 'Fragmente,' 115, 'Der echte philosophische Akt ist

Selbsttödtung; dies ist der reale Anfang aller Philosophie, dahin geht alles Bedürfnis des philosophischen Jüngers, und nur dieser Akt entspricht allen Bedingungen und Merkmalen der transzendenten Handlung.'

44 Werner, *Söhne des Thals*, Part I, Prologue iv: 'Doch dieses stille, friedliche Entsagen / Ist der Vollendung nahe Stufe schon.'

45 Ibid., Part I, II, ii: '– aus diesen dumpfen Massen / Erhebt der reine Phoenix nimmer sich!'

46 Ibid., Part I, II, i: 'Schwand nicht das Scheusal, / als du mit mut'gen Händen es ergriffst?'

47 Jean Paul, *Werke*, VI, 1100: 'Erst jetzo wird die frühere Wassertaufe eine wahre Feuertaufe.'

48 Werner, *Söhne des Thals*, Part II, V, i: 'So musst du auch, willst du den Stoff beherrschen, / Vom eignen dich durch Selbstertödtung scheiden, / Nur wenn dir Geist und Stoff Erscheinung sind, / Gespiegelt im Unendlichen – nur dann / Kannst du ihr launenhaftes Wechselspiel / Mit regelrechtem Willen umgestalten ... Durch Selbstverlierung lernst du anzuschauen.'

49 Werner, *Das Kreuz an der Ostsee*, Teil I, 'Historischer Vorbericht,' 56: 'Ihre Sitten waren so einfach wie ihre Sprache. Für Magen und Seele hatten sie – wie noch die heutigen Litauer und Finanziers – ein und dasselbe, für Tugend und Laster gar kein Wort' (Deutsche Literatur in Entwicklungsreihen, *Romantik*, vol. XX, edited by P. Kluckhohn [Leipzig: Reclam 1937]).

50 This clarifies Carlyle's source, which Harrold in his *Sartor* edition (117), provides with the note: (1) Barrett: 'A Finnish scholar informs me that there is nothing in the Finnish language to support Carlyle's allusion.' Carlyle uses Werner's reference three times in *Sartor* (117, 159, 90) and twice in *Past and Present* (Bk I, ch. 6, and Bk III, ch. 4) In the last citation Carlyle speaks of 'Slavonic dialects.' There is an additional reference in *Essays II*, 'Schiller' (189): 'Does not his Soul, – which in some Sclavonic dialects means his Stomach – sit forever at its ease ...?'

Chapter Seven

1 Horn, *Freundliche Schriften* I, 151: 'Der Zustand des vollendet Göttlichen wäre deshalb ein ewig seliges Ja zu allem Guten, der des vollendet Teuflischen ein ewig unseliges Nein.'

2 Ibid., 152: 'Hier ist denn also der Punkt, von dem aus der Teufel betrachtet werden soll, und so sollten ihn auch die Dichter schildern. Wie viele haben es versucht und wie wenigen ist es gelungen!' Another defi-

nition of the 'ewige Ja' and the 'ewige Nein' is to be found in *Freundliche Schriften*, II, 139, in connection with Shakespeare's Shylock: 'Wer aber den Hass allein hat, ohne Liebe, gleichsam ein ewiges Nein ohne ein ewiges Ja ... der wird sich nur dadurch zu retten suchen, dass er seine Negation zu etwas Positivem zu erheben sucht ... So hier Shylok [sic], dessen Charakter als ein ewiges Nein zu allem Guten and Schönen erscheint' (He who feels hate alone without love, so to speak an eternal No without the eternal Yes ... will only be able to save himself by elevating his negation into something positive ... See Shylock whose character is an eternal No to everything good and beautiful.

3 Horn, 'Diamantene Kutsche,' 160: 'Es ist kein Gott, es ist kein Christus, aber ein Teufel ist.'
4 Ibid., 196: 'Sieh seinen Blick, der ewig Nein spricht zu allem Guten.'
5 Leopold, 'Thomas Carlyle and Franz Horn,' 217
6 E.T.A. Hoffmann 'Kampf der Sänger,' *Werke* VI, 24–63. Carlyle mentions this selection of tales in *German Romance* II, 15.
7 Fouqué, 'Sängerkrieg,' 270: 'Du – Ich – Das sind zwei Gegenbilder, scharf, / Wie Nacht und Tag, wie Jammerschrei und Jubel.'
8 Ibid., 273–4:

MEISTER KLINGSOHR: Donnre Du noch so zürnend dazwischen,
Lügner, Dein trügendes Nein.
Die ewige Wahrheit,
Die ewige Liebe tönt: Ja! –
Was murrst Du in Dir
Wie fern abwetternder Donner
Im fernsten Gebürg?
Was blitzet Dein Auge so trutzig scheu?
Sag's laut!
EGON: Ich will nicht! Bei'm ewigen Nein!
MEISTER KLINGSOHR: Sollst! Sollst! Beim ewigen Ja!

9 Schelling, *Von der Weltseele*, 'Da offenbar entgegengesetzte Materien in unserer Atmosphäre sich das Gleichgewicht halten, so muss irgendwohin das Centrum fallen, auf welches sie beide einwirken.'

Chapter Eight

1 German sources have been discussed only in general terms regarding Palingenesia. Harrold (*Carlyle and German Thought*, 78, 111–12) is totally unspecific, merely mentioning Goethe, Fichte, Schelling in passing. Hill

Shine (*Carlyle and the Saint-Simonians*, ch. 4) gives fuller treatment, if one can call a list of the users of the term just that. It may well be that Carlyle was indebted to the Saint-Simonians, but it should be borne in mind, as Wellek rightly points out (*Confrontations*, 85), that Carlyle was never a Positivist. The fact that he did not use the term 'Palingenesia' before writing *Sartor* is no proof regarding the source. He had read the term in Herder and translated it in Jean Paul. Carlyle nowhere states that Palingenesia is a stage between two cycles as Shine indicates. The fact that he sees eye to eye with the Saint-Simonians in considering the contemporary state of society as deteriorating does not mean that he arrived at this judgment by their reasoning. On the contrary, in his letter to G. d'Eichthal, which Shine quotes (55), one gets the impression that agreement is reached *in spite* of differences: 'Some clearer insights into my view, moral and religious, which are originating from almost the opposite point of vision, yet curiously corresponding.' Carlyle's letter to Goethe (22 January 1831) can hardly be considered as proof to the contrary as he clearly speak of the *false* application of the truth that 'Man is still Man.' Carlyle thus sees the movement as a Sign of the Times, but, it is implied, as a manifestation in the wrong direction. The Editor's remark that Teufelsdröckh might have been abducted by the Society, as a man 'so obnoxious to most of the hostile Sects that convulse our Era' (297), does not testify to a friendly rapprochement or possible cooperation. Furthermore, no mention of the Phoenix is made in any of the sources given by Shine. Wellek (*Confrontations*, 88–9) suggests Palingenesia in Herder's *Ideen* (Book 5, chs. 4–6), where the term itself does *not* occur. The doctrine Herder expounds there is the Great Chain theory, in no way original to him. Throughout *Ideen V*, Herder is concerned with Metempsychosis. Regarding Wellek's reference to Herder's *Zerstreute Blätter*, vol. III, Herder uses the term 'Palingenesia' there in the sense of cultural change. The last passage Wellek refers to (Herder, vol. XIII, 200) deals with immortality; since the word is not used at all. Wellek's reference implying the contrary is misleading: 'the final passage of the fifth book of the *Ideen*, which celebrates both in prose and verse ... the "palingenesis" of the human soul' (*Confrontations*, 89).

2 Harrold (*Carlyle and German Thought*) does not mention Jean Paul at all in this connection. Shine includes him in a list of users of the term 'Palingenesia' (*Carlyle and the Saint-Simonians*, 75). Wellek repeats this reference, but fails to produce the evidence (*Confrontations*, 88).

3 Jean Paul, II (Berend ed.), *Grönländische Prozesse*, 91; *Hesperus*, I, 480; *Selberlebensbeschreibung* VI, 1044; *Siebenkäs*, II, 24 and 370; *Levana*, V, 544 and 580; *Herbst-Blumine*, 299 and 404. See also Tieck, 'Die Elfen,' translated by Carlyle in *German Romance* I, 353, where the image is de-

scribed in fairy-tale context only. Also F. Schlegel (*Geschichte der alten und neuen Literatur*) in connection with the rebirth of Spanish literature 'rising like a Phoenix from the ashes' (*Kritische Ausgabe*, VI, 281).

4 *Methode*, 305: 'diese hat die Wiedergeburt des esoterischen Christentums wie die Verkündigung des absoluten Evangeliums in sich vorbereitet.' Notice the use of the word 'esoteric' also in Carlyle's correspondence: 'As to Kant and Schelling and Fichte, and all those worthies, I confess myself but an esoteric after all' (Carlyle, *Early Letters* I, 333).

5 Schelling distinguishes three periods in history: 1 / that of Nature; 2 / that of Fate or Necessity; and 3 / that of Providence (*Methode*, 290). Fichte, in *Grundzüge*, distinguishes five principle epochs: 1 / State of Innocence; 2 / State of ruling authority; 3 / Liberation; 4 / Knowledge; 5 / Art.

6 Goethe, *Werke*, II, 'Noten zum westöstlichen Divan,' 208: 'Das eigentliche, einzige und tiefste Thema der Welt- und Menschengeschichte, dem alle übrigen untergeordnet sind, bleibt der Konflikt des Unglaubens und Glaubens. Alle Epochen, in welchen der Glaube herrscht, unter welcher Gestalt er auch wolle, sind glänzend, herzerhebend und fruchtbar für Mitwelt und Nachwelt. Alle Epochen dagegen, in welchen der Unglaube, in welcher Form er sei, einen kümmerlichen Sieg behauptet, und wenn sie auch einen Augenblick mit einem Scheinglanze prahlen sollten, verschwinden vor der Nachwelt, weil sich niemand gern mit Erkenntnis des Unfruchtbaren abquälen mag.' References to periods of alternating Unbelief and Belief, or Denial and Faith occur in: 1. *Sartor*, 119, 112; 2. *Diderot*, 248; 3. *French Revolution* I, 10–11; 4. *Heroes*, 77; 126, 172, 204; 5. *Cromwell* I, 83–4; 6. *Characteristics*, 29. See Shine, *Carlyle and the Saint Simonians* (26), for a complete list, including Carlyle's correspondence, where all of the above are included, except the first *Sartor* and the *Characteristics* references, which I added.

7 Carlyle recalls the intensity of his study of these passages (Goethe, *Werke*, VIII, *Wilhelm Meisters Wanderjahre*, Bk. 2, ch. 1), in his 'Inaugural Address' (*Essays IV*, 473): 'I first read it many years ago, and of course, I had to read into the very heart of it while I was translating it.'

8 Goethe, *Werke*, VIII, ibid., 155: 'Das erste ist Ehrfurcht vor dem, was über uns ist ... das Zeugnis von ihnen verlangen, dass ein Gott da droben sei, der sich in Eltern, Lehrern, Vorgesetzten abbildet und offenbart. Das zweite: Ehrfurcht vor dem was unter uns ist. Dann aber heissen wir ihn sich ermannen, gegen Kameraden gewendet nach ihnen sich richten. Nun steht er strack und kühn, nicht etwa selbstisch vereinzelt nur in Verbindung mit seinesgleichen macht er Fronte gegen die Welt.'

9 Werner, *Söhne des Thals*, part II, Epilog, 278: 'Doch konnte er die alte

Form vernichten / Hat wohl die neue längeren Bestand? / ... Entrollt die Bücher aller Weltgeschichten, / Sie sind des steten Wechsels Unterpfand / Mag ewig auch das Heilige bestehen, / Sein irdisch Staubgewand muss untergehen.'

10 Schelling, *Methode*, 308, quotes a slight variation of Goethe's *Faust*, I, ll. 577–8: 'Was ihr den Geist der Zeiten heisst, / Das ist im Grund der Herren eigner Geist.'

11 Schelling, ibid., 309, quotes a slight variation of Goethe's *Faust* I, l. 573: 'Und wie wir's dann so herrlich weit gebracht.'

12 Carlyle, *Sartor*, 119. Compare also the Editor's description of Teufelsdröckh as 'a man who had manfully defied the "Time-prince", or Devil, to his face' (293).

13 Goethe, *Werke* IV, 5 (Cotta edition), Selection 'Gott, Gemüt, und Welt'

14 Goethe, *Werke*, VIII, *Wilhelm Meisters Wanderjahre*, 145: 'Mit allem dem werden Sie mir gestehen, dass der Mensch der Veränderung nicht widersteht, welche die Zeit hervorbringt.'

15 Werner, *Söhne des Thals*, II, 5, iii:

ADAM: Wenn du mir meinen Leinenmantel nimmst,
Und mich in ein Gewand von Sammet kleidest –
Hast du mich umgeschaffen? –
ROBERT: Du verwirrst mich.
ADAM: Sind jene Politik und jene Formen,
In die, wie ein Chamäleon, die Welt
Sich heute so, und morgen anders kleidet –
Sind sie der Kern von unsrer Wesenheit? –
Wie! oder sind sie nicht die Hülle bloss,
Die, mag sie leichter oder schwerer sein,
Den Körper selber nicht verändern kann? –
Kann der Despot die inn're Kraft, dein Selbst,
Das dich zum Abglanz Gottes macht, dir rauben?
Und kann der Freistaat dir den Strahl von oben –
Das Einzige, warum du da bist – geben?

16 Jean Paul, *Werke*, I, 'Preface to *Hesperus*,' 490: 'Ja; es wird zwar ein anderes Zeitalter kommen, wo es Licht wird, und wo der Mensch aus erhabenen Träumen erwacht und die Träume – wiederfindet, weil er nichts verlor als den Schlaf ... Unendliche Vorsicht, du wirst Tag werden lassen. – Aber noch streitet die zwölfte Stunde der Nacht: die Nachtraubvögel ziehen; die Gespenster poltern; die Toten gaukeln; die Lebendigen träumen.' For other Carlyle passages in which this quote is contained, see Appendix to chapter 9.

17 Ibid., V, *Levana*, 567: 'Zum Ziele der Erziehungskunst, das uns vorher klar und gross vorstehen muss ... gehört die Erhebung über den Zeitgeist. Nicht für die Gegenwart ist das Kind zu erziehen ... sondern für die Zukunft, ja oft noch wider die nächste. Man muss aber den Geist kennen den man fliehen will' (Author's English translation).

18 Ibid., 568: 'Was wir Geist der Zeit nennen, hiessen unsere Alten Weltlauf, letzte Zeiten, Zeichen vor dem jüngsten Tage, Reich des Teufels, des Antichrists. Lauter trübe Namen!'

19 Ibid., 570: 'Aus der Welt wurde uns ein Weltgebäude, aus dem Äther ein Gas, aus Gott eine Kraft, aus der zweiten Welt ein Sarg.'

20 It should be stated at the outset that hero-worship is foreign to the North American mentality, except in sports. The reason for this is found in the belief in individual achievement. Generally, the North American does not like to admit that a debt is owed to others on his road to success. Indeed, one may contend that the image of the self-made man interferes with any form of hero-worship and cancels it out. In contrast, the European often desires to relate to an intellectual or spiritual model that affected the pattern of his own life. This search for a *Vorbild*, or prototype of humanity, is especially strong in younger years when life-goals are in the making. The veneration of truly great men, especially poets and teachers, is vouched for by the many monuments erected in their honour, which are largely absent from the North American scene.

21 Schelling, *Über die Methode*, 286: 'Handeln, handeln! Das ist der Aufruf, der von vielen Seiten ertönt, am lautesten von denen, die kein Wissen besitzen.'

22 Ibid., 345: 'Ein Werkzeug der Götter, eine Verkündigerin göttlicher Geheimnisse, die Enthüllerin der Ideen ist.'

23 Werner, *Söhne des Thals*, Part I, Prolog: 'Sie stirbet nicht, die heilige Gemeine; / Denn aus der Asche dämmert erst das Licht.'

24 Goethe, *Tasso*, I, iii: 'Wie gleiches Streben Held und Dichter bindet.'

25 Goethe, *Iphigenie*, II, i: 'Ein jeglicher muss seinen Helden wählen / Dem er die Wege zum Olymp hinauf / Sich nacharbeitet.'

26 Goethe, *Werke*, VII, *Wilhelm Meisters Lehrjahre*, 83: 'Eingeboren auf dem Grund seines Herzens wächst die schöne Blume der Weisheit hervor, und wenn die andern wachend träumen ... so lebt er den Traum des Lebens als Wachender. Und so ist der Dichter zugleich Lehrer, Wahrsager, Freund der Götter und der Menschen.'

27 This attitude to Goethe as an annunciator was to determine Carlyle's view of the periodicity of German literature, as he tells the poet himself: '... till under you and Schiller, I should say, a Third grand Period had evolved itself ... a period of new Spirituality and Belief in the midst of

old Doubt and Denial ... wherein Reverence is again rendered compatible with knowledge, and Art and Religion are one' (*Correspondence between Goethe and Carlyle*, 23 May 1830). Here Carlyle fits Goethe into the cyclic pattern of Belief and Unbelief that the latter had formulated!

28 Goethe, *Werke* VIII, *Wilhelm Meisters Wanderjahre*, 158: 'eine begeisterte Gemeinschaft der Heiligen, welches heisst: der im höchsten Grad Guten und Weisen.'

29 Ibid., 156: 'Ungern entschliesst sich der Mensch zur Ehrfurcht ... es is ein höherer Sinn ... der sich nur bei besonders Begünstigten aus sich selbst entwickelt.'

30 Novalis, *Schriften* (Schlegel-Tieck edition), 'Fragmente,' 219; Carlyle's translation, *Essays II*, 74–5

31 Fichte, *Werke*, *Über das Wesen*, VI, 408: 'Was ist edler als der Trieb zu wirken, Menschen zu begeistern, und gewaltig ihren Blick auf das Heilige zu richten? Und doch kann dieser Trieb zur Versuchung werden, das Heilige gemein darzustellen, damit es an die Gemeinheit komme, und es so zu entheiligen.'

32 Ibid., VI, 396: 'Das Genie wird immer erscheinen als ein besonderes Genie, für Philosophie, Poesie, Naturbeobachtung, Gesetzgebung und dergleichen, keineswegs aber bloss im Allgemeinen als Genie.'

33 Ibid., VI, 406: 'Jene Idee tritt in jedem Zeitalter heraus in einer neuen Gestalt, und begehrt die umgebende Welt nach sich zu gestalten.'

34 Eckermann, *Gespräche*, II, 23 October 1828, 403: 'Aber wissen Sie was? Die Welt soll nicht so rasch zum Ziele, als wir denken und wünschen. Immer sind die retardierenden Dämonen da, die überall entgegentreten, so dass es zwar im ganzen vorwärts geht, aber sehr langsam.'

35 Werner, *Söhne des Thals*, I, Prolog: 'Drum weilet sinnend bei dem schönen Bilde / Der frommen Zeiten, die vorüber sind; / Verschwunden sind die heitern Lustgefilde, / Der Mutterbrust entlaufen ist das Kind. / Es deckt sich mit der Weisheit kaltem Schilde.'

36 Novalis, *Werke*, III, 7 (Kamnitzer edn.): 'wo Europa ein christliches Land war ... ein grosses gemeinschaftliches Interesse verband die entlegensten Provinzen dieses weiten geistlichen Reichs.'

37 Ibid., *Christenheit oder Europa*, 7: 'diese [waren] auserwählte, mit wunderbaren Kräften ausgerüstete Männer wie Kinder des Himmels, deren Gegenwart und Zuneigung mannigfachen Segen verbreitete.'

38 Ibid.: 'Sie waren die erfahrenen Steuerleute auf dem grossen unbekannten Meere, in deren Obhut man alle Stürme gering schätzen und zuversichtlich auf eine sichere Gelandung und Landung an der Küste der eigentlichen vaterländischen Welt rechnen durfte. Die wildesten, gefräs-

sigsten Neigungen mussten der Ehrfurcht und dem Gehorsam gegen ihre Worte weichen.'

39 Ibid., 8: 'Mit welcher Heiterkeit verliess man die schönen Versammlungen in den geheimnisvollen Kirchen, die mit ermunternden Bildern geschmückt, mit süssen Düften erfüllt und von heiliger erhebender Musik belebt waren. In ihnen wurden die geweihten Reste ehemaliger gottesfürchtiger Menschen dankbar in köstlichen Behältnissen aufbewahrt.'

40 Ibid., 9: 'und das eingeschränkte Wissen dem unendlichen Glauben vorziehen und sich gewöhnen würden, alles Grosse und Wunderwürdige zu verachten.'

41 Ibid., 16–17: 'und machte die unendliche schöpferische Musik des Weltalls zum einförmigen Klappern einer ungeheuren Mühle, die, vom Strom des Zufalls getrieben und auf ihm schwimmend, eine Mühle an sich, ohne Baumeister und Müller, und eigentlich ein echtes Perpetuum mobile, eine sich selbst mahlende Mühle sei.'

42 Ibid., 26: 'Wo ist jener alte, liebe alleinseligmachende Glaube an die Regierung Gottes auf Erden, wo ist jenes himmlische Zutrauen der Menschen zueinander, jene süsse Andacht bei den Ergiessungen eines gottbegeisterten Gemüts, jener allesumarmende Geist der Christenheit?'

43 Novalis, ibid., 23: 'Es sind die ersten Wehen; setze sich jeder in Bereitschaft zur Geburt!'

44 Ibid., 18–19: 'Dass die Zeit der Auferstehung gekommen ist, und gerade die Begebenheiten, die gegen ihre Belebung gerichtet zu sein schienen und ihren Untergang zu vollenden drohten, die günstigsten Zeichen ihrer Regeneration geworden sind, dies kann einem historischen Gemüte gar nicht zweifelhaft bleiben. Wahrhafte Anarchie ist das Zeugungselement der Religion. Aus der Vernichtung alles Positiven hebt sie ihr glorreiches Haupt als neue Weltstifterin empor.'

45 Ibid., 19: 'knüpft ihn durch eine höhere Sehnsucht an die Höhen des Himmels, gebt ihm eine Beziehung aufs Weltall.'

46 Ibid., 25: 'Nur die Religion kann Europa wieder aufwecken und die Völker versöhnen und die Christenheit mit neuer Herrlichkeit sichtbar auf Erden in ihr altes friedenstiftendes Amt installieren.'

47 Ibid., 19: 'Der Geist Gottes schwebt über den Wassern, und ein himmlisches Eiland wird als Wohnstätte der neuen Menschen, als Stromgebiet des ewigen Lebens zuerst sichtbar.'

48 Ibid., 7: 'Eine zahlreiche Zunft, zu der jederman den Zutritt hatte ... Jedes Glied dieser Gesellschaft wurde allenthalben geehrt, und wenn die gemeinen Leute Trost oder Hilfe, Schutz oder Rat bei ihm suchten ... so fand es auch bei den Mächtigeren Schutz.'

49 Carlyle had already commented on the Age of Reason in 'Voltaire' (*Essays I*, 396), including the translation of a substantial passage from Novalis's *Christenheit oder Europa*, referring to its author merely as 'a deep observer' (465).

50 Novalis, *Christenheit oder Europa*, 17–18: 'Gott wurde zum müssigen Zuschauer des grossen rührenden Schauspiels, das die Gelehrten aufführten.' See also Goethe, *Werke*, I, 'Die weltanschaulichen Gedichte,' 357: 'Was wär' ein Gott, der nur von aussen stiesse / Im Kreis das All am Finger laufen liesse!'

51 Novalis, *Christenheit oder Europa*, 14–15; Carlyle, *Past and Present*, Bk III, ch. 1, 138

Chapter Nine

1 The arguments of the first school of thought are best presented by Harrold in his Preface to his *Sartor* edition (pp. lix–lx). In *Carlyle and German Thought*, however, he does voice some reservations: 'It may be objected that I have understated the influence of Jean Paul, especially in view of the well-known similarities of their styles' (Preface, vi). Tennyson, in *Sartor Called Resartus* deals with Jean Paul in a footnote to his style chapter 274, fn. 32. Parallels with Jean Paul are presented by Pape ('Jean Paul') with more fervour than accuracy, well argued by Roellinger ('The Early Development') and Smeed ('Thomas Carlyle and Jean Paul Richter'), and also by Wellek (*Confrontations*) in spite of his wavering attitude: 'The great stylistic change ... has to be ascribed to the influence of Jean Paul' (63). For further references see Wellek, *Confrontations*, 62 fn. 77.

2 Froude, *History of the First Forty Years*, vol. 1, 323, and *History of His Life in London*, vol. 1, 40–1. See also Wellek, *Confrontations*, 62.

3 Smeed, 'Carlyles Jean Paul Übersetzungen,' 271

4 Smeed, 'Carlyle and Jean Paul Richter,' 226

5 First quoted by Wellek (*Confrontations*, 63). Originally contained in *Love Letters of Thomas Carlyle and Jane Welsh*, II, 305.

6 Unaware of its true source, Wellek ascribes this comparison to Carlyle (*Confrontations*, 69).

7 Froude, *The First Forty Years*, vol. 2, 38–40. See Roellinger, 'The Early Development of Carlyle's Style,' 945.

8 Jean Paul, *Ästhetik*, *Werke*, V, 96: 'Nämlich das ungeheure, fast hülflose Gefühl, womit der stille Geist gleichsam in der wilden Riesenmühle des Weltalls betäubt steht und einsam. Unzählige unüberwindliche Welt-

räder sieht er in der seltsamen Mühle hintereinanderkreisen – und hört das Brausen eines ewigen treibenden Stromes ... und so steht er verlassen in der allgewaltigen blinden einsamen Maschine.'

9 Jean Paul, *Komet*, *Werke*, VI, 685–6: 'Und das träumende Herz fasste: die Unsterblichkeit wohnte in den Räumen, der Tod nur auf den Welten ... In den Räumen glänzte, tönte, wehte, hauchte nur Leben und Schaffen im Freien des All; die Sonnen waren nur gedrehte Spinnräder, die Erden nur geschossene Weberschiffchen zu dem unendlichen Gewebe des Isis-Schleiers, der über die Schöpfung hing und der sich verlängerte wenn ihn ein Endlicher hob.' Cited text is De Quincey's translation from *Analects*, *Collected Writings*, 292–3

10 Jean Paul, *Siebenkäs*, *Werke*, II, 267: 'Die Kindheit, und noch mehr ihre Schrecken als ihre Entzückungen, nehmen im Traume wieder Flügel und Schimmer an und spielen wie Johanniswürmchen in der kleinen Nacht de Seele. Zerdrückt uns diese flatternden Funken nicht! – Lasset uns sogar die dunkeln peinlichen Träume als hebende Halbschatten der Wirklichkeit! – Und womit will man uns *die* Träume ersetzen, die uns aus dem untern Getöse des Wasserfalls wegtragen in die stille Höhe der Kindheit, wo der Strom des Lebens noch in seiner kleinen Ebene schweigend und als ein Spiegel des Himmels seinen Abgründen entgegenzog?' Cited text is Carlyle's translation from *Essays II*, 'Jean Paul Again,' 156.

11 Jean Paul, *Titan*, *Werke*, III, 965–6: 'Ich trat jetzt trübe und wild auf den Brocken hinaus. Die Sterne brannten den Himmel hinab und schimmerten um das düstere Gebürge. Der Nebel der alten Zeiten tat sich auf, und ich sah darin unten auf der weiten Ebene die unzähligen Scheiterhaufen glühen, welche bloss Unschuldige zernagten. Um mich lagen aufgetürmte Felsklötze wie Quader niedergebrochener Riesenschlösser; und das Renntiermoos der kalten Zone bedeckte als Schimmel der Erde das alte nackte Berghaupt ... Der Sturm schnaubte um mich und mein flatterndes Schifflein herum und fuhr wild unter die Sterne hinaus und schien sie zu rütteln ... im Innersten war mir gross und düster, und ich wünschte jetzt erschiene mir der Teufel ... da war mir plötzlich als sei die ganze Welt und mein Leben in einem Paar Träumen hinweggetropft, und das Ich sagte zu sich selber; ich bin gewiss der Teufel.'

12 See Smeed, 'Carlyle and Jean Paul Richter,' 246, for further details.

Chapter Ten

1 Eckermann, *Gespräche*, vol. I, 11 October 1828

2 Wellek, *Confrontations*, 37
3 Harrold, *Carlyle and German Thought*, 235
4 Eckermann, *Gespräche*, vol. I, 16 December 1828

Select Bibliography

1 With reference to Carlyle's *Sartor Resartus*, C.F. Harrold's edition has been chosen. All other quotes from his works are cited by the J.D. Traill Centenary edition.
2 The main edition used for Goethe is the *Hamburger Ausgabe in* 14 vols. plus 4 vols. of letters.
3 Passages from Jean Paul are quoted from his *Werke* in 6 vols., edited by Norbert Miller, except for his youthful satires, such as *Grönländische Prozesse, Auswahl aus des Teufels Papieren,* and 'Bücherschau: Mme de Staël's *De l'Allemagne'*, all three of which are quoted from *Sämtliche Werke* in 19 vols., edited by E. Berend (Historisch-kritische Ausgabe).
4 Novalis's *Fragmente* and *Christenheit oder Europa* are quoted from *Sämtliche Werke* in 4 vols., edited by E. Kamnitzer.
5 E.T.A. Hoffmann citations refer to *Werke* in 15 Teilen, edited by Georg Ellinger.
6 All Roman numerals following the title of works cited refer to volumes in the various collected works.

Primary Sources

Carlyle, Thomas. *Works*. Centenary Edition. Edited by H.D. Traill, 30 vols. London: Chapman and Hall 1896–9
– *Sartor Resartus*. Edited by C.F. Harrold. New York: Doubleday 1937
– *Lectures on the History of Literature*. Edited by J.R. Greene. New York: Scribner's 1892
– *Unfinished History of German Literature*. Edited by H. Shine. Lexington: University of Kentucky Press 1951
– *Two Notebooks of Thomas Carlyle, 1822–1832*. Edited by C.E. Norton. New York: The Grolier Club 1898
– *Reminiscences by Thomas Carlyle*, 2 vols. Edited by J.A. Froude. London: Longmans 1881

– *Last Words of Thomas Carlyle.* (Contains *Wotton Reinfred*). London: Longmans 1892
– 'Faustus.' *New Edinburgh Review* 2 (1822)
– *Collected Letters of Thomas and Jane Welsh Carlyle.* Haddington Edition. Edited by C.R. Sanders. Durham, NC: Duke University Press 1970–81
– *Early Letters of Thomas Carlyle, 1821–1826,* 2 vols. Edited by C.E. Norton. London: Macmillan 1886
– *Letters of Thomas Carlyle, 1826–1836,* 2 vols. Edited by C.E. Norton. London: Macmillan 1889
– *New Letters of Thomas Carlyle,* 2 vols. Edited by Alex. Carlyle. London and New York: Lane, Bodley Head 1904
– *New Letters and Memorials of Jane Welsh Carlyle,* 2 vols. Edited by Alex. Carlyle. London and New York: Lane Bodley Head 1903
– *Correspondence between Goethe and Carlyle.* Edited by C.E. Norton. London: Macmillan 1887
– *Love Letters of Thomas Carlyle and Jane Welsh.* 2 vols. Edited by Alex. Carlyle. London: John Lane 1909
De Quincey, Thomas. *Collected Writings,* vol. XI. Edited by D. Mason. Edinburge: Black 1890
De Staël Holstein, A.L. *Germany,* 3 vols. London: Murray 1813
Eckermann, J.P. *Gespräche mit Goethe in den letzten Jahren seines Lebens,* 2 vols. Leipzig: Diederich 1902
Fichte, J.G. *Sämmtliche Werke.,* 8 vols. Edited by I.H. Fichte. Berlin: Veit 1846
– *Popular Works,* 2 vols. Translated by W. Smith, London: Trübner 1889
– *Über das Wesen des Gelehrten.* Berlin: Himburg 1806
Forster, G. *Ansichten vom Niederrhein.* Darmstadt: Wiss. Buchges. 1989
Fouqué. Friedrich Baron de la Motte. *Der Sängerkrieg auf der Wartburg: Ein Dichterspiel.* Berlin: Herbig 1828
Goethe, J.W. von. *Goethes Werkes.* Hamburger Ausgabe, 18 vols. Hamburg: Wegner 1963–7
– *Gedenkausgabe der Werke, Briefe und Gespräche,* 24 vols. Edited by E. Beutler. Zürich: Artemis Verlag 1953
Hippel, Fr.Th. von. *Lebensläufe nach aufsteigender Linie,* 4 vols. Berlin: Reimer 1828
Hoffmann, E.T.A. *Werke,* 15 vols. Edited by Georg Ellinger. Berlin: Bong 1912
– *Dichtungen und Schriften.* Gesamtausgabe, 15 vols. Edited by W. Harich, Weimar: Lichtenstein 1924
Horn, Franz. *Die Poesie und Beredsamkeit der Deutschen von Luthers Zeit bis zur Gegenwart,* 4 vols. Berlin: Enslin 1819
– *Umrisse zur Geschichte und Kritik der schönen Literatur Deutschlands, 1700 bis 1818.* Berlin: Enslin 1819

– *Die schöne Literatur Deutschlands während des achtzehnten Jahrhunderts.* Berlin: Nicolai 1812
– *Geschichte und Kritik der deutschen Poesie und Beredsamkeit.* Berlin: Unger 1805
– *Kampf und Sieg,* 2 vols. Bremen: Heyse 1811
– *Novellen,* 2 vols. Berlin: Schüppel 1819
– *Freundliche Schriften,* 2 vols. Nürnberg: Schrag 1817
Hauff, W. *Sämtliche Werke,* 6 vols. Berlin: Knaur. n.d.
Jean Paul [Friedrich Richter]. *Sämtliche Werke.* Historisch-kritische Ausgabe, 19 vols. Edited by Eduard Berend. Weimar: Böhlau 1927
– *Werke,* 6 vols. Edited by Norbert Miller. München: Carl Hanser, 1959–63 (Lizenzausgabe, Wissenschaftliche Buchgesellschaft: Darmstadt)
– *Wahrheit aus Jean Pauls Leben,* 3 vols. Edited by Chr. Otto. Breslau: Max 1826–8
Musäus, J.K.A. *Volksmärchen,* 2 vols. Edited by P. Zaunert. Jena: Diederich 1912
Nicolai, F. *Das Leben und die Meinungen des Herrn Magister Sebaldus Nothanker,* 3 vols. Frankfurt/M: Nicolai 1779
Novalis [Friedrich von Hardenberg]. *Schriften,* 3 vols. Edited by L. Tieck and F. Schlegel. Berlin: Reimer 1826
– *Sämtliche Werke,* 4 vols. Edited by E. Kamnitzer. München: Rösl 1924
– *Werke, Briefe u. Dokumente,* 4 vols. Edited by E. Wasmuth. Heidelberg: Schneider 1953–7
Schelling, F.W.J. *Schriften, 1801–04.* Reprographischer Nachdruck der Cotta Ausgabe von 1859. Darmstadt: Wissenschaftliche Buchgesellschaft 1968
– *Vorlesungen über die Methode des akademischen Studium.* Stuttgart: Cotta 1813
– *Von der Weltseele: eine Hypothese der höheren Physik zur Erklärung des allgemeinen Organismus.* Hamburg: Perthes 1798
Schlegel, A.W., und F. Schlegel. *Athenaeum, 1798–1800,* 3 vols. Reprographischer Nachdruck der 1799 Ausgabe. München: Meyer Jessen 1924
Schlegel, F. *Prosaische Jugendschriften, 1794–1802.* Edited by J. Minor. Wien: Kossegen 1906
– *Kritische Friedrich Schlegel Ausgabe,* vols. 2 and 6. Edited by E. Behler, J.-J. Ansteet, und H. Eichner. München: Schöningen 1967
– *Vorlesungen über die Geschichte der alten und neuen Literatur.* Wien: Schaumburg 1815
– *Philosophische Vorlesungen, insbesondere über Philosophie der Sprache und des Wortes.* Wien: Schaumburg 1830
– *Literary Notebooks, 1797–1801.* Edited by H. Eichner. Toronto: University of Toronto Press 1957
Schleiermacher, F. *Über die Religion.* Berlin: Deutsche Bibliothek n.d.

Tieck, L. *Schriften*, 28 vols. (vol. 22) Berlin: Reimer 1828–46; reprint Berlin: De Gruyter 1966

– *Werke*, 4 vols. Edited by M. Thalmann. Darmstadt: Wissenschaftliche Buchgesellschaft 1967

– *Werke*, 2 vols. Edited by Kasack J. und A. Mohrhenn. Contains Prefaces to Novalis's Works and 'Die altdeutschen Minnelieder.' Berlin: Suhrkamp 1943

Werner, Z. *Die Söhne des Thals*, 2 vols. Berlin: Sander 1807 and 1819.

– *Martin Luther oder: Die Weihe der Kraft*. Wien: Grund 1818

– *Das Kreuz an der Ostsee*. In: *Deutsche Literatur in Entwicklungsreihen. Romantik* XX (Alte Reihe). Leipzig: Reclam 1937

Secondary Material: Books

Albers, L. *Der Gottesbegriff bei Fichte*. Breslau: Fleischmann 1915

Ashton, R. *The German Idea, 1800–1860*. Cambridge: Cambridge University Press 1980

Baumgarten, O. *Carlyle and Goethe*. Tübingen: Mohr 1906

Beach, J.W. *The Concept of Nature in Nineteenth Century English Poetry*. New York: Macmillan 1930

Benz, R. *Die deutsche Romantik*. Leipzig: Reclam 1940

Berend, E. *Jean Paul Bibliographie*. Revised by J. Krogoll. Stuttgart: Klatt 1963

Beyer-Fröhlich, M., ed. *Reihe: Deutsche Selbstzeugnisse*. In: *Deutsche Literatur in Entwicklungsreihen*, vol. I. Leipzig: Reclam 1930

Bielschowsky, A. *Goethe: Sein Leben und seine Werke*, 2 vols. München: Beck 1907

Boeschenstein, H. *Deutsche Gefühlskultur*, vol. I. Bern: Haupt 1954

Brookes, G.H. *The Rhetorical Form of Carlyle's 'Sartor Resartus.'* Berkeley: University of California Press 1972

Bruyn, Günter de. *Das Leben des Jean Paul Friedrich Richter*. Halle: Fischer 1975

Campbell, Ian. *Thomas Carlyle*. New York: Schribner's Sons 1974

Carré, J.-M. *Goethe en Angleterre*. Paris: Bloud 1920

Cazamian, L. *Carlyle*. Paris: Bloud 1913

Clubbe, J., ed. *Carlyle and His Contemporaries: Essays in Honor of C.R. Sanders*. Durham, NC: Duke University Press 1976

Clubbe, J, and Ernest J. Lovell Jr. *English Romanticism*. De Kalb: Northern Illinois University Press 1983

Deile, Gotthold. *Goethe als Freimaurer*. Berlin: Mittler und Sohn 1908

Dyer, I.W. *A Bibliography of Thomas Carlyle's Writings and Ana*. Portland: Southworth Press 1928

Eckloff, L. *Bild und Wirklichkeit by Thomas Carlyle*, vol. 2, Schriften der Albertus Universität. Königsberg: Ost Europa Verlag 1936

Eichner, H. *Friedrich Schlegel.* New York: Twayne 1970
Espinasse, F. *Literary Recollections and Sketches.* London: Hodder 1893
Fichte, I.H. *Johann Gottlieb Fichtes Leben und literarischer Briefwechsel,* 2 vols. Leipzig: Brockhaus 1862
Fielding, K.J., and R.L. Tarr, eds. *Carlyle Past and Present: A Collection of New Essays.* New York: Barnes and Noble 1976
Flügel, E. *Thomas Carlyles religiöse und sittliche Entwicklung und Weltanschauung.* Leipzig: Grunow 1887
Fridell, E. *Novalis als Philosoph.* München: Bruckman 1904
Froude, J.A. *Thomas Carlyle: A History of the First Forty Years of His Life, 1795–1835,* 2 vols. London: Longmans 1882
– *Thomas Carlyle: A History of His Life in London, 1834–1881,* 2 vols. New York: Harper 1885
Garnett, R. *Life of Thomas Carlyle.* London: Walter Scott 1887
Grützmacher, L. *Franz Horn: Ein Nachfahre der Romantik.* Münster: Universitas 1928
Hallamore, G.J. *Das Bild Laurence Sternes in Deutschland. Germanische Studien,* Heft 172. Berlin: Ebering 1936
Harich, W. *Jean Paul.* Leipzig: Haessel 1925
Harrold, C.F. *Carlyle and German Thought: 1819–1834.* New Haven: Yale University Press 1934
Haym, R. *Die Romantische Schule in Deutschland: Ein Beitrag zur Geschichte des deutschen Geistes.* Darmstadt: Wissenschaftliche Buchgesellschaft 1961
Haywood, B. *Novalis: The Veil of Imagery.* 's Gravenhage: Mouton 1959
Heilborn, E. *Novalis der Romantiker.* Berlin: Reimer 1901
Heimsoeth, H. *Fichte.* München: Reinhart 1923
Henkel, A. *Entsagung: Eine Studie zu Goethes Altersroman.* Tübingen: Niemeyer 1964
Hensel, P. *Thomas Carlyle.* Stuttgart: Fromanns Verlag 1902
Hettner, H. *Die romantische Schule in ihrem inneren Zusammenhang mit Goethe und Schiller.* Braunschweig: Vieweg 1865
Howe, S. *Wilhelm Meister and His English Kinsmen.* New York: Columbia University Press 1930
Huch, R. *Die Romantik: Ausbreitung, Blütezeit und Verfall.* Tübingen: Wunderlich 1951
Joachimi, M. *Die Weltanschauung der deutschen Romantik.* Jena: Diederichs 1905
Johnson, W.S. *Thomas Carlyle: A Study of His Literary Apprenticeship.* New Haven: Yale University Press 1911
Kluckhohn, P. *Die deutsche Romantik.* Bielefeld und Leipzig: Reclam 1924
– *Die Auffassung der Liebe in d. Lit. d. 18 Jhd. u. in der deutschen Romantik.* Tübingen: Niemeyer 1966

Kaplan, F. *Thomas Carlyle: A Biography*. Ithaca: Cornell University Press 1983
Kellner, L. *Die englische Literatur im Zeitalter der Königin Viktoria*. Leipzig: Tauchnitz, 1909. 'Carlyle,' Chapter V
Korff, H.A. *Der Geist der Goethezeit*, Part 3: *Frühromantik*. Leipzig: Koehler 1966
Koziełek G. *Das dramatische Werk Zacharias Werners*, Wrocław: Polskiej Akademii Nauk 1967
Lassky A.E. *Tieck's Approach to Romanticism*. Leipzig: Universitätsverlag, 1925
– *Tieck's Romantic Irony*. Chapel Hill: University of North Carolina Press 1932
Lehman, B.H. *Carlyle's Theory of the Hero: Its Sources, Development, History, and Influence on Carlyle's Work*. Durham: Duke University Press 1928
Linscheid, J.E. 'Carlyle's Translation of the German Narratives.' Diss., University of Kansas, 1935
Lotter, Karl. 'Carlyle und die deutsche Romantik.' Diss., University of Erlangen, 1925
Lukács, G. *Goethe und seine Zeit*. Bern: Francke 1947
MacCunn, J. *Six Radical Thinkers*. London: Arnold 1907
Marx, K., und F. Engels. *Über Kunst und Literatur*. Edited by M. Lifschitz. Berlin: Henschel 1948
Marx, Olga. 'Carlyle's Translation of Wilhelm Meister.' Diss., Johns Hopkins University 1925
Mason, E.C. *Deutsche und englische Romantik*. Göttingen: Vandenhoeck 1959
Maulsby, D.L. *The Growth of Sartor Resartus*. Tuft's College Studies, no. 1. Malden, MA, 1899
Meyer, H. *Der Sonderling in der deutschen Dichtung*. München: Hauser 1963
Minor, J. *Studien zu Novalis*. Wien: Kossegen 1911
Müller, J., ed. *Gestaltung, Umgestaltung: Festschrift für H.A. Korff*. Leipzig: Koehler 1957
Neff, E. *Carlyle*. London: Allen 1932
– *Carlyle and Mill: Mystic and Utilitarian*. New York: Columbia University Press 1926
Nerrlich, P. *Jean Paul, sein Leben und seine Werke*. Berlin: Weidman 1889
Noack, L. *Schelling und die Philosophie der Romantik*. Berlin: Mittler 1859
Pape, H. 'Jean Paul als Quelle von Thomas Carlyles Anschauungen und Stil.' Diss., University of Rostock, 1904
Pascal, Roy. *Die Autobiographie*. Stuttgart: Kohlhammer 1965
Pixberg, H. *Novalis als Naturphilosoph*. Gütersloh: Bertelsmann 1928
Plagens, H. 'Carlyles Weg zu Goethe.' Diss., University of Berlin 1938

Rasch, W. *Die Erzählweise Jean Pauls.* München: Carl Hanser 1961
Reiss, H.S. *The Political Thought of the German Romantics, 1793–1815.* Oxford: Blackwell 1955
Roe, F.W. *Thomas Carlyle as a Critic of Literature.* New York: Columbia University Press 1910
Rosenberg, Ph. *Thomas Carlyle and the Theory of Radical Activism.* Cambridge, MA: Harvard University Press 1974
Schmitz, W. *Die Empfindsamkeit Jean Pauls.* Heidelberg: Winters Universitätsbuchhandlung 1930
Schrimpf, H.J. *Das Weltbild des späten Goethe.* Stuttgart: Kohlhammer 1956
Shine, H. *Carlyle's Early Readings to 1834.* Includes Introductory Essay on his Intellectual Development. Lexington: University of Kentucky Libraries 1953
– *Carlyle's Fusion of Poetry, History and Religion by 1834.* Chapel Hill: University of North Carolina Press 1938
– *Carlyle and the Saint-Simonians: The Concept of Historical Periodicity.* Baltimore: Johns Hopkins University Press 1941
Smeed, J.W. *Jean Paul's Dreams.* Oxford: Oxford University Press 1966
Spazier, R.O. *Jean Paul Friedrich Richter: Ein biographischer Commentar zu dessen Werken,* 4 vols. Leipzig: Brüggemann 1833
Spenlé, J.H. *Novalis: Essai sur l'Idéalisme Romantique en Allemagne.* Paris: Colin 1904
Stefansky, G. *Das Wesen der deutschen Romantik.* Stuttgart: Metzler 1923
Storrs, M. 'The Relation of Carlyle to Kant and Fichte.' Diss., Bryn Mawr College, 1929
Streuli, W. *Thomas Carlyle als Vermittler deutscher Litteratur und deutschen Geistes.* Zürich: Schulthess 1895
Strich, F. *Deutsche Klassik und Romantik.* München: Beck'sche Verlagsbuchhandlung 1928
Tarr, R.L. *Thomas Carlyle: A Descriptive Bibliography.* Pittsburgh, PA: University of Pittsburgh Press 1989
Tennyson, G.B. *Sartor Called Resartus.* Princeton, NJ: Princeton University Press 1965
Vijn, J.P. *Carlyle and Jean Paul: Their Spiritual Optics.* Amsterdam/Philadelphia: Benjamin 1982
Walzel, O. *Deutsche Romantik.* Leipzig: Teubner 1908
Wead, M.E., ed. *A Catalogue of the Dr. Samuel A. Jones Carlyle Collection.* Ann Arbor: University of Michigan Press 1919
Wellek R. *Immanuel Kant in England: 1793–1838.* Princeton, NJ: Princeton University Press 1931
– *Confrontations: Studies in the Intellectual and Literary Relations between*

Germany, England, and the United States during the Nineteenth Century. Princeton, NJ: Princeton University Press 1965
– *A History of Modern Criticism, 1750–1950,* vols. I and III. New Haven, CT: Yale University Press 1965
Wiese, Benno von. *Der deutsche Roman,* vol. 1. Düsseldorf: Bagel 1963
Zeydel, E.H. *Ludwig Tieck and England.* Princeon, NJ: Princeton University Press 1931

Secondary Material: Articles and Parts of Books

Alexander, W.J. 'Sartor Resartus,' *Univ. of Toronto Monthly* 3 (1903), 149–55, 195–204
Baker, Lee C.R. 'The Open Secret of *Sartor Resartus*: Carlyle's Method of Converting His Reader.' *Studies in Philology* 83 (1986), 218–35
Beinard, Ch. 'Rebelling from the Right Side: Carlyle's Struggle against the Dominant Nineteenth-Century Rhetoric.' *Studies in Scottish Lit.* 22 (1987), 142–56
Berend, E. 'Jean Pauls Ästhetik.' *Forschungen zur neueren Literaturgeschichte* 35 (1909), 200ff.
– 'Der Typus des Humoristen.' In *Die Ernte: Festschrift für Franz Muncker,* 95–115. Halle: Niemeyer 1926
Boeschenstein, H. 'On Rereading Jean Paul.' *GR* 29 (1954), 119–30
Boyesen, H.H. 'Goethe and Carlyle.' In *Essays on German Literature.* London: Fisher Unwin 1892
Brie, F. 'Carlyle and Goethe's *Symbolum.*' *Anglia* 66 (1942), 228–54
Brinkmann, R. 'Romantische Dichtungstheorie in Fr. Schlegels Frühschriften,' *DVj* 32 (1958), 344–71
Burnett, P.B. 'The Language of Carlyle as affected by the German.' *PMLA* 11 (1896), 76–7
Carr, C.T. 'Carlyle's Translations from German,' *MLR* 42 (1947), 223–32
Carré, Jean-Marie. 'Quelques lettres inédites de William Taylor, Coleridge et Carlyle.' *Revue Germanique* 8 (1912), 34–49
Czerny, J. 'Sterne, Hippel und Jean Paul.' *Forschungen zur neueren Literaturgesch.* 27 (1904), 1–86
Dilthey, W. 'Thomas Carlyle.' *Archiv f. Geschichte d. Philosophie* 4 (1891), 260–85
Durand, W.Y. 'De Quincey and Carlyle in Their Relation to the Germans,' *PMLA* 22 (1907), 521–30
Eichner, H. 'Fr. Schlegel's Theory of Romantic Poetry,' *PMLA* 71 (1956), 1018–41
Fehr, B. 'Der deutsche Idealismus in Carlyles *Sartor Resartus.*' *GRM* 5 (1913), 81–101

Fife, R.H. 'Jean Paul Fr. Richter and E.T.A. Hoffmann,' *PMLA* 22 (1907), 1–32

Geissendoerfer, T. 'Carlyle and Jean Paul Friedrich Richter.' *JEGP* 25 (1926), 540–53

Geissler, E. 'Jean Paul als Erzieher zum dentschen Stil.' *Hesperus* 19 (1960), 42–55

Harding, A. 'Sterling, Carlyle, and German Higher Criticism.' *VS* 26 (1983), 269–85

Harrold, C.F. 'Carlyle and Novalis.' *SP* 27 (1930), 47–63

– 'The Nature of Carlyle's Calvinism.' *SP* 33 (1936), 475–86

– 'The Mystical Element in Carlyle: 1827–34.' *MP* 29 (1932), 459–75

– 'Carlyle's Interpretation of Kant.' *PQ* 7 (1928), 345–57

Hatch, M.G. 'The Development of Goethe's Concept of the Calling in *Wilhelm Meisters Lehrjahre* and *Wanderjahre*.' *GQ* 32 (1959), 217–26

Henel, H. 'Fr. Schlegel u. d. Grundlagen d. modernen literarischen Kritik.' *GRM* 20 (1945), 81–93

Holl, K. 'Goethes Vollendung in ihrer Beziehung zu Byron u. Carlyle.' *GRM* 9 (1921), 75–87

Immerwahr, R. 'Fr. Schlegel's Essay on Goethe's *Meister*,' *Monatshefte* 49 (1957), 1–21

Jeffers, Th. 'Forms of Misprision: The Early and Mid-Victorian Reception of Goethe's *Bildungsidee*.' *U. of T. Quarterly* 57 (1988) 501–5

Kraeger, H. 'Carlyles deutsche Studien u. der *Wotton Reinfred*.' *Anglia*, Beiblatt 9 (1898), 193–219

– 'Zu Carlyles *Sartor Resartus*,' *Anglia*, Beiblatt 10 (1899), 12–13

– 'Carlyles Stellung zur deutschen Sprache und Literatur.' *Anglia* 22 (1899), 145–342

Krüger, A. 'Wuz und Quintus Fixlein.' *Hesperus* 21 (1961), 38–45

Küchler, F. 'Carlyle und Schiller.' *Anglia* 26 (1903), 1–93, 393–446

Lange, V. 'Friedrich Schlegel's Literary Criticism.' *Comp. Lit.* 7 (1955), 298–305

Leopold, W. 'Die religiöse Wurzel von Carlyles literarischer Wirksamkeit,' *Studien z. engl. Philologie* 62 (1922), 1–114

– 'Thomas Carlyle and Franz Horn,' *JEGP* 28 (1929), 215–19

– 'Carlyle's Handbooks on the History of German Literature.' In Harrold, *Carlyle and German Thought*, Appendix, 238–47

Lloyd, T. 'Towards Natural Supernaturalism: Carlyle and Dual Vision, 1823–29.' *PQ* 65 (1986), 479–94

Metzger, L. 'Sartor Resartus: A Victorian *Faust*.' *Comp. Lit.* 13 (1961), 316–31

Minor, J. 'Classiker und Romantiker.' *GJB*, 10 (1889), 212–32

Moore, C. 'The Persistence of Carlyle's "Everlasting Yea." ' *MP* 54 (1956–7), 187–96

– '*Sartor Resartus* and the Problem of Carlyle's "Conversion."' *PMLA* 70 (1955), 662–81

Morgan, W. 'Carlyle and German Thought.' *QQ* 22 (1916), 438–52

Murphy, E.M. 'Carlyle and the Saint-Simonians.' *SP* 33 (1936), 93–118

Orsini, G.N.G. 'Coleridge and Schlegel Reconsidered.' *Comp. Lit.* 16 (1964), 97–118

Plard, H. 'Le *Sartor Resartus* de Carlyle et Jean Paul.' *Etudes Germaniques* 18 (1963), 114–28

Rabb, J.D. 'The Silence of Thomas Carlyle.' *ELN* 26 (1989), 70–81

Roellinger, F.X., Jr. 'The Early Development of Carlyle's Style.' *PMLA* 22 (1957), 936–51

Röhl, H. 'Charaktere in d. deutschen Dichtung des 19. Jhd.' *ZfDk* 35 (1921), 369–77, 454–63; 36 (1922), 213–21

Schmidt, W. 'Fichtes Einfluss auf die deutsche Romantik.' *Euph.* 20 (1913), 435–58, 647–81

Schröder, R. 'Thomas Carlyles Abhandlung über den Goetheschen "Faust."' *AfnSpr* 96 (1896), 241–68

Shine, H. 'Carlyle's Views on the Relation between Religion and Poetry up to 1832,' *SP* 33 (1936), 57–92

– 'Carlyle's Views on the Relation between Poetry and History up to 1832.' *SP* 33 (1936), 487–506

– 'Carlyle and the German Philosophy Problem during the Year 1826–27.' *PMLA* 50 (1935), 807–27

Smeed. J.W. 'Thomas Carlyle and Jean Paul Richter.' *Comp. Lit.* 16 (1964), 226–53

– 'Carlyles Jean Paul Übersetzungen.' *DVj* 35 (1961), 262–79

Sonstroem, D. 'The Double Vortex in Carlyle's *Hero and Hero-Worship.*' *PQ* 59 (1980), 531–40

Stock, I. 'A View of Wilhelm Meister's Apprenticeship.' *PMLA* 72 (1957), 84–103

Tennyson, G.B. 'Carlyle: Beginning with the Word.' In *The Victorian Experience: The Prose Writers*, edited by R.A. Levine, 1–21. Athens: Ohio University Press 1982

Vaughan, C.E. 'Carlyle and His German Masters.' In *Essays and Studies by Members of the English Association*, vol. 1, 168–96. Oxford: Clarendon Press 1910

Index

www.ingramcontent.com/pod-product-compliance
Lightning Source LLC
Chambersburg PA
CBHW050240110726
47898CB00007B/2216